Kieler Studien • Kiel Studies 337
Dennis Snower (Editor)
Kiel Institute for the World Economy

Stéphanie M. Stolz

Bank Capital and Risk-Taking

The Impact of Capital Regulation, Charter Value, and the Business Cycle

Springer

Dr. Stéphanie M. Stolz
3517 17th Street, N.W.
Washington, D.C. 20010

Library of Congress Control Number: 2006935424

ISSN 0340-6989
ISBN 978-3-540-48544-5 Springer Berlin Heidelberg New York

Springer is a part of Springer Science+Business Media
springeronline.com

Printed in Germany

Cover design: Erich Kirchner, Heidelberg

Printed on acid-free paper 42/3180 - 5 4 3 2 1 0

To My Parents

Preface

The year-long consultations on Basel II mirror the international popularity of capital requirements as a regulatory instrument. Yet, the impact of capital requirements on banks' behavior is not fully understood. The aim of this study is to contribute to this understanding by answering the following questions: How do banks adjust capital and risk after an increase in capital requirements? How do banks adjust their regulatory capital buffer over the business cycle? And what is the impact of banks' charter value on the regulatory capital buffer?

The research undertaken for this study has benefited from support in terms of ideas, research facilities, and, not least, financial funding. My thanks go first of all to Claudia M. Buch for her constant encouragement, her continuous guidance, and her confidence in my research ideas. My thanks go also to the Kiel Institute for World Economics and its staff for providing a very fertile academic ground for my research and for providing excellent research facilities. In fact, conducting this study would not have been possible without the support of my colleagues at the Kiel Institute and elsewhere. In particular, I am grateful to Horst Siebert for providing me the freedom to pursue this topic. My special thanks go to Jörg Breitung, Kai Carstensen, and Dieter Urban for providing input on econometric issues. I am also grateful to Andrea Schertler for the long and productive discussions I had on various parts of this study. I am especially indebted to Paul Kramer, who introduced me to *parallelism* and other secrets of the English language. My thanks go also to Kerstin Stark for sharing her editorial expertise with me and to Itta Schulte not only for the same reason but also for holding up the Swabian flag in the Swabian diaspora in Kiel. I am also grateful to my former colleagues Ralph Heinrich, Christian Pierdzioch, and Julius Spatz, who offered detailed comments on earlier drafts of key chapters. I also want to thank Michael Kötter and Thorsten Nestmann for mutual support and encouragement.

The empirical work presented here is based mainly on confidential supervisory data provided by Deutsche Bundesbank in Frankfurt. Hence, I would like to thank Thilo Liebig and his team for the fruitful cooperation and for always welcoming me so warmly during my various stays. The idea of this study was born during a stay at the Prudential Supervision Division of the European Central Bank. Hence, I would like to express my gratitude to Andrea Enria, Jukka Vesala, and Giuseppe Vulpes for drawing my attention to the topic and for providing respective research impulses. I would also like to thank Philip

Bartholomew of the IMF and Tom Lutton of the Office of Federal Housing Enterprise Oversight for their comments on various aspects of my research.

The research for Chapter 5 was partly financed under the 6th EU framework (Contract No. SCS8-CT-2004-502642). Hence, my thanks go also to the European Commission DG Research, DG ECFIN, and DG ESTAT, the cooperation partners, and the team leaders of *FINPROP*.

And last, but not least, my thanks go to my coauthors Frank Heid, Daniel Porath, and Michael Wedow for the productive time we spent together working on the papers that were the basis for Chapters 3 and 4.

Of course, I am solely responsible for all remaining errors and inaccuracies in this study.

Frankfurt, April 2007 Stéphanie M. Stolz

Contents

1 Introduction **1**

2 Theoretical Literature **7**

2.1 Moral Hazard in Banking 7

2.2 Capital Regulation in Models of Moral Hazard 10

2.3 The Disciplining Effect of Charter Value 13

2.4 A Model with Charter Value and Endogenous Capital 16

2.5 Further Considerations 21

2.6 Hypotheses on … 25

2.6.1 Capital and Risk Adjustments after an Increase in Capital Requirements 25

2.6.2 Capital and Risk Adjustments over the Business Cycle 27

2.6.3 The Disciplining Effect of Charter Value on Risk-Taking 28

3 Capital and Risk Adjustments after an Increase in Capital Requirements **30**

3.1 Introduction 30

3.2 The Empirical Model 32

3.2.1 A Simultaneous Equations Model with Partial Adjustment 33

3.2.2 Hypotheses 34

3.2.3 Methodology 35

3.2.4 Measures of Capital and Risk 38

3.2.5 Variables Affecting the Optimum Levels of Capital and Risk 40

3.3 Data Description 42

3.4 Regression Analysis 47

3.4.1 Dummy Variable Approach in a Pooled Regression 47

3.4.2 Subsample Approach 53

3.4.3 Rolling Window Approach 56

3.4.4 Dummy Variable Approach in a Dynamic Panel Regression 59

3.5 Conclusion 63

3.6 Appendix 1: Descriptive Statistics 64

3.7 Appendix 2: Robustness Checks 68

4 Capital and Risk Adjustments over the Business Cycle 78

4.1 Introduction 78

4.2 The Empirical Model 80

4.2.1 A Partial Adjustment Model 80

4.2.2 Hypotheses 83

4.2.3 Methodology 84

4.2.4 Measures of the Capital Buffer, Regulatory Capital, Risk-Weighted Assets, and Business Cycle Fluctuations 85

4.2.5 Bank-Specific Control Variables 86

4.3 Data Description 88

4.4 Regression Analysis 90

4.4.1 Adjustments in the Capital Buffer 92

4.4.2 Asymmetries 94

4.4.3 Adjustments in Regulatory Capital and Risk-Weighted Assets 97

4.4.4 Robustness Checks 102

4.5 Conclusion 103

4.6 Appendix 1: Descriptive Statistics 104

4.7 Appendix 2: Robustness Checks 107

5 The Disciplining Effect of Charter Value on Risk-Taking 111

5.1 Introduction 111

5.2 The Empirical Model 113

5.2.1 A Two-Step Dynamic Model 114

5.2.2 Hypotheses 114

5.2.3 Methodology 115

5.2.4 Definitions of Charter Value and Risk-Taking 116

5.2.5 Bank-Specific and Macroeconomic Control Variables 118

5.3 Data Description 121

5.4 Regression Analysis 122

5.4.1 Charter Value 123
5.4.2 Risk-Taking 125
5.4.3 Robustness Checks 129
5.5 Conclusion 132
5.6 Appendix 1: Descriptive Statistics 134
5.7 Appendix 2: Robustness Checks 139

6 Final Remarks 140

References 144

List of Tables

Table 1: Levin–Lin–Chu (2002) Panel Unit-Root Test 37

Table 2: The Basel Capital Ratio of German Savings and Cooperative Banks and Its Components, 2003 45

Table 3: Pooled 3SLS Estimates for Specifications with Regulatory Dummy and Interactions Terms, 1994–2004 48

Table 4: Pooled 3SLS Estimates for Two Subsamples, 1993–2004 54

Table 5: Blundell–Bond Two-Step GMM Estimates for Specifications with Regulatory Dummy and Interaction Terms, 1995–2001 61

Table 6: Blundell–Bond Two-Step System GMM Estimates for the Capital Buffer—All Banks, Savings Banks, and Cooperative Banks, 1995–2003 93

Table 7: Blundell–Bond Two-Step System GMM Estimates for the Capital Buffer—Savings Banks and Cooperative Banks, 1995–2003 96

Table 8: Blundell–Bond Two-Step System GMM Estimates for Capital Savings—Banks and Cooperative Banks, 1995–2003 98

Table 9: Blundell–Bond Two-Step System GMM Estimates for Risk-Weighted Assets—Savings Banks and Cooperative Banks, 1995–2003 99

Table 10: Blundell–Bond Two-Step System GMM Estimates for Charter Value, 1997–2003 124

Table 11: Blundell–Bond Two-Step System GMM Estimates for Risk-Taking (Charter Value Modeled as Exogenous Variable), 1997–2003 127

Table 12: Blundell–Bond Two-Step System GMM Estimates for Risk-Taking (Charter Value Modeled as Endogenous Variable), 1995–2003 128

Table A1: Definition of the Bank-Specific (Control) Variables 64

Table A2: Descriptive Statistics for the Pooled Sample 64

Table A3: Variable Means for Each Year of the Observation Period 65

Table A4: Correlations between Variables 66

Table A5: Variable Means for Banks with Low and High Capital Buffers 67

Table A6: Pooled 3SLS Estimates for Specifications with Regulatory Dummy and Interactions Terms (definition of *dyREG* based on the 25th percentile capital buffer), 1993–2004 68

Table A7: Pooled 3SLS Estimates for Specifications with Regulatory Dummy and Interactions Terms (definition of *dyREG* based on the median capital buffer), 1993–2004 70

Table A8: Pooled 3SLS Estimates for Two Subsamples, 1993–2004 72

Table A9: Blundell–Bond Two-Step GMM Estimates for Specifications with Regulatory Dummy and Interaction Terms, 1995–2001 74

Table A10: Definition of the Business Cycle Indicators 104

Table A11: Definition of the Bank-Specific (Control) Variables 104

Table A12: Descriptive Statistics for the Business Cycle Indicators 105

Table A13: Descriptive Statistics for the Bank-Specific (Control) Variables 105

Table A14: Correlation Matrix 106

Table A15: Fixed Effects and Pooled OLS Estimates for the Capital Buffer—Savings and Cooperative Banks, 1995–2003 107

Table A16: Pooled OLS Estimates—Savings and Cooperative Banks, 1995–2003 108

Table A17: Blundell–Bond Two-Step System GMM Estimates for the Capital Buffer (ROA, SIZE, LIQUID, and LLOSS Modeled as Endogenous Variables)—Savings Banks and Cooperative Banks, 1995–2003 109

Table A18: Blundell–Bond Two-Step System GMM Estimates (Interaction Terms Modeled as Endogenous Variables)—Savings Banks and Cooperative Banks, 1995–2003 110

Table A19: Description of the Bank-Specific and Macroeconomic Variables 134

Table A20: Composition of Observations and Banks by Country 135

Table A21: Descriptive Statistics 135

Table A22: Variable Means for Each Year of the Observation Period 136

Table A23: Correlations between the Variables of the First-Step Regression 137

Table A24: Correlations between the Variables of the Second-Step Regression 138

Table A25: Blundell–Bond Two-Step System GMM Estimates for the Absolute Capital Buffer, 1997–2003 139

List of Figures

Figure 1: Capital, Incentives for Risk-Taking, and Charter Value 19

Figure 2: Optimum Capital Buffer and Charter Value 21

Figure 3: Estimated Coefficients for a Rolling Window of 750 Banks, 1993–2004 58

Figure 4: Capital Buffers of German Savings and Cooperative Banks over the Business Cycle, 1993–2003 91

Figure A1: Estimated Coefficients for a Rolling Window of 750 Banks, 1993–2001 76

1 Introduction

Capital regulation in the form of minimum capital requirements is the most popular instrument in current banking regulation. The prevalence of minimum capital requirements is the result of a process of deregulation starting in the 1970s. In the course of deregulation, regulators have subsequently abolished, among other instruments, limitations on eligible banking activities and deposit rate ceilings. In order to limit the probability of default, they continued to require banks to hold a certain amount of capital measured as a percentage of total assets. The rationale was that capital acts as a buffer: As bank owners' claims are subordinate to depositors' claims, banks are solvent if their asset value is at least as high as depositors' claims. In order to guarantee that funds are still available to pay back depositors and other creditors of a bank in the case of financial distress, minimum capital requirements introduce a higher artificial insolvency threshold. In the Savings and Loan Crisis in the US and in the Latin-American crisis, it became, however, apparent that minimum capital requirements that do not depend on banks' asset risk are not sufficient to limit the probability of default. Hence, regulators tried to bind minimum capital requirements to banks' asset risk by measuring capital as a percentage of risk-weighted assets.

At the same time, it also became apparent that banks were extending their activities beyond their traditional national activities. They were becoming increasingly active internationally and were competing with banks from other jurisdictions.[1] As funding through capital is relatively costly compared with funding through deposits, minimum capital requirements affect the profitability of banks and, thus, their international competitiveness. Hence, regulators tried to level the playing field of international banks by harmonizing minimum capital requirements. The resulting international initiative, the Basel Capital Accord of 1988, required international banks to hold a minimum of 8 percent capital-to-risk-weighted assets. In 1993, the Basel Capital Accord was implemented in the EU by an EU directive that, since then, has required *all* banks, national and international, to comply with the Basel minimum capital requirements.

The 1988 Basel Capital Accord seems to have been successful in reaching its two principle aims: ensuring an adequate level of capital in the international

---

1 For example, foreign assets (liabilities) of German commercial banks vis-à-vis OECD countries increased by more than 880 (710) percent in real terms between 1983 and 1999 (Buch 2003).

banking system and creating a level playing field in competitive terms (Basel Committee on Banking Supervision 2001). This led to its role as an accepted world standard, with well over 100 countries applying the Basel framework to their banking system. However, the 1988 Basel Capital Accord exhibited a major shortcoming: It did not sufficiently link capital requirements to economic risk, thus opening up the opportunity for regulatory capital arbitrage.[2] This tended to reduce the average quality of bank loan portfolios (Basel Committee on Banking Supervision 2001).

In June 1999, the Basel Committee on Banking Supervision, thus, released a first consultative package on a new, more risk-sensitive accord. A first revised version was published in January 2001 and a second in April 2003. In June 2004, the Basel Committee on Banking Supervision published a preliminary final version and intends for the Accord to be available for implementation as of 2007. Basel II consists of three reinforcing pillars: a minimum capital requirement, a supervisory review process, and market discipline. However, the calculation of minimum capital requirements is still the focus of Basel II: 146 of the 251 pages of the Basel II document are devoted solely to the calculation of minimum capital requirements.

The prevalence of minimum capital requirements in banking regulation has stirred up a hot debate among academics about whether banks should be regulated and whether capital requirements are the right regulatory instrument. Yet, the theoretical literature controversially discusses the incentive effects of minimum capital requirements. Hence, it is ultimately an empirical question how banks behave in the light of minimum capital requirements. In the following, I shortly review the theoretical underpinnings of capital requirements before I state the hypotheses to be tested in this study. Finally, I sketch out the plan of the study.

The Theoretical Underpinnings

The prevalence of minimum capital requirements is based mainly on the assumption that banks engage in moral hazard behavior. Information asymmetries and inadequately priced deposit insurance, by shielding banks from the disciplining control of depositors, give banks the incentive to decrease capital and increase asset risk (Merton 1977). Whether this incentive problem is mitigated by the introduction of minimum capital requirements is not undisputed (Sharpe 1978; Koehn and Santomero 1980; Kim and Santomero 1988; Furlong and Keeley 1989; Rochet 1992). However, the prediction of theory that banks engage

2 Banks could increase their risk without increasing required capital by keeping the allocation between buckets constant and substituting low-risk for high-risk assets within a bucket.

in extreme risk-taking does obviously contrast with the behavior of real banks. First, banks hold a capital buffer that is substantially in excess of the regulatory minimum capital requirements (the "capital buffer"). And second, the majority of banks seems to have a very low probability of default (Santomero and Vinso 1977; Marcus and Shaked 1984).

These empirical findings have inspired the literature to search for an incentive that could moderate the moral hazard behavior of banks. Such an incentive has been found in banks' charter value (Marcus 1984). The charter value is the net present value of future rents. This charter value would be lost in the case of bankruptcy and, hence, represents banks' private cost of failure. The higher banks' charter value is, the higher banks' private cost of asset risk and leverage is. Hence, banks hold a capital buffer to cushion negative capital shocks and, thus, to protect their charter values. However, holding capital is costly compared to holding insured deposits. This trade-off determines the optimal capital buffer that bank owners aim at holding above the regulatory minimum (Milne and Whalley 2001).

Hypotheses to Be Tested in This Study

The theoretical literature, in particular the capital buffer theory, provides three hypotheses, which I test in this study. First, the classical models of moral hazard make rivaling predictions with regard to adjustments in capital and risk after an increase in the minimum regulatory capital requirement. Hence, I test whether banks increase or decrease risk when capital requirements force them to hold higher capital levels. In particular, I test whether adjustments in capital and risk depend on banks' capital buffer, as predicted by the capital buffer theory.

Second, the capital buffer theory predicts that banks' optimum capital buffers depend positively on asset risk. If banks have a higher asset risk, they need a higher capital buffer to be fully insured against violating the regulatory minimum. As loans are traditionally banks' most important asset category, credit risk is one of the main drivers of asset risk. To the degree that credit risk fluctuates over the business cycle, optimum capital buffers also fluctuate over the business cycle. Whether capital buffers fluctuate procyclically or countercyclically depends on whether banks provide for materializing credit risk in a downturn by already building up capital buffers in an upturn. Hence, I test whether banks' capital buffers fluctuate procyclically or countercyclically over the business cycle.

Third, the theoretical literature predicts that charter value has a moderating effect on banks' incentives for risk-taking. Hence, I test whether banks with high charter values have a lower probability of default as given by higher capital (buffers) and lower asset risk.

The Plan of the Study

This study is intended as a positive analysis of bank behavior in the light of minimum capital requirements. Chapter 2 provides the unifying theoretical framework for the three empirical chapters 3–5. In Chapter 2, I begin my analysis by reviewing the theoretical literature on minimum capital requirements. In particular, I outline the Milne and Whalley (2001) model, which introduces charter value into a moral hazard model and additionally endogenizes capital. From the reviewed literature, I then derive the hypotheses to be tested in the empirical chapters 3–5. These empirical chapters are structured as self-contained chapters with their own introduction, their own description of the data and the methodology, and their own conclusion. They also refer to the relevant empirical literature and very shortly again refer to the relevant theoretical literature reviewed extensively in Chapter 2.

In Chapter 3, I test whether adjustments in capital and risk are positively or negatively related after an increase in the minimum regulatory capital requirement and whether the relationship depends on the size of banks' capital buffers. The analysis is based on confidential supervisory micro data for German savings banks in the period 1993–2004. I estimate a modified version of the model developed by Shrieves and Dahl (1992). The simplest way to account for the size of a bank's capital buffer is to use dummy variables that are unity for banks with a capital buffer below a certain threshold and zero else. In addition to this standard dummy approach in a pooled regression used in the literature (Shrieves and Dahl 1992; Jacques and Nigro 1997; Aggarwal and Jacques 2001; Rime 2001), I use dynamic panel data techniques (Arellano and Bond 1991; Blundell and Bond 1998) as a robustness check. Compared to former research, I impose fewer restrictions with regard to the impact of regulation on capital and risk adjustments. I complement this dummy approach with a rolling window approach. The rolling window approach has the advantage that it does not impose ad hoc restrictions with regard to the impact of regulation on capital and risk adjustments. Furthermore, this approach allows the impact of regulation to change continuously depending on the amount of capital the bank holds in excess of the regulatory minimum.

I find evidence that the coordination of capital and risk adjustments depends on banks' capital buffers. For banks with low capital buffers, adjustments in capital and risk are negatively related, while they are positively related for banks with high capital buffers. These findings are in line with the predictions of the capital buffer theory.

In Chapter 4, I test whether banks' capital buffers fluctuate procyclically or countercyclically over the business cycle. In addition, I decompose the capital buffer into its two components, regulatory capital and risk-weighted assets, and I also regress the components on the business cycle. This analysis is based on confidential supervisory micro data for German savings and cooperative banks in the period 1993–2003. I use dynamic panel data techniques (Arellano and Bond 1991; Blundell and Bond 1998).

I find that capital buffers fluctuate countercyclically over the business cycle. Ayuso et al. (2004) argue that a countercyclical fluctuation is evidence for banks' shortsightedness: If banks fail to build up capital buffers in a business cycle upturn when they expand their loan portfolio, their capital buffers cannot absorb the materializing credit risks in a business cycle downturn. Hence, they may be forced to build up their capital buffers in a business cycle downturn through a reduction in risk-weighted assets, i.e., their loan supply. In contrast to Ayuso et al. (2004), I argue that regressing banks' capital buffers on the business cycle cannot distinguish between banks' deliberate capital buffer decisions, i.e., supply-side effects, and demand-side effects working through loan demand. As loan demand is known to fluctuate procyclically over the business cycle, demand-side effects may also lead to a countercyclical behavior of capital buffers through their effect on risk-weighted assets. However, this countercyclical behavior of capital buffers does not correspond to banks being shortsighted. Effects of banks' capitalization on the behavior of capital buffers, however, indicate the existence of supply-side effects. Hence, I also test for asymmetries with respect to the capitalization of banks. I indeed find evidence for such asymmetries. Surprisingly, however, banks with low capital buffers do not reduce their risk-weighted assets in a business cycle downturn by more than their well-capitalized peers, but rather by less. Cooperative banks even increase their risk-weighted assets.

In Chapter 5, I test whether banks' charter values have a disciplining effect on banks' risk-taking. In line with the empirical literature (Keeley 1990; Demsetz et al. 1996; Gropp and Vesala 2004), I regress banks' charter value on various measures of leverage and asset risk. The analysis is based on micro data for EU commercial banks in the period 1997–2003 derived from the BankScope database. I use dynamic panel data techniques (Arellano and Bond 1991; Blundell and Bond 1998).

In contrast to the literature, I do not find an effect of banks' charter value on asset risk. Further, I cannot reject that banks' charter values have a negative effect on banks' capital buffers. While this is in contrast to the empirical literature, the finding that banks' charter values have a negative effect on banks' capital buffers is in line with the prediction of Milne and Whalley (2001) for banks with high charter values: banks with high charter values can cushion negative capital shocks by retaining earnings and, hence, may hold lower capital buffers. Further, the capital buffer theory predicts the relationship between banks' charter value and banks' capital buffer to be nonlinear and the effect of charter value on asset risk to work through its effect on the impact of capital on asset risk. Hence, I test for these two nonlinearities. Finally, increasing competition has often been suggested to be behind the perceived increase in banks' instability: competition drives down banks' charter values, thereby reducing the disciplining effect of charter value on banks' risk-taking. Hence, I additionally test whether increased competition in the EU has indeed decreased banks' charter values. Yet, of all my competition measures, only the country-specific spread between lending and deposit rates has a significant effect on banks' charter value. Thus, my research lends only weak support to this hypothesis.

2 Theoretical Literature

2.1 Moral Hazard in Banking

If financial markets are assumed to be complete and depositors are perfectly informed about the failure risk of banks, the Modigliani and Miller (1958) indeterminacy principle applies. This, however, requires that owners do not have the possibility to exploit depositors. To illustrate this problem, let us assume that bank managers act in the interest of owners, who seek to maximize the value of equity. If the bank is a corporation (as most banks are), the bank owners' liabilities are limited to the amount of their investments. This means that the owners' losses are limited, but their gains are not: Once, the value of the bank is greater than the fixed amount owed to depositors, gains fully fall to owners. Due to this convex payoff function of owners, banks prefer risky to save investments.

However, if depositors are perfectly informed about the bank's investment strategies, they will demand deposit rates that fully reflect the bank's risk. Hence, shareholders cannot exploit their controlling position, and maximizing the value of equity is equivalent to maximizing the bank's total value. Thus, the value-maximizing portfolio is always chosen, and the market value of a bank is independent of its capital structure. In this framework, banks would always choose socially optimal risk levels and, hence, there would be no need for regulation.

However, the Modigliani–Miller theorem is unlikely to be applicable to banks (Sealey 1985; Baltensperger and Milde 1987): In a Modigliani–Miller world with complete markets and without any frictions, there would not be a need for the existence of financial intermediaries. However, information asymmetries between small depositors and firms make it hard for depositors to discriminate between good and bad investments. Moreover, depositors may want to invest their funds on a short-term basis, while firms seek long-term funding. These two problems in channeling funds from savers to firms are solved by the existence of banks, as banks fulfill delegated monitoring and liquidity transformation functions. However, while the delegated monitoring function renders depositors unable to monitor banks, the liquidity transformation function renders depositors unwilling to monitor banks, both giving rise to moral hazard. I will elaborate this issue in the following.

Information theories suggest that a primary rationale for the existence of banks is that they have an information advantage over depositors in monitoring firms. Hence, depositors deposit their funds at banks, thereby delegating the monitoring of firms to banks. However, the information advantage of banks also means that depositors lack the information to fully assess banks' asset risks. Thus, depositors are not able to efficiently monitor and discipline banks.

The information advantage of banks gives rise to moral hazard (Jensen and Meckling 1976): If information is not equally distributed (or alternatively, if debt holders cannot later intervene into the firm's actions and/or they cannot sign perfect contracts with the firm managers), equity holders have an incentive to pretend to invest in a low-risk asset, but after having sold bonds at a high price, to increase asset risk or to issue additional debt. In a banking context, this means that if depositors cannot intervene into the bank's activity and/or cannot observe the bank's actions, interest rates fail to fully reflect the risk of bankruptcy. Moral hazard arises, i.e., banks have an incentive to decrease capital and increase asset risk.[3]

In addition to depositors' inability to monitor banks due to the delegated monitoring function of banks, depositors may also be unwilling to monitor banks due to the liquidity transformation function of banks and, hence, the existence of deposit insurance. The liquidity transformation function of banks refers to the fact that banks take in short-term deposits and finance long-term investments (loans). While this is a function that is valuable for the process of channeling funds from depositors to firms, it, however, makes banks prone to bank runs. Deposit insurance is the only effective measure to prevent bank runs without preventing banks from fulfilling their liquidity transformation function (Diamond and Dybvig 1986). This has also been acknowledged by regulators and, hence, most countries have set up deposit insurance facilities in one or the other form.

However, if deposit insurance premia are mispriced, i.e., if they do not fully reflect the riskiness of banks' assets, the existence of deposit insurance gives rise to moral hazard:[4] Under a system of deposit insurance, depositors do not incur any risk by depositing their funds with a bank. Thus, their payoff is deterministic and independent of banks' asset risk and they lose any incentive to monitor banks' behavior. As the deposit rates demanded by the fully insured depositors do not reflect asset risk, banks will again have an incentive to increase asset risk.

This can also be seen within an option-pricing framework. The payoff of equity, C, can be interpreted as the payoff of a European call option on a bank's

---

3 See also Galai and Masulis (1976) and Green (1984), who describe the hidden action phenomenon for firms which are financed both with equity and debt.

4 For verbal discussions, see Benston et al. (1986) and Kane (1985); for analytical discussions within a state-preference framework, see Sharpe (1978), Kareken and Wallace (1978), Dothan and Williams (1980).

asset value, A, with a strike price of the same value as the liabilities, D, owed to depositors. At the maturity date, T, the value of the bank's equity, C, is

(1) $V_T(C) = \max[A - D, 0]$.

Assume the following diffusion process:

(2) $dA = RAdt + \sigma Adz$,

where R is the instantaneous expected growth rate of A, σ is the instantaneous standard deviation of the rate of return, and dz is a Wiener process.

Applying the formula derived by Black and Scholes (1973), today's value of the bank's equity is as follows:

(3) $V_0(C) = [A_0 N(d_1) - e^{rT} DN(d_2)]$,

where r is the risk-free interest rate, $d_1 = [\log(A_0 / D) + (r + \sigma^2 / 2) / T] / \sigma\sqrt{T}$, $d_2 = d_1 - \sigma\sqrt{T}$, and $N(\cdot)$ is the cumulative standard normal distribution.

The first derivates of $V_0(C)$ with respect to equity and asset risk shed light on the shareholders' incentives. Additions to capital increase the market value of bank capital at rate $\partial V_0(C) / \partial A$ and increase current owners' wealth at rate $\partial V_0(C) / \partial A - 1$. Evaluating this expression, I obtain

(4) $\partial V_0(C) / \partial A - 1 = N(d_1) - 1$.

This expression is necessarily negative. Hence, shareholders can increase the value of equity by decreasing capital. Likewise, the first derivative of the value of equity with respect to asset risk is given by

(5) $\partial V_0(C) / \partial \sigma = A_0 \sqrt{T} n(d_1)$,

where $n(\cdot)$ is the standard normal density function. This expression is necessarily positive. Hence, in addition to decreasing capital, shareholders can also increase the value of equity by increasing risk.

Within the same analytical framework, the value of the deposit insurance guarantee can be analyzed. Merton (1977) shows that the value of the deposit insurance guarantee is equal to a European put option issued on a bank's asset value, with the payment promised to the depositors being the strike price.[5]

---

5 The interests of the deposit insurance system parallel those of a private bond holder because the deposit insurance system, not the insured depositors, stands to lose in the event of a bank failure. Thus, regulatory capital requirements and other portfolio restrictions could be viewed as being similar to private bond covenants (see Black et al. (1978) for a discussion of why bank regulation is analogous to the contractual enforcement of private lending agreements by private debt holders).

Pyle (1984) shows that when deposit insurance underprices risk, as flat deposit insurance premia do, banks seeking to maximize the value of their stockholders' equity by decreasing capital and increasing asset risk attempt to maximize the option value of deposit insurance. The associated beneficial wealth effect to bank owners is often referred to as a *deposit insurance subsidy*.

However, properly priced risk-sensitive premia can eliminate the incentive to take excessive risks, since the bank will then internalize the externality associated with returns in states of bankruptcy (e.g., Rochet 1992).

Kane (1989) points out an extreme case of moral hazard due to deposit insurance in which *zombie banks* gamble for their resurrection. Insured depositors do not have an incentive to force actually insolvent banks into bankruptcy, and thus such banks can stay in business. On the contrary, depositors are even willing to provide further funding, as they do not incur any risk. The bank in turn invests these new funds in risky assets hoping to become profitable if the gamble succeeds and to leave the losses with the deposit insurance if the gamble fails.

Further, concerns are often expressed with regard to moral hazard and large banks. According to this *too-big-to-fail* argument, large banks, knowing that they are systemically important, might count on a public bailout should they become financially distressed. Thus, they have an incentive to take higher risks and, thereby, to exploit this implicit public guarantee.

2.2 Capital Regulation in Models of Moral Hazard

As bank defaults are a threat to the proper functioning of the financial intermediation process, and as the costs of bank defaults are socialized by way of the deposit insurance system, there is a widely perceived need for bank regulation among both academics and practitioners (e.g., Santos 2000). While regulators have been relying mainly on capital regulation since the process of deregulation in the 1970s, the theoretical banking literature does not unanimously praise capital requirements as the ultima ratio: Although the literature widely agrees that the probability of failure may be excessively high due to a moral hazard problem in banking, it disagrees on the effectiveness of capital regulation in reducing this moral hazard problem (e.g., Merton 1977; Kim and Santomero 1988; Keeley and Furlong 1990; Hellmann et al. 2000).[6] In the following, the discussion within the literature is outlined.

6 This section focuses mainly on the effectiveness of capital requirements in reducing the moral hazard behavior of banks due to risk-insensitive funding rates (Benston and Kaufman 1996; Buser et al. 1981). In addition to capital requirements countering the adverse effects from moral hazard, the literature seems to give three other theoretical

The bulk of the literature on bank regulation argues within a one-period framework of pure moral hazard. In such a framework, banks do not have an incentive to hold capital. Hence, when minimum capital requirements are introduced, banks hold exactly as much capital as required by the regulation. In such a framework, capital requirements do not have an effect on asset risk: choosing the highest risk portfolio is always optimal for banks, irrespective of the (required) level of capital. To limit the probability of failure in such models of moral hazard, capital requirements have to be combined with asset portfolio regulation. In contrast, risk-based capital requirements can eliminate the adverse incentive effect to the same degree as risk-based deposit insurance premia (Sharpe 1978). The question is then why capital regulation should be implemented at all if correct pricing of deposit insurance could eliminate moral hazard. However, if the insurer is unable to exactly observe bank risks, these alternative pricing mechanisms are no longer equivalent and a combination of both instruments would minimize the errors in private-sector allocation (Flannery 1991; Giammarino et al. 1993).

Furlong and Keeley (1989) contradict the view that flat minimum capital requirements do not have a moderating effect on bank risk-taking. They point out that under deposit insurance, the incentive to decrease capital-to-asset ratios and to increase asset risk depends on the level of capital and risk.[7] An increase in the capital requirement reduces the value of the deposit insurance put option, thereby reducing the incentive for banks to increase asset risk levels. Therefore, more stringent capital regulation reduces moral hazard and, thus, the probability of bank failure.

This argument, however, is not undisputed. Gennotte and Pyle (1991) show within the same option pricing framework as Furlong and Keeley (1989) that capital regulation may even increase both portfolio risk and the probability of bank failure. This result is primarily due to their assumption of decreasing returns to investment in risky bank assets. Decreasing returns can be justified by the information-intensive, nonmarketable nature of the loans in which banks typically specialize. In the Gennotte and Pyle model, an increase in the capital requirement may then induce a bank to simultaneously decrease the size of its

reasons justifying minimum capital requirements: (i) they minimize the social cost of bank failure (Berger et al. 1995); (ii) they counter the effects of market failure due to information asymmetry between banks and depositors (Miles 1995); (iii) they protect small depositors (Tirole 1994). See Santos (2000) and Bhattacharya et al. (1998) or Chapter 9 in Freixas and Rochet (1997) for an elaborate justification of capital regulation.

7 Technically speaking, the marginal value of the deposit insurance option with respect to increasing asset risk is decreasing in the capital-to-asset ratio. Likewise, the marginal benefit from decreasing the capital-to-asset ratio is decreasing in the level of asset risk incurred by the bank.

portfolio and increase its asset risk. Thus, with capital regulation, the probability of failure may even be higher than without regulation.[8] The possibility that flat capital requirements may not only be ineffective, but that they may even have an *adverse* incentive effect on banks is actually a result for which another strand of the literature is known. This strand of the literature models banks within the framework of portfolio models as opposed to the state-preference and option pricing models reviewed above.

Portfolio models assume that the bank's objective is to maximize the expectation of a von Neumann–Morgenstern utility function that describes the preferences of the risk-averse owner-manager. To break it down to a mean-variance framework, one has to either assume a quadratic utility function or a probability distribution that can be described by its first two moments. Most work done in this field assumes a single-period framework. Equity and deposits are modeled as securities with fixed returns. Thus, banks face the Markowitz portfolio selection problem with additional restrictions on the sign of the shares invested in equity (negative), deposits (negative), and assets (positive).

Building on earlier work such as Hart and Jaffee (1974) and Kahane (1977), Koehn and Santomero (1980) analyze the effect of flat capital regulation. As higher required capital levels mean a loss in the expected return, banks try to make up for this loss by investing in higher-risk assets. The magnitude of this increase in asset risk and, thus, the change in the probability of failure depends on the degree of risk aversion. For sufficiently risk-averse banks, the probability of failure declines, as the relatively low increase in asset risk is outweighed by the higher capital level. For banks with low risk aversion, insolvency becomes more likely if stricter capital regulation is imposed. Hence, capital regulation alone may fail to reduce the probability of failure. To be effective, capital requirements may have to be combined with asset regulation.

However, Kim and Santomero (1988) show that risk-sensitive capital requirements may be an effective means of preventing banks from increasing asset risk in reaction to the imposition of capital requirements. Rochet (1992) comes to the same conclusion in a similar framework. He shows that the correct risk weights are proportional to the systematic asset risk and are thus independent of individual risk aversion.

---

8 However, the expected costs imposed on the insurer are generally lower even when the probability of failure is higher, since the value of the deposit insurance put option actually decreases. Higher expected costs imposed on the insurer result only if an increase in expected deadweight liquidation costs from the higher probability of failure outweighs the decrease in the put option value. However, it may be noted that if some extreme assumptions are made about the distribution of asset returns, examples may be found in which increased capital requirements result in higher put option values and a higher probability of failure without deadweight liquidation costs.

Keeley and Furlong (1990) note that the Koehn and Santomero (1980) and the Kim and Santomero (1988) type of portfolio models neglect the deposit insurance subsidy, thereby mischaracterizing both the risk-return frontier and the shift in the risk-return frontier after an increase in capital requirements. Keeley and Furlong (1990) show that when incorporating the deposit insurance subsidy into this type of portfolio models, an increase in capital requirements does not cause banks to increase asset risk. This occurs because an increase in capital reduces the value of the deposit insurance put option, thereby reducing the incentive for banks to increase asset risk levels.

While the standard portfolio models abstract from the limited liability of banks, Rochet (1992) shows that, with the introduction of bankruptcy into these models, the relationship between the utility of shareholders and asset returns is no longer uniformly convex or concave. Given low capital requirements, banks tend to choose risky investments because of moral hazard. For higher capital requirements, this strategy is, however, deterred due to risk aversion. To avoid risk-loving behavior, capital requirements should thus be set at sufficiently high levels.[9]

2.3 The Disciplining Effect of Charter Value

The traditional banking literature reviewed above has identified a moral hazard problem at banks, as depositors, the largest source of funds, are likely to be unable and/or unwilling to monitor banks' investment strategies. This irresponsiveness of funding costs to banks' risks gives rise to moral hazard behavior on the part of banks: banks have an incentive to decrease capital-to-asset ratios and to increase asset risk, thereby increasing their probability of default and extracting wealth from the deposit insurance system. Hence, regulation has to set minimum capital requirements, thereby forcing banks to hold more capital and, thus, placing more of their own funds at risk. Whether introducing flat capital requirements increases or decreases incentives for risk-taking is not undisputed. Risk-sensitive capital requirements may in principle eliminate the adverse incentive effect on banks if the risk weights are correctly chosen.[10]

---

9 However, as Stiglitz and Weiss (1981) have noted in the context of credit rationing, in the presence of diminishing risk aversion, high capital requirements may lead to the selection of agents with lower levels of risk aversion and thus preferences for higher risk investments.

10 However, determining market-based risk weights may be difficult or even impossible. Information theories suggest that a primary rationale for the existence of banks is that they have an information advantage in monitoring firms. Hence, the market

Two implications of this theory of moral hazard in banking obviously do not correspond to the real behavior of banks. First, the theory predicts that banks do not have an incentive to hold capital in excess of the regulatory minimum. This prediction obviously contrasts with the empirical finding that banks hold a buffer above the regulatory minimum capital requirements (the "capital buffer"). For instance, in the United States, banks held a regulatory capital buffer of 4.04 percentage points at the end of the 1990s, compared to 3.3 in Germany and 3.81 in Japan (Barth et al. 2001).

Second, the theory of moral hazard in banking predicts that banks try to extract wealth from the deposit insurance system. However, empirical evidence suggests that the majority of banks do not exploit the deposit insurance system. Santomero and Vinso (1977) show that the probability of default of a typical US bank is almost negligible. Marcus and Shaked (1984) find that most US banks have such a low probability of default that they extract virtually no wealth from the deposit insurance system. They find that the riskiest five percent of banks account for virtually the total contingent liability of the deposit insurance system.

These empirical findings have inspired the literature to search for an incentive that could moderate the moral hazard behavior of banks. Such an incentive has been found in intertemporal considerations absent in the traditional moral hazard literature. Marcus (1984) shows that incorporating intertemporal considerations into banks' shareholder value maximization may have a moderating effect on moral hazard. While the theory of pure moral hazard is derived for a competitive bank in a static setting, he assumes that banks can generate rents. Such rents could result from differing monitoring costs or imperfect competition. In a dynamic setting, the present value of such expected future rents represents the bank's charter value. This charter value would be lost in the case of bankruptcy and, hence, represents the bank's private cost of failure. The higher the bank's charter value, the higher the bank's private cost of asset risk and leverage is (Suarez 1994).

Given this intertemporal, nonperfectly competitive setting, the value of the bank's equity, C, at the maturity date, T, additionally includes the bank's charter value, CV, as compared to (1):

$$(6) \qquad V_T(C) = \max[A - D + CV, 0].$$

values of bank assets are not directly observable. Thus, market-based capital regulation cannot readily be imposed on banks. A related point is the fact that a large part of bank assets are nonmarketable loans. In the light of increasing securitization, this argument may, however, lose relevance (Rochet 1992). But incorrect risk weights may allow for asset substitution and, thus, provide new risk-increasing incentives.

Assuming the same diffusion process as above (see (2)), today's value of the bank's equity now additionally includes the present value of the charter value as compared to (3):

$$(7) \qquad V_0(C) = [AN(d_1) + e^{-rT} DN(d_{2)})] + e^{-rT} CVN(d_2),$$

where d_1 and d_2 equal the same expressions as in the Merton (1977) model without charter value. Let us again analyze the bank's risk-taking incentives. Additions to capital now increase current owners' wealth at rate

$$(8) \qquad \partial V_0(C)/\partial A - 1 = N(d_1) + e^{-rT} CVn(d_2)/(A\sigma\sqrt{T}) - 1\,.$$

In contrast to the model of pure moral hazard, this expression is indeterminate. While an increase in equity reduces the probability of default and the associated loss of the charter value, it also reduces the value of the deposit insurance subsidy. For high enough charter value, *CV*, though, the first effect dominates the latter. Hence, a large charter value gives the bank an incentive to hold capital.

Further, the first derivative of the value of equity with respect to asset risk now becomes

$$(9) \qquad \partial V_0(C)/\partial\sigma = A_0\sqrt{T} n(d_1) - e^{-rT} CV d_1 n(d_2)/\sigma\,.$$

This expression is again indeterminate. The first term is the original risk incentive effect (see (5)), which is necessarily negative. The second term, representing the loss in the value of the charter due to an increased probability of default, is positive for $A > D$. When capitalization and, thus, d_1 is sufficiently large, $\partial V_0(C)/\partial\sigma$ is negative and value maximization dictates the protection of the charter value by decreasing asset risk. Further, banks with high charter values are more apt to avert risk. As the value of the charter value falls, the high asset risk strategy is, however, more apt to dominate.

In sum, charter value has a moderating effect on moral hazard incentives and, thus, gives banks the incentive to maintain reasonable capital levels and moderate risk levels also in the absence of capital regulation. In contrast, in the traditional models of pure moral hazard, capital regulation has to force banks to hold capital, which in turn may or may not moderate risk-taking incentives.

The literature has also tried to explain the increase in bank failures in the United States during the 1980s as being the result of the erosion of banks' charter value. Hellmann et al. (2000) study the effect of competition in this context in a state-preference model. They show that if competition erodes the bank's charter value, then the bank decreases capital and increases asset risk. They also show that capital requirements themselves may reduce the bank's charter value. Apart from forcing the bank to put more of its funds at risk, minimum capital requirements also have an adverse incentive effect: increased financing through expensive capital lowers profits in every period, thereby reducing the bank's charter value and, thus, the cost of bankruptcy. For shortsighted banks, i.e., banks that give less weight to periods more distant in the future, this loss in charter value is relatively small and can be outweighed by the positive capital-at-risk effect. Flat capital requirements can, thus, eliminate moral hazard for shortsighted banks. The minimum capital requirement, however, will be inefficiently high. Repullo (2004) shows that, in contrast, risk-sensitive capital requirements are an efficient means of eliminating moral hazard.

In a related model, Boot and Greenbaum (1993) argue that not only may capital regulation and competition erode charter values, the existence of a deposit insurance system may also do so. They argue that reputational considerations have become increasingly important against the background of eroding monopoly rents due to increasing competition in the banking sector. In their model, banks have an incentive to avoid risk by putting greater effort into monitoring. Better monitoring improves banks' reputation, thereby, lowering their funding costs. These funding-related reputational benefits have the same positive incentive effect as monopolistic rents in the Hellmann et al. (2000) model. This funding benefit is, however, only available to uninsured institutions whose depositors pay attention to the risks incurred. Deposit insurance, thus, has the effect of destroying the funding-related benefits of reputation. Boot and Greenbaum (1993), therefore, argue that fixed-rate deposit insurance premia might only be viable when low competition alone encourages optimal monitoring. Monopoly rents will then limit moral hazard due to deposit insurance. However, when competition increases, banks reduce their monitoring efforts and incur higher risks. Capital requirements will not have an alleviating effect on this excessive risk-taking. In contrast, they may even aggravate it.

Milne and Whalley (2001) extend these models of charter value by modeling banks' capital decisions as being an endogenous response to the imposition of minimum capital requirements. As the hypotheses tested in the later chapters can be derived from this option-pricing model, it is outlined in more detail in the following section.

2.4 A Model with Charter Value and Endogenous Capital

Milne and Whalley (2001) develop a continuous-time dynamic option-pricing model that explains the incentives of banks to hold a capital buffer above the regulatory minimum capital requirement. The model builds on the following trade-off, which banks face when deciding upon their optimum capital levels: Violating the regulatory minimum capital requirement is costly to banks, as they have to chose between fixed costs of recapitalization or the loss of their charter value when the supervisor discovers the violation. Hence, banks hold a capital buffer to cushion negative capital shocks and, thus, to protect their charter values. However, holding capital is costly compared to holding insured deposits. This trade-off determines the optimum capital buffer of banks.[11]

Milne and Whalley (2001) assume the same diffusion process for the bank's assets as Merton (1977). However in Milne and Whalley (2001), the bank keeps the amount of assets fixed.[12] The bank funds these assets by holding capital at the amount C (book equity) and raising zero-cost short-term deposits of the amount $D = A - C$. Thus, the change in capital is given by

$$(10) \quad dC = (RA - \theta)dt + \sigma dz = -dD ,$$

where θ is the dividend the bank pays to its shareholders and dz is a Wiener process.

The shareholder value is given by the present value of future dividends:

$$(11) \quad V(C) = \max_{\theta,\sigma} E\left\{\int_t^{\infty} \theta e^{-\rho\tau} d\tau\right\},$$

where V is the value function and ρ is the discount factor. ρ also represents the cost of equity relative to the zero-cost deposits. The bank aims at maximizing shareholder value subject to (10) by choosing θ and σ. Hence, banks decide on their dividend payments, thereby deciding on their capital levels, and on their asset risk. The restrictions are $\theta \geq 0$, i.e. dividends are nonnegative, and $\sigma \in [\sigma_1, \sigma_2]$, i.e., banks can set their asset risk within an interval with an exogenously given upper and lower bound.

The bank is regularly audited by a supervisor. Following Merton (1978), the audit is modeled as a stochastic Poisson process with the parameter q. qdt is the probability of an audit in each period, dt. During an audit, the supervisor compares C to the regulatory minimum capital requirement, $\tilde{C}$. If $C < \tilde{C}$, the regulator gives the bank the choice to recapitalize at the cost $\chi + \Delta C$ (where χ is the fixed cost of recapitalization) or to close down. If the bank chooses to close down, the deposit insurance system repays the depositors, and the shareholders receive nothing.

To solve this problem of dynamic stochastic optimization, standard techniques are applied. First, the Hamilton–Jacobi–Bellman differential equation is derived from arbitrage arguments:

---

11 This trade-off is an adapted version of the Kraus and Litzenberger (1973) trade-off in the corporate finance literature.

12 Hence, R is no longer the instantaneous expected growth rate of A, but the continuous expected rate of return of the assets.

$$(12)\quad \rho V = \begin{cases} \max\limits_{\theta,\sigma\in[\sigma_1,\sigma_2]} \left[\theta + (RA-\theta)V_C + 0.5\sigma^2 V_{CC}\right] & \text{if } C > \tilde{C} \\ \max\limits_{\theta,\sigma\in[\sigma_1,\sigma_2]} \left[\theta + (RA-\theta)V_C + 0.5\sigma^2 V_{CC}\right] + \\ q\left[\max\left(\max\limits_{\Delta C>\tilde{C}-C} \{V(\Delta C + C) - \Delta C - \chi\}, 0\right) - V(C)\right] & \text{if } C > \tilde{C}\,. \end{cases}$$

As long as banks hold capital in excess of the regulatory minimum, they set θ and σ such that the expected instantaneous gain in shareholder value is maximized. The expected instantaneous gain in shareholder value is given by the sum of current dividends, θ, and the expected instantaneous capital gain, $\theta + (RA-\theta)V_C + 0.5\sigma^2 V_{CC}$. If the bank falls below the regulatory minimum and the supervisor notices this violation during an audit, the bank can either recapitalize or close down. The recapitalization, ΔC, is optimal if the gain in shareholder value, $V(\Delta C + C) - V(C)$, is higher than the cost of recapitalization, $\Delta C + \chi$.

Second, the boundary and side conditions, such as continuity and smoothness of $V(C)$ at the minimum capital requirement, $\tilde{C}$, are derived from arbitrage arguments. For instance, a jump in the value function at $\tilde{C}$ would allow market participants to set up a portfolio that generates a profit with a positive probability at zero investment, thereby putting pressure on the market and, thus, eliminating the discontinuity.

Finally, the differential equation is solved subject to the boundary and side conditions. This is a tractable problem with analytical, but not always closed form, solutions. Hence, in the case of nonclosed-form solutions, numerical solutions are derived by applying the Newton–Raphson procedure.

The most important results can be summarized as follows. If the charter value, given by RA/ρ, exceeds a certain threshold, the bank aims at holding an optimum capital buffer, C^*, above the regulatory minimum in order to reduce the expected cost of violating the regulatory minimum. C^* is a function of risk, charter value, audit frequency, recapitalization costs, and the cost of equity relative to deposits. The bank adjusts towards C^* by retaining all earnings as long as $C < C^*$ and paying out all earnings as dividends if $C = C^*$. If the charter value falls below this threshold, the banks' strategy reverses completely: The bank pays out dividends at the highest rate possible for all levels of C and liquidates immediately if an audit takes place. Hence, the bank is no longer concerned with future earnings and the bank's behavior is the same as in a static model of moral hazard.

Further, the model has implications for the effect of capital on the bank's incentives for risk-taking. These are given in Figure 1, in which the model parameters are set as follows: $\tilde{C} = 0$, $\rho = 5$ percent per annum, $\sigma_1 = 0.5$,

Figure 1:
Capital, Incentives for Risk-Taking, and Charter Value

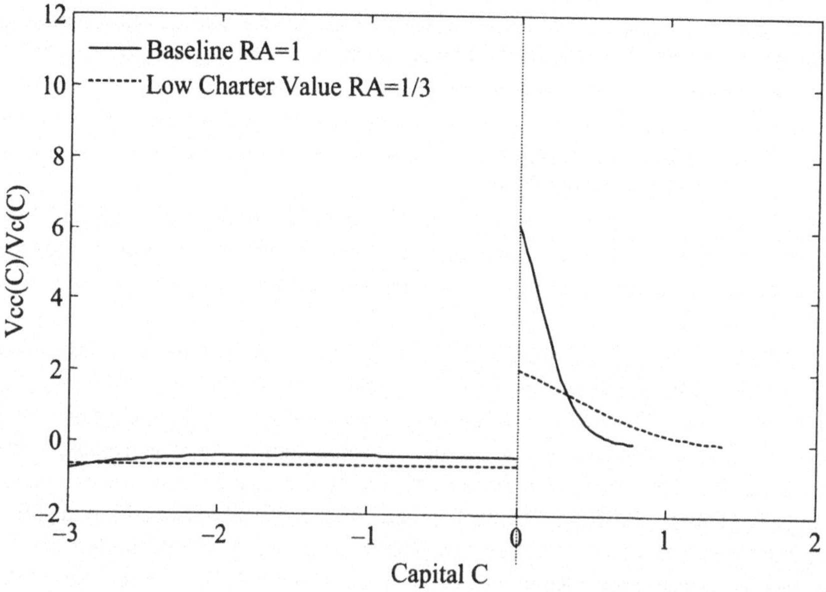

$\sigma_2 = 2$, $q = 1$, and $\chi = 6.666$. The value of σ_1 is chosen such that a bank with *RA*=1 (the baseline case, i.e., the average bank) has a negative cash flow one year in 20, which is approximately the average observed performance of OECD banks. The choice of σ_2 is arbitrary, but reflects the idea that greater increases in cash-flow uncertainty would certainly alert supervisory authorities. $q = 1$ means that, after one period, half of the population of banks will have been audited. As the bank's charter value is given by RA/ρ, the charter value equals 20 for the average bank. The cost of recapitalization χ is set such that it equals a third of the charter value. $\tilde{C}$ is set equal to zero for expositional reasons.

If $C = C^*$, shareholder value is found to equal the bank's charter value. This means that shareholders are fully insured against the future cost of liquidation or recapitalization, the cost of this insurance being the forgone dividend of $C^* - \tilde{C}$. Hence, banks are risk-neutral, as given by the Arrow–Pratt measure of absolute risk aversion $-V_{CC}(C)/V_C(C)$.

However, if $C < C^*$, banks are less than fully insured against the future cost of liquidation or recapitalization and, thus, are risk averse. Their risk aversion increases, as their capitalization, *C*, decreases towards the regulatory minimum, $\tilde{C}$. However, the increase in risk aversion is less pronounced for banks with low expected earnings, i.e., low charter values. In this situation, it is optimal for banks to choose the lowest asset risk σ_1, as there is no trade-off between asset risk and expected earnings.

If a bank's capitalization falls below the regulatory minimum, the bank becomes risk loving and gambles for resurrection: As the audit is random, it is optimal for the bank to choose the highest portfolio risk, σ_2, and, thus, to try to increase earnings in order to increase capital levels above $\tilde{C}$ before the supervisor discovers the bank's violation of the regulatory minimum. It is never optimal for the bank to recapitalize or close down voluntarily, thereby incurring the cost of liquidation or recapitalization.

If, however, the supervisor discovers the bank's violation of the regulatory minimum, the bank chooses to recapitalize if the charter value is higher than the cost of recapitalization, $\Delta C + \chi$. If the bank recapitalizes, it is always optimal to restore capital to the optimum capital level, C^*.

Further, the model has implications for the effect of the bank's charter value on its optimum capital buffer, $C - \tilde{C}$. Figure 2 shows that the relationship is highly nonlinear. For banks with high expected earnings, i.e., high charter values (as charter value is given by RA/ρ), the optimum capital buffer increases, as the charter value decreases. The reason for this is that banks with lower charter values have lower expected earnings and are, hence, less able to cushion negative capital shock out of current earnings. Hence, they need to hold higher capital buffers as an insurance against negative capital shocks. If the charter value falls to close to the fixed cost of recapitalization, the relationship is, however, reversed: the incentive to protect charter value is eroded and the optimum capital buffer falls rapidly towards zero. Only in the extreme case when the charter value is close to zero is it optimal for the bank to maximize risk and to transfer as much capital as possible to shareholders.

Finally, the model has implications for the effect of a change in the capital requirement on capital and asset risk. It finds that the optimum capital buffer is independent of the capital requirement and that the risk attitude of banks depends only on the capital buffer, not on the capital requirement. Hence, in the long-run, a change in the capital requirement does not have an effect on bank behavior: after an increase in the regulatory minimum, banks restore their optimum capital buffers to old levels and, once they have restored them, they hold the same asset risk as before.

This prediction is in direct conflict with the prediction of Hellmann et al. (2000) that an increase in capital requirements may lower charter values and, hence, increase incentives for risk-taking. These different predictions are due to capital being exogenous in Hellman et al. (2000) and endogenous in Milne and Whalley (2001). With capital being exogenous, an increase in capital requirements forces portfolio reallocations, which reduce banks' charter value, while,

Figure 2:
Optimum Capital Buffer and Charter Value

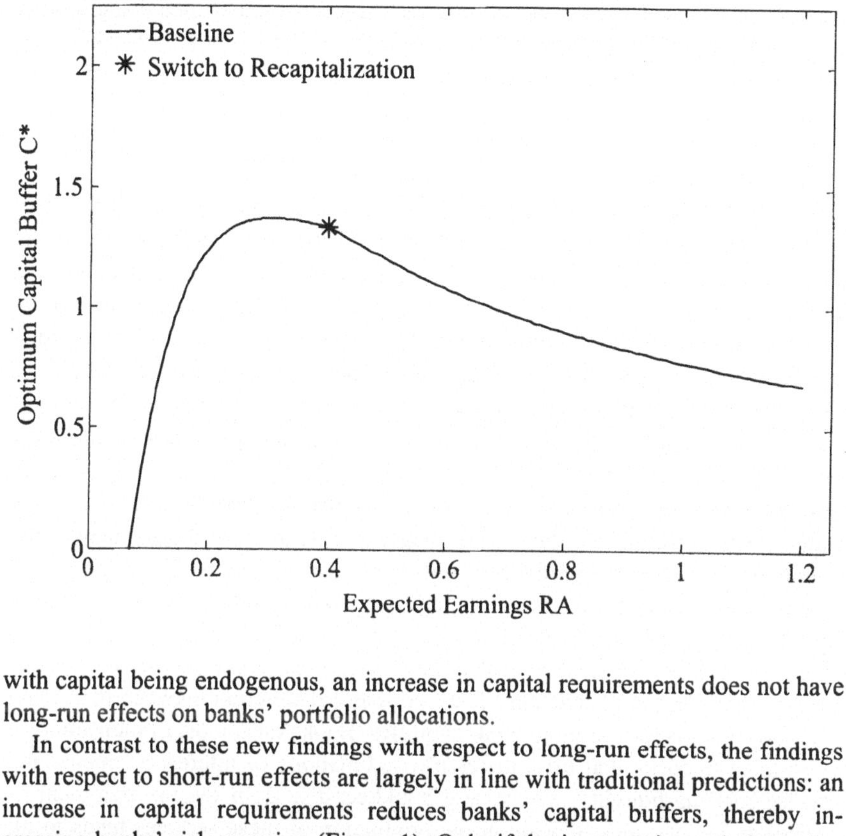

with capital being endogenous, an increase in capital requirements does not have long-run effects on banks' portfolio allocations.

In contrast to these new findings with respect to long-run effects, the findings with respect to short-run effects are largely in line with traditional predictions: an increase in capital requirements reduces banks' capital buffers, thereby increasing banks' risk aversion (Figure 1). Only if the increase in capital requirements renders banks' actual capital buffers negative do banks become risk loving.

2.5 Further Considerations

The traditional banking literature has identified a moral hazard problem at banks that derives from the irresponsiveness of funding costs to the bank's risks. Hence, banks have an incentive to decrease capital-to-asset ratios and to increase asset risk. The literature has also identified charter value as having a moderating effect on this moral hazard behavior: As banks lose their charter value in the case of bankruptcy, they try to protect it by holding adequate capital-to-asset ratios and by accepting moderate asset risks. While the main strand of the literature discusses charter value as a disciplining factor, a few studies also discuss other factors that could explain why banks deviate from the extreme risk-taking behavior predicted by the moral hazard theory. These studies are reviewed in the following.

Tax Considerations

First of all, the classical tax arguments of the corporate finance literature (Kraus and Litzenberger 1973; DeAngelo and Masulis 1980; Miller 1977) may give rise to an optimum capital structure: As interest payments are tax deductible and dividend payments are not, debt financing has a tax advantage over equity. Without bankruptcy costs, firms would, therefore, finance themselves through debt. With bankruptcy costs, increased use of debt entails the increased risk of costly bankruptcy. The optimal capital structure is then reached when the marginal tax advantage is equal to the marginal disadvantage due to bankruptcy costs. In a banking context, this means that optimum capital levels may result from trade-offs between the tax advantage of deposit financing and leverage related costs identified as the disadvantages due to reserve requirements, diseconomies of scale in the production of deposit services, and bankruptcy costs.

While this literature has interesting implications for the banking sector, Orgler and Taggart (1983) want to see it applied to banks with caution: banks and nonfinancial firms exhibit fundamental differences, which contribute to a large disparity in their degree of leverage. The first major distinction between banks and other industries is the nature of bank liabilities. Banks raise most of their funds in the form of deposits that offer different combinations of interest payments and services such as liquidity, safety, and bookkeeping. Both the tax treatment of services and economies of scale in the production of these services tends to increase the aggregate amount of deposits in equilibrium. The second major difference between banks and nonfinancial firms is the regulatory environment. Banks are more closely regulated and supervised than any other industry. This specificity reduces the agency costs borne by depositors and, thus, also leads to greater bank leverage in equilibrium.

Buser et al. (1981) explicitly refer to banks and additionally take deposit insurance into consideration. They find that optimal capital level results from the value maximization of banks that optimize over the tax advantage of deposits, bankruptcy costs, and (implicit and explicit) deposit insurance premia. As a result, banks operate at leverage levels slightly above the regulatory minimum. In this model, regulatory authorities adjust implicit costs associated with asset risk and bank capital levels in order to elicit desired changes. As a result, changes in regulation allow a bank whose capital level has increased to pursue riskier investments, and a higher risk level in effect forces a bank (through regulatory pressure) to increase its capital level. Thus, regulatory action would result in de facto risk-based capital standards, and a positive association between changes in risk and capital levels among those banks for which regulatory mandates represent binding constraints.

Information Asymmetries

Apart from this traditional corporate finance literature, another strand of the literature rationalizes optimum capital structure in the presence of information asymmetries. Several authors have shown that firms may use their capital structure as a signal of variables that are not directly observable by outsiders. Ross (1977), for instance, assumes that managers have inside information about the value of their firms. Thus, they can use the capital structure as a valid signal to convey information to investors. Accordingly, firms issue equity when they have poor prospects, and they issue debt when their prospects are good. Stated simply, a firm with poor prospects wants to share its downside risk with new claimants and, thus, prefers the issuance of stock, while a firm with good prospects does not want to share its upside "risk" with new claimants and, thus, prefers the issuance of debt.

Ross's paper and similar analyses by Leland and Pyle (1977) and Myers and Majluf (1984) suggest that capital regulation may impose a real cost on banks, as they lose their ability to signal their true value to the market. The cost is higher, the more the banks' future prospects are above average, as the market is unable to distinguish good from bad banks.

Besanko and Kanatas (1996) show that the application of the Jensen and Meckling (1976) agency problem between inside investors (i.e., owner-managers who only hold part of the equity) and outside investors (shareholders) to banking predicts an increase in asset risk after the imposition of capital requirements. In the Besanko and Kanatas (1996) model, insiders supply effort that increases the likelihood of the successful loan repayment. Solvent, but capital constrained banks are forced by the regulator to substitute equity for deposit financing, thus reducing the expected surplus available to bank stockholders. As a result of the reduction in the insiders' portion of the surplus, they provide less effort, thereby increasing asset risk. Further, the model has an interesting prediction for the reaction of share prices. The new stockholders anticipate the insiders' behavior and only pay lower prices for their shares. Thus, while recapitalization increases the amount of book capital, it decreases its value via negative incentive effects. The model suggests that the decline in the stock price is greater, the smaller the initial equity ownership of insiders. Thus, situations may exist in which the bank's issue of equity may reduce the market value of equity.

Saunders et al. (1990) study the idea that bank managers may have preferences that diverge from shareholders' interests. They argue that managers may prefer a lower level of default risk than shareholders. Managers are assumed to be compensated with risky fixed claims on the bank and to have firm- and industry-specific human capital. Thus, they have a lot to lose if they default. Their disutility is therefore increasing in asset risk and leverage. As managers will try to balance risk and leverage, portfolio risk and capital are positively related. Managerial risk-aversion might, therefore, at least act to alleviate shareholders' adverse incentive effects.

Finally, Dewatripont and Tirole (1994) follow a very different approach. Their theory builds on the standard managerial moral hazard within a firm. Thus, managers' choice of effort is not observable and, hence, managers lose the incentive to monitor banks' lending activities. Formal incentive schemes are assumed to be limited by imperfect verifiability of firm performance. Consequently, additional incentives are provided by the possibility that outsiders such as equityholders or debtholders may be externally involved in management. As managers dislike interference, discipline is best provided by promising a low level of interference in case of good performance and a high level of interference in case of a mediocre one. Since equityholders have a convex and debtholders a concave return structure and interference per assumption leads to a decrease in risk, debtholders are more prone to interfere than equityholders. Thus, control should shift from equityholders to debtholders in case of mediocre performance. As depositors lack the knowledge to take over control, another institution, for instance, the regulator, should assume this task (this is the so called "representation hypothesis").

Dewatripont and Tirole (1994) argue that capital regulation is a rough substitute for the optimum banking governance structure, as it shifts control to the regulator when the bank's solvency falls under some threshold. Managers, thus, balance their disutility of interference and their costs of monitoring the assets. As the probability of violating the minimum capital requirement is increasing in the capital requirement, managers monitor the assets better, thereby lowering asset risk. They also increase capital if shareholders are willing to recapitalize. Therefore, capital requirements are able to lower default risk.

A Theory of Bank Capital

Compared to the literature that studies firms' capital structure, the literature on banks' capital structure is underdeveloped. Diamond and Rajan (2000) are the first to present a model that simultaneously rationalizes the asset and the liability side of banks. In their model, greater capital reduces the probability of financial distress, but also reduces liquidity creation. The quantity of capital influences the amount a bank can induce borrowers to pay. Optimum bank capital, thus, trades off effects on liquidity creation, costs of bank distress, and the ability to force borrower repayment. Risk and capital are, therefore, positively related. A rise in the binding capital requirement renders the bank safer, but also increases the bank's rents, reduces the amount the bank can pledge to outsiders, and raises the bank's effective cost of capital. But in this framework, capital requirements also have more subtle effects, such as changing the bank's horizons, distributional effects, and the possibility of a bank run. Thus, capital requirements affect the flow of credit and can even make the bank riskier.

2.6 Hypotheses on ...

The moral hazard theory and the capital buffer theory have three main predictions for banks' behavior. The first prediction regards adjustments in capital and asset risk after an increase in the capital requirements. The second prediction regards the impact of business cycle fluctuations on adjustments in capital and asset risk. And the third prediction regards the impact of charter value on banks' risk-taking. The three predictions are outlined in the following subsections.

2.6.1 Capital and Risk Adjustments after an Increase in Capital Requirements

The classical models of moral hazard come to ambiguous predictions with regard to adjustments in capital and asset risk after an increase in the minimum regulatory capital requirement. While Koehn and Santomero (1980) predict that banks may increase their asset risk after a forced increase in capital, Furlong and Keeley (1989) argue that forcing banks to hold more capital has moderating effects on banks' asset risk. Further, the literature argues that risk-based capital regulation may completely eliminate adverse incentive effects. However, this result depends crucially on the correct risk weights. Incorrect risk weights may allow for asset substitution and, thus, provide new risk-increasing incentives.

The Milne and Whalley (2001) setting adds an intertemporal aspect to the discussion whether adjustments in capital and risk after an increase in the minimum regulatory capital requirement are positively or negatively related. It predicts that as long as banks' capital buffers remain positive after an increase in the regulatory minimum, banks continue to choose the lowest possible asset risk. This finding is driven by the simplifying assumption that there is no trade-off between asset risk and expected earnings. Without this assumption, the model could no longer be solved analytically. However, if a trade-off between asset risk and expected earnings is assumed, the Arrow–Pratt measure of absolute risk aversion is an indicator of banks' risk-taking incentive and the following adjustment is predicted. An increase in the capital requirement equals a decrease in banks' capital buffers. Hence, banks' risk aversion increases. If banks cannot adjust asset risk instantaneously, banks stretch the necessary decrease in asset risk over several periods. At the same time, banks rebuild capital towards optimum capital levels. The increase in capital decreases banks' risk aversion and, thus, increases optimum risk levels. As soon as actual asset risk and desired asset risk are equal again, the bank again increases both capital and asset risk until it reaches the optimum capital level, C^*. Hence, the extended Milne and Whalley (2001) model predicts that banks first increase capital and decrease asset risk after an increase in the regulatory minimum and, after a period of adjustment, as soon as capital buffers are restored to some extent, increase both capital and risk.

As the theories come to rivaling predictions for capital and risk adjustments after an increase in the regulatory minimum capital requirement, what actually happens is ultimately an empirical question. In line with the literature, I test whether banks increase or decrease risk when capital requirements force them to hold higher capital levels. In addition, I test the prediction of the capital buffer theory that adjustments in capital and risk depend on banks' capital buffer. Hence, taking as the null hypothesis that capital and risk adjustments are not interrelated, Chapter 3 tests the following hypotheses:

H_1: Adjustments in capital and asset risk are positively related for banks with high capital buffers.

H_2: Adjustments in capital and asset risk are negatively related for banks with low capital buffers.

In addition and in line with the empirical literature, Chapter 3 also tests the hypothesis that banks with low capital buffers adjust capital and risk faster than banks with high capital buffers. Hence, taking as the null hypothesis that banks with low capital buffer do not adjust capital and risk faster, Chapter 3 also tests the following hypotheses:

H_3: Banks with low capital buffers adjust capital faster than banks with high capital buffers.

H_4: Banks with low capital buffers adjust risk faster than banks with high capital buffers.

2.6.2 Capital and Risk Adjustments over the Business Cycle

In the Milne and Whalley (2001) model, the optimum capital buffer depends positively on asset risk. If banks have a higher asset risk, they need a higher capital buffer to be fully insured against a violation of the regulatory minimum. As loans are traditionally banks' most important asset category, credit risk is one of the main drivers of asset risk. To the degree that credit risk fluctuates over the business cycle, optimum capital buffers also fluctuate over the business cycle.[13] For a forward-looking bank, this leads to the following expected behavior of the capital buffer: During business cycle upturns, when banks expand lending, potential risks tend to rise and banks increase their capital buffers in order to account for these increasing risks. In business cycle downturns, when risks materialize, banks can then draw on these higher capital buffers. Hence, capital buffers are expected to fluctuate procyclically over the business cycle if banks are forward looking.

However, the finding that capital buffers fluctuate countercyclically over the business cycle can be evidence for two competing arguments. It may point to shortsightedness: banks have to increase their capital buffers during business cycle downturns to account for the increasing credit risks, as they have not built up their capital buffers during business cycle upturns. Alternatively, a negative sign may also indicate demand-side effects because increasing (decreasing) loan demand decreases (increases) banks' capital buffers in business cycle upturns (downturns).

Taking as the null hypothesis that business cycle fluctuations do not have an effect on the change in banks' capital buffers, Chapter 4 starts by testing the following alternative hypotheses:

H_5: *Banks' capital buffers fluctuate procyclically over the business cycle.*

H_6: *Banks' capital buffers fluctuate countercyclically over the business cycle.*

In the case that H_2 cannot be rejected, I will not be able to directly distinguish whether demand-side effects alone are behind the countercyclical fluctuation of capital buffers or whether supply-side effects also drive this result. Hence, I additionally test whether, in a business cycle downturn, banks with low capital buffers increase their risk-weighted assets by less than banks with high capital buffers. This would lend support to the existence of supply-side effects, as in a business cycle downturn, banks with low capital buffers may be forced to increase their capital buffers relative to banks with high capital buffers by de-

---

[13] For instance, Altman et al. (2005) show that, apart from corporate default probabilities, recovery rates also fluctuate procyclically over the business cycle.

creasing their risk-weighted assets. Hence, taking as the null hypothesis that banks with low capital buffers decrease their risk-weighted assets in a business cycle downturn by the same amount as banks with higher capital buffers, I can state my hypotheses as follows:

H_7: During business cycle downturns, banks with low capital buffers increase their risk-weighted assets by less than banks with higher capital buffers.

H_8: During business cycle downturns, banks with low capital buffers increase their risk-weighted assets by more than banks with higher capital buffers.

While H_7 lends support to the claim that there are supply-side effects and, hence, that banks are shortsighted, H_8 does not lend support to banks' shortsightedness. However, it still lends support to supply-side effects, yet in an unexpected way. It indicates that banks may face some restrictions on adjusting their loan portfolio. These restrictions may also be behind their low capitalization.

2.6.3 The Disciplining Effect of Charter Value on Risk-Taking

The literature suggests that charter value has a moderating effect on banks' incentives for risk-taking. Further, increasing competition has often been suggested to be behind the perceived increase in banks' instability (e.g., Hellman et al. 2000; Keeley 1990): competition drives down banks' charter value, thereby reducing the disciplining effect of charter value on banks' risk-taking. Hence, I test the following two hypotheses. First, I test whether competition decreases banks' charter values. Hence, taking as the null hypothesis that competition does not have an effect on banks' charter value, I test the following hypothesis:

H_9: Competition has a negative effect on banks' charter value.

In line with the empirical literature, I test whether banks with high charter values have a lower probability of default as given by higher capital (buffers) and lower asset risk. Hence, taking as the null hypothesis that charter value does not have an effect on banks' capital and asset risk, Chapter 5 tests the following alternative hypothesis:

H_{10}: Banks' charter value has a positive (negative) effect on capital (asset risk).

While a negative effect of banks' charter value on banks' capital buffers would be in contrast to the findings of the existing empirical literature, such a negative effect would be in line with the prediction of Milne and Whalley (2001) for banks with high charter values. In their model, charter value gives banks the incentive to hold a capital buffer. In this sense, charter value has a disciplining effect on banks' risk-taking. However, the effect of banks' charter value on banks' capital buffer is nonlinear: for banks with high charter values, the optimum capital buffer increases, as the charter value decreases (see Figure 2). Only if the charter value falls close to the fixed cost of recapitalization is the relationship reversed.

The problem with testing this nonlinearity is that banks' cost of recapitalization is not observable. Further, observable characteristics of banks that are highly correlated with the cost of recapitalization are hard to find. Against this background of lacking alternatives, I test, without controlling for the cost of recapitalization, whether the effect of banks' charter value on optimum capital buffers depends on the size of banks' charter value.

Further, with respect to asset risk, the Milne and Whalley (2001) model predicts that the effect of charter value on asset risk works through its effect on the impact of capital on asset risk: asset risk depends positively on capital, the positive effect being more pronounced the higher the charter value (Figure 1). Hence, I test whether the effect of banks' capital buffer on banks' asset risk depends on the size of banks' charter value.

3 Capital and Risk Adjustments after an Increase in Capital Requirements

3.1 Introduction

Since the process of deregulation of banks in the 1970s, the supervision of banks has relied mainly on minimum capital requirements. This prominent role of minimum capital requirements is particularly reflected in the Basel Capital Accord of 1988 and the current process of its revision (Basel II). However, the importance attached to capital requirements in the supervision of banks raises several questions: How do banks react to capital requirements? Do they increase capital when their capital ratio approaches the regulatory minimum? Do they also adjust risk and how are these adjustments interrelated? And finally, Do minimum capital requirements also have an effect on well-capitalized banks?

A growing branch of the theoretical literature has tried to assess the effects of minimum capital requirements on banks' capital and asset risk. This literature argues mainly within a framework of moral hazard in banking in which information asymmetries and deposit insurance shield banks from the disciplining control of depositors. This irresponsiveness of funding costs to the risk of banks gives rise to moral hazard behavior on the part of banks: Merton (1977) shows that banks have an incentive to decrease capital-to-asset ratios and to increase asset risk, thereby increasing the probability that they will default and extract wealth from the deposit insurance system. Furlong and Keeley (1989) show that—by exposing banks' own funds to potential risks—flat capital requirements can reduce, but do not eliminate, moral hazard incentives. This is mainly because the amount of capital a bank has to set aside against credit risk does not depend on the bank's asset quality. In contrast, Koehn and Santomero (1980) argue that flat capital requirements may even increase risk-taking incentives instead of lowering them: as the forced increase in expensive capital financing reduces a bank's expected return, the bank, in turn, tries to increase its profitability by investing in riskier assets. Other authors show that risk-based capital requirements can, however, eliminate risk-taking incentives if risk weights are correctly chosen (Sharpe 1978; Kim and Santomero 1988; Rochet 1992). Incorrect risk-weights may, however, allow for asset substitution and, thus, provide new risk-increasing incentives.

While the traditional theory of moral hazard predicts that banks hold just as much capital as required by regulation, another branch of the literature predicts that banks hold safety cushions above the regulatory capital requirement: banks may not be able to adjust capital or risk instantaneously due to adjustment costs or illiquid markets. Furthermore, under asymmetric information, raising equity capital could be interpreted as a negative signal with regard to a bank's value (Myers and Majluf 1984), rendering it unable or reluctant to react to negative capital shocks instantaneously. However, to breach regulations triggers costly supervisory actions, possibly even leading to a bank's closure. Hence, banks have an incentive to hold more capital than required (a "capital buffer") as an insurance against violation of the regulatory minimum capital requirement (Milne and Whalley 2001).

The moral hazard theory and the capital buffer theory have different implications for how banks adjust capital and risk after an increase in the regulatory capital requirement. The moral hazard theory predicts that, when an increase in the regulatory capital requirement forces banks to increase capital, they react by either increasing or decreasing risk (Koehn and Santomero 1980; Furlong and Keeley 1989). The capital buffer theory adds an intertemporal aspect to the discussion whether adjustments in capital and risk are positively or negatively related after an increase in the minimum regulatory capital requirement (Milne and Whalley 2001). It predicts that as long as banks' capital buffers remain positive after the increase in the regulatory minimum, banks continue to choose the lowest possible asset risk. This finding is driven by the simplifying assumption that there is no trade-off between asset risk and expected earnings. With such a trade-off, the following adjustment is predicted: an increase in the capital requirement decreases banks' capital buffers, thereby increasing their risk aversion. If banks cannot adjust risk instantaneously, banks stretch the necessary decrease in asset risk over several periods. At the same time, banks rebuild capital towards optimum capital levels. The increase in capital decreases banks' risk aversion and, thus, increases optimum risk levels. As soon as actual asset risk and desired asset risk are equal again, the bank again increases both capital and risk until it reaches the optimum capital level. Hence, the extended Milne and Whalley (2001) model predicts that banks first increase capital and decrease risk after an increase in the regulatory minimum and, after a period of adjustment when banks have rebuilt their capital buffers to some extent, increase both capital and risk.

An increasing number of empirical papers (Shrieves and Dahl 1992; Jacques and Nigro 1997; Aggarwal and Jacques 2001; Rime 2001) have tested whether banks increase or decrease asset risk when capital requirements force them to hold higher capital levels. Most papers find a positive relationship between capital and risk adjustments, indicating that banks that have built up capital have, at the same time, also increased asset risk. This finding has been interpreted as supporting the adverse incentive effects of capital requirements.

This chapter contributes to this empirical literature in four ways. First, to the best of my knowledge, this chapter is the first to test the capital buffer theory empirically. Second, while former studies define dummy variables depending on the capital ratio of banks to capture the impact of regulation, this chapter complements the standard dummy approach with a rolling window approach to overcome the problem that the definition of dummy variables is always arbitrary. In addition, the rolling window approach allows the impact of banks' capital buffer to change *continuously* depending on the capital position of the bank. In contrast, earlier research assumed a regime shift when banks crossed a threshold arbitrarily chosen by the respective author. Third, in addition to pooling the data and running 2SLS and 3SLS regressions as done in the literature, this chapter also uses dynamic panel data techniques in order to account explicitly for bank-specific effects. And fourth, as most of the literature studies US banks, this chapter contributes by providing further evidence based on non-US banks. This chapter uses a new supervisory dataset on German savings banks, collected by Deutsche Bundesbank. I focus on savings banks, as they are the largest and most homogeneous banking group in Germany.

This chapter is organized as follows. Section 3.2 specifies the empirical model, the hypotheses to be tested, and the methodology. Section 3.3 describes the data. Section 3.4 shows the regression results. Section 3.5 concludes.

3.2 The Empirical Model

As explained in the introduction, the aim of this chapter is to test the predictions of the capital buffer theory (Marcus 1984; Milne and Whalley 2001) with respect to capital and risk adjustments after an increase in the regulatory minimum capital requirement. This section describes the empirical model and the estimation strategy used here. First, it derives the empirical model. Second, it states the hypotheses to be tested. Third, it describes the empirical methodology. Fourth, it defines the measures of the variables of interest, i.e., banks' capital and asset risk. Finally, it defines the measures and the impact of the bank-specific control variables.

3.2.1 A Simultaneous Equations Model with Partial Adjustment

The capital buffer and the moral hazard theory discussed above presume that banks simultaneously determine capital and asset risk. Empirical tests of the relationship between capital and asset risk must recognize this simultaneity. Hence, I use a simultaneous equations model that builds on earlier work by Shrieves and Dahl (1992). The two equations used in the model explain adjustments in capital and risk.[14] As the observed adjustments are the result not only of the discretionary behavior of banks but also of exogenous shocks, adjustments are modeled as the sum of a discretionary component and an exogenous random shock:[15]

(13) $\Delta CAP_{i,t} = \Delta CAP^{d}_{i,t} + u_{i,t}$,

(14) $\Delta RISK_{i,t} = \Delta RISK^{d}_{i,t} + w_{i,t}$,

where $\Delta CAP_{i,t}$ and $\Delta RISK_{i,t}$ are the total observed changes, $\Delta CAP^{d}_{i,t}$ and $\Delta RISK^{d}_{i,t}$ are the endogenously determined adjustments, and $u_{i,t}$ and $w_{i,t}$ are the exogenous random shocks in capital and risk levels, respectively, for bank i in period t.

The capital buffer theory additionally assumes that banks face rigidities and adjustment costs that may prevent them from making instantaneous discretionary adjustments. Hence, I model the discretionary part of observed adjustments in capital and risk in a partial adjustment framework. This framework assumes that banks aim at establishing optimum capital and risk levels, the "target levels." Since exogenous shocks drive actual levels away from target levels, banks then adjust capital and risk to meet the target. However, full adjustment may be too costly and/or infeasible. Hence, banks adjust levels only partially towards the target levels. The partial adjustment framework assumes that the adjustment is proportional to the difference between optimum and actual levels:

---

14 Most empirical models do not try to explain absolute levels of capital and risk. Instead, they explain adjustments in capital and risk. The first reason for this is the fact that a theory of the optimal capital structure for banks does not exist. The theories referred to above, rather, have implications for how individual banks adjust capital in reaction to adjustment in risk (and vice versa). To understand the second reason for this specification, let us assume a mean-variance framework such as in Kim and Santomero (1988). Banks with relatively low risk aversion will then choose relatively high leverage and relatively high asset risk. I would, thus, expect to observe a negative cross-sectional correlation between the level of asset risk and capital ratios due to cross-sectional variation in risk preferences.

15 With respect to capital, exogenous shocks can be the result of unanticipated changes in earnings. With respect to risk, exogenous shocks are mainly the result of unanticipated economic developments, such as changes in asset or loan quality or changes in the value of loan collaterals (Hart and Jaffee 1974; Marcus 1983).

(15) $\Delta CAP^{d}_{i,t} = \alpha(CAP^{*}_{i,t} - CAP_{i,t-1})$,

(16) $\Delta RISK^{d}_{i,t} = \alpha(RISK^{*}_{i,t} - RISKP_{i,t-1})$,

where α and β are the speeds of adjustment, $CAP^{*}_{i,t}$ and $RISK^{*}_{i,t}$ are the optimum levels, and $CAP_{i,t-1}$ and $RISK_{i,t-1}$ are the actual levels of capital and risk, respectively, in the previous period.

Substituting (15) and (16) into (13) and (14) and accounting for the simultaneity of capital and risk decisions, the observed adjustments in capital and risk can be written as

(17) $\Delta CAP_{i,t} = \alpha(CAP^{*}_{i,t} - CAP_{i,t-1}) + \phi\Delta RISK_{i,t} + u_{i,t}$,

(18) $\Delta RISK_{i,t} = \beta(RISK^{*}_{i,t} - RISK_{i,t-1}) + \varphi\Delta CAP_{i,t} + w_{i,t}$.

Hence, the observed adjustments in capital and risk in period t are a function of the optimum levels and the lagged levels of capital and risk, respectively, as well as a function of exogenous shocks.

The problem with estimating the partial adjustment model presented in (17) and (18) is that the optimum capital and risk levels are not readily observable. Hence and in line with the literature, they are modeled as depending on observable bank-specific variables other than capital and risk.

3.2.2 Hypotheses

I test two different effects of the size of the capital buffer on capital and risk adjustments. First, I test the prediction of the capital buffer theory (Milne and Whalley 2001) that, after an increase in capital requirements, capital and asset risk are initially negatively related as long as capital buffers are low, while they are positively related as soon as capital buffers have recovered. Second and in line with Aggarwal and Jacques (2001), I test whether banks with low capital buffers adjust capital and risk faster than banks with high capital buffers.

Taking as the null hypotheses that adjustments in capital and risk do not impact on one another and that the (speeds of) capital and risk adjustments are equal for banks with high and low capital buffers, respectively, I can state my hypotheses in terms of the coefficients as follows:

H_1: $\phi|_{low\ capital\ buffer} < 0$ and $\varphi|_{low\ capital\ buffer} < 0$. Adjustments in capital and risk are negatively related for banks with low capital buffers.

H_2: $\phi|_{low\ capital\ buffer} > 0$ and $\varphi|_{low\ capital\ buffer} > 0$. Adjustments in capital and risk are positively related for banks with high capital buffers.

H_3: $\alpha|_{low\ capital\ buffer} > \alpha|_{high\ capital\ buffer}$. *Banks with low capital buffers adjust capital faster than banks with high capital buffers.*

H_4: $\beta|_{low\ capital\ buffer} > \beta|_{high\ capital\ buffer}$. *Banks with low capital buffers adjust risk faster than banks with high capital buffers.*

3.2.3 Methodology

In line with the literature (Shrieves and Dahl 1992; Jacques and Nigro 1997; Aggarwal and Jacques 2001; Rime 2001), I pool the cross-sectional data over all the twelve years in the observation period. The time dimension is taken into account by including dummy variables for each but one year in the observation period.

Given the simultaneous equations model of (17) and (18), the estimation strategy has to account for the endogeneity of the regressors $\Delta RISK$ and ΔCAP. In contrast to the ordinary least squares estimator, the two- and three-stage least squares (2SLS/3SLS) estimators take account of this endogeneity and, hence, produce consistent estimates.[16] 3SLS produces asymptotically more efficient estimates than 2SLS, as 3SLS uses the information that the disturbance terms in the two structural equations are contemporarily correlated (Zellner and Theil 1962). As 2SLS and 3SLS produce quite similar estimates for my sample, I present only the 3SLS estimates.

The pooled 3SLS is the standard approach taken by the empirical literature. This procedure, however, assumes that the unobserved heterogeneity, i.e., bank-specific effects, is negligible. If this assumption is incorrect, the coefficient estimates of the 3SLS regression are biased. Although I have tried to reduce the problem of unobserved heterogeneity by choosing the most homogeneous banking group in Germany, I additionally model the behavior of banks in a dynamic panel data context as a robustness check.

---

16 2SLS and 3SLS are instrumental variables approaches that use a linear combination of all exogenous and predetermined variables as instruments for the endogenous regressors. In my case, these are *SIZE*, *ROA*, *LLOSS*, CAP_{t-1}, and $RISK_{t-1}$. In the specifications where I include *dyREG**$\Delta RISK$ and *dyREG**ΔCAP among the regressors, I also use instrumental variables for these interaction terms. As a combination of all exogenous variables uses the most information possible in the construction of an instrument, 2SLS and 3SLS produce both consistent and efficient estimates. The potential bias due to bank-specific effects is addressed in the next subsection. With respect to the potential endogeneity of *dyREG*, I run robustness checks. As the results are qualitatively the same when modeling *dyREG* as an endogenous variable, I do not show the results.

Hence, I now assume that the error terms in (5) and (6) consist of a bank-specific effect and white noise, i.e., $u_{i,t} = \mu_i + \varepsilon_{i,t}$ and $w_{i,t} = \eta_i + v_{i,t}$, with $\mu_i \sim IID(0,\sigma_\mu^2)$, $\eta_i \sim IID(0,\sigma_\eta^2)$, $\varepsilon_i \sim IID(0,\sigma_\varepsilon^2)$, and $v_i \sim IID(0,\sigma_v^2)$, independent of each other and among themselves.

Unlike previous empirical studies of the Shrieves and Dahl type, I employ dynamic panel data techniques that control for the bank-specific effects μ_i and η_i. The within estimator is known to produce biased estimates when the lagged dependent variable appears as a regressor.[17] The bias will approach zero as T goes to infinity (Nickell 1981). In my case, T is relatively small compared to N. Hence, I have basically two possibilities: either to correct the Nickell bias or to use an instrumental variable approach. Monte Carlo simulations suggest that the within estimator with the Kiviet (1995) correction outperforms all other estimators in small samples (Judson and Owen 1999). Yet, this estimator has the shortcoming that standard errors are not readily available, so that bootstrapping has to be employed. Hence, as my sample is not too small, I use an instrumental variables approach in accordance with the vast majority of empirical studies.

I take the first difference of the model in order to eliminate the individual effects, μ_i, and try to find suitable instruments for $CAP_{i,t-1} - CAP_{i,t-2}$.[18] Arellano and Bond (1991) suggest a generalized method of moments (GMM) estimator that uses the entire set of lagged values of CAP_i as instruments. However, in models with endogenous regressors, using too many instruments in the later cross-sections could result in seriously biased estimates. Hence, I only use a subsample of the whole history of the series as instruments in the later cross-sections. To determine the optimal lag length of the instruments, I use the procedure suggested by Andrews and Lu (2001). I start by using the full set of moment conditions and reduce them step by step. For each set of moment conditions, I compare the Hansen test to the Hansen test of the last regression. As the Hansen test starts to increase in significance, I stop and take the last specification, which then has the highest p-value for the Hansen statistic. To further re-

---

17 Since $\Delta CAP_{i,t}$ is a function of μ_i, $CAP_{i,t-1}$ is also a function of μ_i. Hence, $CAP_{i,t-1}$, a right-hand regressor in (7), is correlated with the error term. This renders the 2SLS and 3SLS estimator biased and inconsistent. For the fixed effects estimator, the within transformation eliminates the μ_i, but $(CAP_{i,t-1} - \overline{CAP}_{i.-1})$, where $\overline{CAP}_{i.-1} = \sum_{t=2}^{T} CAP_{i,t-1}/(T-1)$, will still be correlated with $(\varepsilon_{i,t} - \bar{\varepsilon}_i)$, as $CAP_{i,t-1}$ is correlated with $\bar{\varepsilon}_i$ by construction. $\bar{\varepsilon}_i$ contains $\varepsilon_{i,t-1}$, which is correlated with $CAP_{i,t-1}$. Therefore, the fixed effects estimator is biased (Nickell 1981). Besides, the random effects GLS estimator is also biased because, before applying GLS, quasi-demeaning is performed.

18 I use the capital equation as an example in what follows. The same considerations in the choice of instruments hold for the risk equation.

duce the problem of biased estimates, I add together the columns of the optimal instrument matrix and, hence, use only one instrument for each variable and lag distance, rather than one for each time period, variable, and lag distance (Roodman 2005).

Yet, the Arellano and Bond (1991) estimator is found to have large finite sample bias and poor precision in simulation studies if the data generating process is highly persistent and if the number of time-series observations is small (Alonso-Borrego and Arellano 1996). The loss in asymptotic efficiency of the Arellano and Bond (1991) estimator intuitively makes sense, as in the light of persistence, levels are only weakly correlated with changes. This weak instrument problem is likely to be relevant for my dataset, as the pooled 3SLS estimations find low speeds of adjustment, i.e., a high persistence in the data series for capital and risk.

The high persistence and the trend in the data for *CAP* and *RISK* could also indicate a unit root. Hence, I additionally test for a unit root in *CAP* and *RISK*. Most panel unit-root tests are designed for macro panels with a long time series, though. For instance, the Im–Pesaran–Shin test assumes an individual AR(1) for each cross-section unit (Im et al. 2003). Hence, *N* individual AR(1) coefficients are estimated based on *T* observations each and, thus, the asymptotic properties of the test depend on *T* being large. However, my dataset has a short time series and a large cross-section dimension. Hence, for my dataset, the most suitable test is the Levin–Lin–Chu (LLC) panel unit-root test, which assumes that each cross-section unit shares the same AR(1) (Levin et al. 2002). This assumption seems rather restrictive at first, but I use the most general specification possible by allowing for individual effects, for time effects, for a time trend, and for serial correlation in the errors. The null hypothesis is that of nonstationarity (I(1) behavior). The test results are given in Table 1.

Table 1:
Levin–Lin–Chu (2002) Panel Unit-Root Test

Variable	Probability
Regulatory capital to total assets ratio (*CAP*)	0.000***
Risk-weighted assets to total assets ratio (*RISK*)	0.000***
Absolute capital buffer (*BUF*)	1.000
First difference of the absolute capital buffer (ΔBUF)	0.000***

Notes: The null hypothesis of the Levin–Lin–Chu Panel Unit-Root Test is that there is a common unit-root process for all individual banks. *** indicates statistical significance at the 1 percent level.

The LLC test rejects the hypothesis of a common unit root both for *CAP* and for *RISK*. Interestingly, it does not reject a common unit root for the absolute capital buffer, *BUF*, although *CAP* and *RISK* are the determinants thereof. Yet, the first difference of the absolute capital buffer is stationary again. Hence, in this chapter, I proceed with the levels of *CAP* and *RISK*, while in the next chapter, where I try to explain *BUF*, I first-difference *BUF* to account for the unit-root characteristic.

While the null hypothesis of nonstationarity is rejected, I still have to account for the high persistence in the process of *BUF* and, hence, the weak-instrument problem. For highly persistent processes, Blundell and Bond (1998) suggest using a so-called system GMM estimator. They use the fact that, where instruments are available that are uncorrelated with the individual effect, these variables can be used as instruments for the equations in levels. Hence, lagged differences of CAP_i are used as instruments for equations in levels, in addition to lagged levels of CAP_i that are used as instruments for equations in first differences. As, for my sample, the one- and two-step Blundell–Bond system GMM estimators produce quite similar estimates, I present only the two-step estimates, as they are asymptotically more efficient. However, the two-step estimates of the standard errors tend to be severely downward biased (Arellano and Bond 1991; Blundell and Bond 1998). To address this issue, I use the finite-sample correction to the two-step covariance matrix derived by Windmeijer (2005).

In order to account for the simultaneity of (17) and (18), I model $\Delta RISK$ in the capital equation and ΔCAP in the risk equation as endogenous variables. Hence, for the capital equation, I use *LLOSS* and lagged levels of *RISK* as instruments for $\Delta RISK_{i,t} - \Delta RISK_{i,t-1}$ in the difference equations and first differences as instruments for $\Delta RISK_{i,t}$ in the level equations in addition to lagged levels of *CAP* as instruments for $CAP_{i,t-1} - CAP_{i,t-2}$ in the difference equations and first differences as instruments for $CAP_{i,t-1}$ in the level equations. For the risk equation, I use *ROA* and lagged *CAP* as instruments to account for the endogeneity of ΔCAP.

I do not, however, account for the contemporaneous correlations between the two equations. Hence, my procedure is more comparable to the pooled 2SLS estimator than to the pooled 3SLS system estimator. In this sense, the name *system* GMM estimator may be misleading, as it may be confused with the pooled 3SLS *system* estimator.

3.2.4 Measures of Capital and Risk

I measure capital, *CAP*, as the ratio of total regulatory capital to total assets, TCTA. Total capital consists of all liable capital components permitted under the

German Banking Act and is comparable to the definition used in the Basel Capital Accord.

The measurement of risk is more problematic. Data to calculate more advanced measures of risk, such as value at risk, are unfortunately not available. The same holds for the volatility of the market price of a bank's assets, as savings banks are neither listed on a stock exchange, nor are most of their assets marketable. Thus and in line with the empirical literature, I measure asset risk, *RISK*, as the ratio of risk-weighted assets to total assets, *RWATA*. The rationale for this is that the allocation of bank assets among risk categories is the major determinant of a bank's asset risk.[19] However, Shrieves and Dahl (1992) point out that, apart from allocation, a bank's asset risk is also determined by the quality of loans. To account for this, I also experiment with a system of three equations in which I introduce a second risk equation based on nonperforming loans. However, the results based on the system of three equations are inconclusive and, thus, I return to a system of two equations with *RWATA* being the only risk measure. Using *RWATA* as the only risk measure is also defended by Jacques and Nigro (1997), who argue that the *RWATA* captures the allocation as well as the quality aspect of portfolio risk. And Avery and Berger (1991) argue that, in any case, *RWATA* is at least positively correlated with banks' asset risk.

Another reason why I use *TCTA* and *RWATA* as measures of capital and asset risk, respectively, is the following. The Basel I minimum capital requirement is defined as the ratio of total capital to total risk-weighted assets. In order to comply with the 8 percent regulatory minimum, banks can adjust the numerator and/or the denominator of the Basel capital ratio. In the definitions chosen in this chapter, ΔCAP reflects adjustments in the numerator (capital), while $\Delta RISK$ reflects adjustments in the denominator (risk-weighted assets). Hence, *CAP* and *RISK* can be interpreted as the two variables banks have at their discretion to manage their Basel capital ratio. This interpretation is logically independent of whether or not *RISK* is a correct measure of asset risk. The interpretation as a measure of asset risk is correct only if the risk weights correctly reflect the economic risk of the assets. Empirical evidence, however, shows that the Basel I risk weights and the economic risk of an asset are only weakly correlated (Avery and Berger 1991). Yet, regardless of whatever additional risk measures they use in their daily business, all banks still have to obey regulatory rules. Thus, they have to manage their "regulatory" risk. Despite the shortcomings of RWATA as a measure of asset risk and in line with the literature, I interpret *RISK* as a measure of asset risk in the remainder of the chapter. However, skeptical readers might want to replace "asset risk" with "risk-weighted assets" in what follows.

---

19 Support for this measure can be found in Chessen (1987) and Keeton (1989).

3.2.5 Variables Affecting the Optimum Levels of Capital and Risk

The partial adjustment model presented in (17) and (18) above suggests that banks aim at establishing optimum capital and risk levels. These optimum levels are not readily observable. They depend on other variables specific to the individual bank. For comparability reasons, I use variables similar to those used in the literature. In the following, these explanatory variables and their expected impact on the observed adjustments in capital and risk are presented. The exact variable definitions are also given in Table A1 in Appendix 1 of this chapter.

Size may have an effect on a bank's target capital level, as the size of a bank is an indicator of the bank's access to capital. German law prohibits savings banks from raising Tier 1 capital via equity markets. Hence, savings banks depend on retained earnings and capital injections from their public owners. However, big savings banks use subordinated debt issues to raise Tier 2 capital (see below). Thus, larger savings banks are more flexible in raising capital, which renders their optimum capital levels smaller than the optimum capital levels of smaller banks. Further, economies of scale in screening and monitoring have the same implications for the effect of size on the optimum capital level: unexpected losses are in part due to asymmetric information between banks and their borrowers. Screening and monitoring reduce this asymmetry, but are costly and, thus, banks balance the cost and gains from these activities against holding expensive capital. If there are economies of scale in screening and monitoring, large banks should hold relatively less capital and instead undertake more monitoring and screening. In addition, size may also have an effect on a bank's optimum risk level, as the size of a bank affects its investment opportunities and diversification possibilities. The sign of this effect is, however, undetermined (Acharya et al. 2006). Hence, I include the natural log of total assets, *SIZE*, in the capital and risk equations to capture size effects.

Savings banks rely mainly on retained *earnings* to increase capital. Hence, I include the bank's return on assets, *ROA*, in the capital equation as a measure of profits with an expected positive sign.

Current loan losses affect the ratio of risk-weighted assets to total assets, as they reduce the nominal amount of risk-weighted assets. Building on Rime (2001), I approximate these losses, *LLOSS*, with the ratio of new net provisions to total assets and include *LLOSS* in the risk equation with an expected negative sign.

In addition, I include dummy variables in the capital and risk equation. First, the savings banking sector has seen a *merger* wave in the last years. When a savings bank faces financial troubles, it is merged with a healthy bank in the neighborhood. I therefore expect to observe a decrease in capital and an increase in risk for the takeover bank in the year of the merger. In order to capture these effects, I include a merger dummy variable, *dyMERGER*, in the regression equations which is unity in the year a savings bank takes over another bank and zero otherwise. Second, I also include time dummy variables that capture year-specific macroeconomic effects.

Apart from including time dummy variables, I also experiment with including macroeconomic variables directly. As savings banks are the main lenders to local firms, I expect local firm insolvencies to have a negative impact on capital and a positive impact on risk. Hence, I approximate these local insolvencies with the ratio of firm insolvencies to the total number of firms in the German state where the savings bank is located. However, firm insolvencies turn out to be insignificant throughout all of my specifications. Hence, I do not show these regression results. Apart from firm insolvencies, I also experiment with GDP. However, the results with respect to capital and risk adjustments do not change when including GDP in the regression. Further, Chapter 4 treats the impact of GDP on banks' capital buffers, capital, and risk in extension. Hence, the results are not quoted in this chapter.

Last but not least, I have to find a criterion to distinguish between banks with high capital buffers and banks with low capital buffers. The criterion used by the majority of the literature builds on the capital buffer measured as the absolute difference between the actual Basel capital ratio and the 8 percent regulatory minimum capital requirement (the "absolute capital buffer").

In order to test the predictions of the capital buffer theory, another criterion that is based on the standardized capital buffer is, however, more appropriate. Let us assume the existence of two banks, A and B, both having the same absolute capital buffer. However, Bank A's capital buffer is less volatile than Bank B's capital buffer. Hence, Bank A is better insured against a possible violation of the regulatory minimum in spite of both banks' holding the same absolute capital buffer. To capture this effect, I divide the absolute capital buffer by the bank-specific standard deviation of the absolute capital buffer (the "standardized capital buffer"). Based on this criterion, I use a capitalization dummy, *dyREG*, that is unity if a bank has a standardized capital buffer equal to or less than a certain cutoff value and zero otherwise. I name this dummy *dyREG*, as it captures the impact of banks' regulatory capital buffer. As a cutoff value, I use the 10th percentile of the standardized capital buffer in the pooled sample. As a robustness check, I also use the 25th percentile and the median of the standardized capital buffer. As a further robustness check, I also define a capitalization dummy on the basis of the absolute capital buffer. However, in contrast to the regression results based on the standardized capital buffer, the regression results based on the absolute capital buffer turn out to be inconclusive and, thus, are not further referred to.

In order to test my hypotheses on the coordination of capital and risk, I interact *dyREG* with *ΔRISK* and *ΔCAP* and additionally include these interaction terms, *dyREG*ΔRISK* and *dyREG*ΔCAP*, in the regression. Analogously, I interact *dyREG* with CAP_{t-1} and $RISK_{t-1}$ and additionally include these interaction terms, $dyREG * CAP_{t-1}$ and $dyREG * RISK_{t-1}$, in the regression to test whether banks with low capital buffers adjust capital and risk faster than banks with high capital buffers. Further, I also allow the intercept to differ for banks with low capital buffers and, hence, I additionally include *dyREG* in the regression.

According to the discussion above, the empirical model is then specified as follows:

$$(19) \quad \begin{aligned} \Delta CAP_{i,t} &= \alpha_0 + \alpha_1 dyREG_{i,t} + \alpha_2 ROA_{i,t} + \alpha_3 SIZE_{i,t} \\ &+ \alpha_4 \Delta RISK_{i,t} + \alpha_5 dyREG_{i,t} \Delta RISK_{i,t} - \alpha_6 CAP_{i,t-1} - \alpha_7 dyREG_{i,t} CAP_{i,t-1} \\ &+ \alpha_8 dyMERGER + time\,dummies + u_{i,t}, \end{aligned}$$

$$(20) \quad \begin{aligned} \Delta RISK_{i,t} &= \beta_0 + \beta_1 dyREG_{i,t} + \beta_2 LLOSS_{i,t} + \beta_3 SIZE_{i,t} \\ &+ \beta_4 \Delta CAP_{i,t} + \beta_5 dyREG_{i,t} \Delta CAP_{i,t} - \beta_6 RISK_{i,t-1} - \beta_7 dyREG_{i,t} RISK_{i,t-1} \\ &+ \beta_8 dyMERGER + time\,dummies + w_{i,t}. \end{aligned}$$

3.3 Data Description

The German banking system is highly fragmented and heterogenous. Hence, coefficients may not be stable across the different banking groups. To avoid this problem, I consider savings banks only. Savings banks are the largest banking group in Germany, representing 36 percent (48 percent) of the balance sheet total of all banks (universal banks) (according to the Bundesbank Banking Statistics).

In the following, I first describe how I clean the data. I then provide descriptive statistics for the dataset used in the remainder of the chapter. And finally, I provide statistics and arguments in favor of savings banks being suitable to test the capital buffer theory.

Apart from focusing on savings banks only, I further clean the dataset to have an even more homogeneous group of banks. First of all, I exclude the central giro institutions from the sample, as their portfolio is very different from those of local savings banks.[20] The remaining dataset still shows several outliers, which turn out to have a high impact on my regression results. Instead of dropping single outliers arbitrarily, I drop all observations outside the 1st and 99th percentile of my endogenous variables ΔCAP and $\Delta RISK$.[21] While this procedure is adequate for the pooled regressions, it causes problems in the dynamic panel regressions, as it creates missing values in the time dimension. Hence, for the dynamic panel regressions, I drop a bank entirely if it has observations outside the 1st and 99th percentile.

As a result, my sample for the pooled regressions consists of about 570 local German savings banks over the 1993–2004 period, as 1993 is the earliest year for which data on risk-weighted assets are available. 2004 is the latest year for which data is currently available. For the pooled regressions, the observations for 1993 are lost due to the dynamic specification. For the dynamic panel regressions, another year is lost due to first-differencing and instrumenting. The data were kindly provided by Deutsche Bundesbank, which collects bank-level data as part of its supervisory function.

Appendix 1 provides some descriptive statistics of the variables. Table A2 shows that, throughout the observation period, the savings banks under review held an average capital buffer of 2.48 standard deviations above the 8 percent regulatory minimum. The lowest (highest) capital buffer in the sample was –1.60 (49.82).[22] Excluding the lowest and the highest 5 percent from the sample leaves the capital buffers ranging between 0.43 and 4.61. Further, Table A3 gives the mean values of the variables for each year. The mean values show that *CAP* and *RISK* exhibit a positive trend over the observation period. As will be seen below, this trend causes estimation problems in the dynamic panel regressions.

Table A4 gives the pairwise correlations between the variables based on the pooled sample. Two findings are worth mentioning. First, absolute and standardized capital buffers are not as highly correlated as may be expected, the correlation being only 0.39. This low correlation justifies the classification of banks according to their standardized capital buffer, as the absolute capital buffer is likely to render a very different ranking. Second, both the correlation between

20 Private savings banks (so-called independent savings banks) are also excluded from the sample, as they are not subject to regional investment restrictions and therefore have more degrees of freedom in deciding upon their loan portfolio.

21 ΔCAP ranges between –0.0254 and 0.0306 before the cleaning procedure and between –0.0068 and 0.0131 afterwards, while $\Delta RISK$ ranges between –0.3250 and 0.3380 before the cleaning procedure and between –0.0548 and 0.0729 afterwards.

22 The sample contains 27 observations with negative capital buffers. While these banks may be under the control of supervisors and, hence, may not be able to take deliberate capital and risk decisions, dropping these observations from the sample does not change the regression results.

levels of *CAP* and *RISK* and the correlation between first differences of *CAP* and *RISK* are positive. This finding stands in contrast to Shrieves and Dahl (1992), who—based on data for US banks—find a negative correlation between levels and a positive correlation between first differences. They argue that the negative correlation between levels is due to cross-sectional variation in risk preferences: banks with low risk aversion choose low capital ratios and high risk, whereas banks with high risk aversion choose high capital ratios and low risk. However, in this chapter, savings banks were deliberately chosen, as they are a rather homogeneous group of banks. Hence, the absence of cross-sectional variation in risk aversion is not surprising.

Finally, Table A5 gives the mean values of the variables separately for banks with high and low capital buffers. I use three classification criteria. The criterion used the most in this chapter is whether banks have capital buffers below or above the 10th percentile, which is at 0.7413 standard deviations above the 8 percent regulatory minimum for my sample. As a robustness check of my regression analysis, I also use the median (25th percentile) of the standardized capital buffer, which is at 2.4372 (1.4921) standard deviations.

In the remainder of this subsection, I contradict potential critics that argue that the predictions of the capital buffer theory cannot be tested based on savings banks. These critics may argue that, first, savings banks cannot deliberately adjust their capital buffer, as they cannot raise equity at the capital markets. And second, they have different incentives than private banks. In particular, they do not aim at maximizing profits. In the following, I contradict this view and argue that, despite the institutional characteristics of savings banks, the predictions of the capital buffer theory can indeed be tested using German savings banks.

First, German savings banks can and do adjust their Basel capital ratio. Banks in Germany, as in most other industrialized countries, have to comply with the Basel Capital Accord. Hence, they have to hold regulatory capital of at least 8 percent of their risk-weighted assets. To manage their Basel capital ratio, banks can adjust regulatory capital and/or risk-weighted assets.

Regulatory capital consists of core (Tier 1) and supplementary (Tier 2) capital. Hence, banks can adjust both components subject to the condition that Tier 2 capital is only eligible up to the same amount as Tier 1 capital. With respect to raising Tier 1 capital, German savings banks are restricted, as they cannot raise equity through external capital markets. In principle, the municipalities as the owners of the respective local savings bank can increase equity. However, in practice, they rarely do so due to budget constraints. Hence, savings banks can only increase Tier 1 capital by retaining earnings. However, private banks also rely mainly on retained earnings to increase Tier 1 capital.

With respect to Tier 2 capital, savings banks can—and very actively do—issue subordinated debt. German savings banks are among the main players in European subordinated debt markets (Basel Committee on Banking Supervision 2003).

Descriptive statistics also provide evidence that savings banks adjust Tier 1 and Tier 2 capital similarly to private banks. An ideal benchmark is given by German cooperative banks as they have similar portfolio structures and compete directly with local savings banks. But in contrast to savings banks, they are privately organized.

Table 2 shows that, for both banking groups, Tier 2 capital amounts to about 50 percent of Tier 1 capital. In this sense, the average bank has scope to increase its Basel capital ratio by increasing Tier 2 capital. Indeed, only 1.75 percent of savings banks and 0.95 percent of cooperative banks are constrained in this sense, as they hold Tier 2 capital in equal amounts as Tier 1 capital. Table 2 also shows that, while savings banks adjust both Tier 1 and Tier 2 capital over time, the adjustment is higher for Tier 2 capital (with respect to its mean) as given by the coefficient of variation. Further, Table 2 shows that the adjustment is similar for savings banks and cooperative banks.

With respect to risk-weighted assets, banks can adjust the total amount of investments and/or the relative investment in asset classes with different risk weights (e.g., increase government lending to the expense of corporate lending). These two adjustments are reflected in the variation of total assets and the average risk weight, respectively. Table 2 shows that savings banks adjust both total assets and their average risk weight over time. Again, the variation over time is similar for savings banks and for cooperative banks.

Table 2:
The Basel Capital Ratio of German Savings and Cooperative Banks and Its Components, 2003

	Savings banks		Cooperative banks	
	Mean	Average coef. of variation	Mean	Average coef. of variation
Basel capital ratio	10.86	0.09	11.41	0.10
Tier 1 capital	58.68	0.22	10.84	0.25
Tier 2 capital	31.24	0.37	5.66	0.31
Total assets	1,473.33	0.16	244.01	0.18
Average risk weight (*RISK*)	0.55	0.07	0.61	0.06

Notes: The Basel capital ratio is defined as regulatory capital divided by total risk-weighted assets in percent. Tier 1 capital, Tier 2 capital, and total assets are given in millions of euros. Average risk weight is defined as total risk-weighted assets divided by total assets. Mean refers to means within the respective banking group. Average coefficient of variation refers to the average coefficient of variation of banks over time.

Hence, German savings banks do adjust Tier 1 capital, Tier 2 capital, and (risk-weighted) assets over time in order to manage their regulatory capital ratio. Both the adjustment of the single components as well as of the Basel capital ratio is similar for public savings banks and for private cooperative banks.

Second, German savings banks have incentives similar to those of private banks. German local savings banks are owned by the local municipalities, which were fully liable for the local savings banks' liabilities due to the legal institutions of "Anstaltslast" and "Gewährträgerhaftung" during the observation period. However, in practice, municipalities are not in a financial position to settle the debtors' claims where local savings banks are insolvent. Hence, insolvencies are normally settled by merging the insolvent savings bank with a healthy savings bank in the respective region. Therefore, while municipalities are fully liable in principle, they are liable only to a limited extent in practice. Limited liability implies a convex payoff structure, which gives rise to potential moral hazard behavior.

Further, although savings banks are required to follow economic principles, profit maximization is not an explicitly defined objective.[23] Their public mandate is enshrined in the savings bank law of the relevant federal state government and comprises general tasks like guaranteeing banking services in all regions, fostering savings, supporting the local economic structure, or acting as the local authorities' house bank (Oellerking and Holzgrabe 1990). Yet, they seem to aim at maximizing profits (Hartmann-Wendels et al. 1998). This is not surprising though, as in the long run, they have to make profits to survive. Also, as public coffers are empty, municipalities would clearly like to see savings banks make profits that can be distributed to the municipality.

Apart from the owners' incentives, the management's incentives are also similar for savings bank and for private banks. When a savings bank is insolvent, the supervisory authority takes over the control of the bank and dismisses the management. This is the same distress resolution procedure as with a private bank.

In sum, German savings banks can and do adjust their Basel capital ratio and they have similar incentives as private banks. Hence, the capital buffer theory can indeed be tested using German savings banks, despite their institutional particularities.

---

23 See, for instance, Section 3(3) of the Savings Bank Act of the State of North Rhine-Westphalia.

3.4 Regression Analysis

This section presents the regression results. In order to test the hypotheses posited in Section 2.2, I first employ a dummy variable approach, allowing the coefficients of interest to vary depending on whether banks hold high or low capital buffers. In line with the literature, I begin by employing pooled three-stage least squares regressions that disregard bank-specific effects. Second, I use a subsample approach, allowing *all* coefficients to vary depending on whether banks hold high or low capital buffers. Third, I use a rolling window approach, allowing all coefficients to vary continuously depending on the size of banks' capital buffers. Fourth and finally, as a robustness check, I employ dynamic panel regressions that account for the unobserved bank-specific effects.

3.4.1 Dummy Variable Approach in a Pooled Regression

In this subsection, I present the pooled 3SLS estimates for (19) and (20), accounting for the effect of banks' capitalization by including capitalization dummy variables. The results of estimating the simultaneous system of (19) and (20) are given in Table 3. I show three different specifications that vary in the way the regulatory variable affects the capital and risk decisions of banks. Moving from the least complex to the more advanced approaches, Specification 1 allows adjustments in capital and asset risk to depend on whether banks have low or high capital buffers (inclusion of *dyREG*). Specification 2 additionally allows for higher speeds of adjustment in capital and asset risk (inclusion of $dyREG*CAP_{t-1}$ and $dyREG*RISK_{t-1}$, respectively). Finally, Specification 3 additionally allows for differences in the coordination of capital and risk adjustments (inclusion of $dyREG*\Delta RISK$ and $dyREG*\Delta CAP$, respectively).

Table 3 shows that all of the variables are significant in at least one specification. As expected, the return on assets, *ROA*, has a statistically highly significant and positive effect on capital. Hence, savings banks seem to rely strongly on retained earnings in order to increase capital. This finding is also in line with the findings of other empirical papers (Aggarwal and Jacques 2001; Rime 2001). Loan losses, *LLOSS*, have the expected significant and negative effect on asset risk only in Specification 2. The insignificance of *LLOSS* in most specifications is in line with the finding of Rime (2001), who cannot find a significant effect of loan losses on risk-weighted assets for Swiss banks. In contrast, Aggarwal and Jacques (2001) find that US banks with higher loan loss provisions have higher risk-weighted assets. Bank size (*SIZE*) has a negative effect on both capital and asset risk and is significant in most specifications. The negative effect on capital is in line with the empirical literature and means that larger banks increase capi-

Table 3:
Pooled 3SLS Estimates for Specifications with Regulatory Dummy and Interactions Terms, 1994–2004

a) Capital Equation

	1	2	3
Dependent variable	ΔCAP	ΔCAP	ΔCAP
dyREG	–0.0026***	0.0012	0.0030**
	(10.70)	(1.08)	(2.45)
ROA	0.2229***	0.3030***	0.2138***
	(6.33)	(7.36)	(5.52)
SIZE	–0.0000	–0.0003***	–0.0000
	(0.25)	(3.65)	(0.21)
$\Delta RISK$	0.0023	–0.1674***	0.0159
	(0.08)	(6.04)	(0.47)
*dyREG**$\Delta RISK$			–0.1974***
			(4.68)
CAP_{t-1}	–0.0335***	–0.0619***	–0.0302***
	(4.40)	(7.85)	(3.58)
*dyREG**CAP_{t-1}		–0.0694***	–0.0807***
		(2.80)	(3.56)
dyMERGER	0.0002	0.0013***	0.0001
	(0.45)	(3.17)	(0.40)
Constant	0.0048***	0.0118***	0.0046***
	(3.04)	(6.86)	(2.68)
Year dummies	yes	yes	yes
# Observations	5,909	5,909	5,909

Notes: The capital equation (Panel a) and the risk equation (Panel b, below) are estimated simultaneously using the three-stage least squares procedure. The dependent variable is $\Delta CAP_{i,t}$. *CAP* is defined as total regulatory capital over total assets. *dyREG* is a dummy variable that is unity if the bank has a standardized capital buffer equal to or less than the 10th percentile and zero otherwise. *ROA* is the return on assets. *SIZE* is defined as the natural log of total assets. *RISK* is defined as total risk-weighted assets over total assets. *dyMERGER* is a dummy variable, which is unity in the year a bank has taken over another bank and zero otherwise. Δ indicates the first difference. ***, **, and * indicate statistical significance at the 1, 5, and 10 percent level, respectively, in a two-tailed *t*-test.

Table 3 continued

b) Risk Equation

	1	2	3
Dependent variable	$\Delta RISK$	$\Delta RISK$	$\Delta RISK$
dyREG	0.0132***	0.0201***	0.0315***
	(6.71)	(3.75)	(5.12)
LLOSS	0.0378	–0.1259**	0.0479
	(0.54)	(2.03)	(0.66)
SIZE	–0.0013***	–0.0014***	–0.0012***
	(4.41)	(4.74)	(3.97)
ΔCAP	3.3232***	0.6182	3.5195***
	(5.76)	(1.33)	(5.82)
$dyREG*\Delta CAP$			–6.4938***
			(6.46)
$RISK_{t-1}$	–0.0172***	–0.0169***	–0.0154***
	(6.07)	(6.31)	(5.10)
$dyREG*RISK_{t-1}$		–0.0268***	–0.0266**
		(2.72)	(2.49)
dyMERGER	0.0066***	0.0067***	0.0059***
	(3.74)	(3.88)	(3.22)
Constant	0.0285***	0.0393***	0.0253***
	(4.18)	(6.11)	(3.58)
Year dummies	yes	yes	yes
# Observations	5,909	5,909	5,909

Notes: The capital equation (Panel a) and the risk equation (Panel b) are estimated simultaneously using the three-stage least squares procedure. The dependent variable is $\Delta RISK_{i,t}$. *RISK* is defined as total risk-weighted assets over total assets. *dyREG* is a dummy variable that is unity if the bank has a standardized capital buffer equal to or less than the 10th percentile and zero otherwise. *LLOSS* is defined as new provisions over total assets. *SIZE* is defined as the natural log of total assets. *CAP* is defined as total regulatory capital over total assets. *dyMERGER* is a dummy variable, which is unity in the year a bank has taken over another bank and zero otherwise. Δ indicates the first difference. ***, **, and * indicate statistical significance at the 1, 5, and 10 percent level, respectively, in a two-tailed *t*-test.

tal by less than smaller banks. A possible explanation for this is that larger savings banks have access to the bond market. Hence, the optimum capital buffer (measured relative to total assets) of larger banks is smaller than the optimum capital buffer of smaller banks because larger savings banks have access to alternative funds. Another possible explanation is that large banks have economies of scale in screening and monitoring and, hence, they prefer to undertake more monitoring and screening than hold high levels of expensive capital. However, the negative effect of bank size on risk is in contrast to most other papers and means that larger banks have lower optimum risk levels than smaller banks. An alternative explanation is that large savings banks hold higher portfolio shares of shares and bonds, which tend to have lower risk-weights than loans.

Specification 1 shows that the parameter estimate of $\Delta RISK$ in the capital equation is insignificant, while the parameter estimate of ΔCAP in the risk equation is significant and positive. This means that banks increase risk when capital increases. However, they do not adjust capital when risk changes. In contrast, Specification 2 shows that, when controlling for different speeds of adjustment for banks with low capital buffers, the parameter estimate of $\Delta RISK$ in the capital equation becomes significant and negative, while the parameter estimate of ΔCAP in the risk equation becomes insignificant. The picture becomes more coherent, though, when I allow for differences in the coordination of capital and risk adjustments (Specification 3). I discuss these results in more detail when I talk about the impact of banks' capital buffer on capital and risk adjustments (see below).

Further, Specification 1 shows that the parameter estimates of lagged capital and risk are statistically highly significant. They show the expected negative sign and lie in the required interval of $[0;-1]$. Hence, they can be interpreted as speeds of capital and risk adjustment. The speed of capital adjustment (0.0514) is almost four times higher than the speed of risk adjustment (0.0197). The estimated speeds of adjustment mean that shocks to capital and risk are halved after 20 and 40 years, respectively. Hence, the estimated speeds of adjustment are very slow, mirroring the fact that the average bank built up capital and risk over the observation period. If I shorten the time series by dropping data for 2003 and 2004, the estimated speeds increase to about 0.1 for capital and 0.03 for risk.

Moreover, specifications 1–3 show that mergers, *dyMERGER*, have a positive effect on both capital and risk adjustments. However, in the capital equation, the estimated coefficient of *dyMERGER* is not significant in two out of three specifications. While the positive effect on *RISK* is intuitive (the risk-weighted assets of an acquiring bank increase when taking over a problem bank), the positive effect on *CAP* is counterintuitive. As bigger banks have lower capital (and higher risk), a plausible reason for the positive effect may be that the statistics indicate the bigger bank is the acquirer.

Specifications 1–3 provide interesting results with respect to the impact of banks' capital buffer on the adjustment of capital and risk. In Specification 1, I control for banks' capital buffers by simply including the capitalization dummy *dyREG*. I find that, contrary to expectations, banks with low capital buffers increase capital by less, and risk by more, than banks with high capital buffers. However, when I control for the impact of banks' capital buffers on the speed of adjustment and the coordination of capital and risk adjustments in Specification 3, *dyREG* is found to have the expected significant and positive effect on capital.

With respect to the impact of banks' capital buffers on the speed of capital adjustment, specifications 2 and 3 show that the interaction term $dyREG * CAP_{t-1}$ is negative and significant. The estimated coefficients indicate that banks with low capital buffers adjust capital twice (Specification 2) or even almost four times as fast (Specification 3) as banks with high capital buffers. Further, the interaction term $dyREG * RISK_{t-1}$ is also found to be significant, indicating that banks with low capital buffers adjust risk almost three times as fast as banks with high capital buffers.

Finally, Specification 3 provides interesting results with respect to the impact of banks' capital buffer on the coordination of adjustments in capital and risk. In accordance with hypotheses H_1 and H_2, I expect that for banks with low capital buffers, adjustments in capital and risk will be negatively related, while for banks with high capital buffers, adjustments in capital and risk will be positively related. Therefore, adjustments in capital and risk are expected to have a negative (positive) sign in both equations for banks with low (high) capital buffers.

The estimation results support my expectations. I find that the estimated coefficient of $\Delta RISK$ is insignificant, while the estimated coefficient of ΔCAP is significant and positive. While the one-way coordination is surprising (I expected the coordination to be two-way), the findings nevertheless indicate that capital and risk adjustments are positively correlated for banks with high capital buffers. Further, I find that the estimated coefficient of $dyREG*\Delta RISK$ is significant and negative, while the estimated coefficient of $dyREG*\Delta CAP$ is significant, negative, and larger (in absolute terms) than the coefficient of ΔCAP. This finding indicates capital and risk adjustments are negatively correlated for banks with low capital buffers.

The standardized beta coefficients show that the coefficients are also economically significant. Banks with high capital buffers react to an increase in capital of one standard deviation by increasing asset risk by 0.54 standard deviations, while banks with low capital buffers react by decreasing asset risk by 0.45 standard deviations. In addition, banks with low capital buffers react to a decrease in asset risk of one standard deviation by increasing capital by 1.30 standard deviations.

The one-way coordination for banks with high capital buffers may be explained by the fact that adjustments in capital are more costly than adjustments in risk. Hence, banks with a relatively large safety buffer adjust risk in accordance with capital, but not vice versa. In contrast, banks with a low safety buffer are forced to coordinate capital and risk adjustments in both directions.

My findings with respect to the impact of banks' capitalization on the speed and coordination of capital and risk adjustments are confirmed when using the 25th percentile and the median value instead of the 10th percentile as threshold values to distinguish between banks with high and low capital buffers. The results for the two alternative thresholds are given in tables A6 and A7 in Appendix 2. Yet, the higher the threshold value, the more better capitalized banks migrate into the category of banks with low capital buffers. Hence, the capitalization dummy is more likely to capture also banks that behave as expected of banks with high capital buffers. Therefore, when using the median capital buffer as the threshold value, it is not surprising that the sum of the coefficients of $dyREG^{*}\Delta CAP$ and ΔCAP is no longer negative although the estimated coefficient of $dyREG^{*}\Delta CAP$ is still negative. A Wald test also confirms that the sum is significant and positive.

In summary, the dummy approach suggests that banks' capital buffer has an impact on the speed of capital and risk adjustment and the coordination of capital and risk. Banks with low capital buffers adjust capital and risk much faster. In addition, they increase capital and decrease risk, thereby rebuilding their capital buffer. In contrast, banks with high capital buffers increase risk when capital increases. However, they do not adjust capital when risk changes. This finding indicates that, for banks with high capital buffers, the coordination of capital and risk adjustments runs only from capital to risk and not vice versa. Although I did not expect this coordination to be one-way, the findings are in line with the capital buffer theory.

Readers who feel uncomfortable with *RISK* as a measure of asset risk and who thus prefer to interpret *RISK* as risk-weighted assets can interpret the regressions as follows. Milne and Whalley (2001) predict that banks adjust their capital buffers to optimum levels. As my measures of capital and asset risk correspond to the numerator and denominator of the banks' Basel capital ratio, respectively, the finding that, for banks with low (high) capital buffers, adjustments in capital and risk are negatively (positively) related suggests the following: banks with low capital buffers try to build up regulatory capital buffers by increasing capital and reducing risk-weighted assets, while banks with high capital buffers try to maintain their capital buffers by adjusting capital and risk-weighted assets in the same direction.

3.4.2 Subsample Approach

The dummy approach used in Section 4.1 is based on the restrictive assumption that banks with low capital buffers differ from banks with high capital buffers only with respect to the intercept, the speed of adjustment, and the coordination of capital and asset risk. With respect to the other variables, however, the same model is assumed to be applicable to both groups of banks. I could expand the dummy approach by interacting all variables with the regulatory dummy and including all interaction terms in the regression. This approach would allow all coefficients to vary depending on whether the bank holds a high or low capital buffer. An alternative approach, which I shall follow in the sequel, is to stratify the sample.

I split the sample according to whether the bank holds a high or low capital buffer. I then estimate the following system of equations:

$$(21)\quad \Delta CAP_{i,t} = \alpha_0 + \alpha_1 ROA_{i,t} + \alpha_2 SIZE_{i,t} + \alpha_3 \Delta RISK_{i,t} - \alpha_4 CAP_{i,t-1} + \alpha_5 dyMERGER_{i,t} + time\,dummies + u_{i,t}$$

$$(22)\quad \Delta RISK_{i,t} = \beta_0 + \beta_1 LLOSS_{i,t} + \beta_2 SIZE_{i,t} + \beta_3 \Delta CAP_{i,t} - \beta_4 RISK_{i,t-1} + \beta_5 dyMERGER_{i,t} + time\,dummies + w_{i,t}$$

where the regulatory dummy and the interaction terms have been eliminated compared to (19) and (20). I compare the coefficient estimates of the two subsamples and interpret different estimates as being due to the different capital buffers. As the allocation of the banks into the two subsamples is endogenous, a fully econometrically valid test of whether the estimates are statistically different for the two subsamples is not straightforward. Hence, as rule of thumb, I compare the respective confidence intervals and interpret two estimates as different if the 95 percent confidence intervals do not overlap.

In analogy to the dummy approach, I use the 10th percentile to distinguish between banks with high and low capital buffers. However, when doing so, the subsample of banks with low capital buffers is relatively small. Hence, the confidence intervals become relatively large and my rule of thumb is not able to distinguish between the two coefficients. Thus, I complement the results for the 10th percentile threshold with the results for the median threshold.

Table 4 gives the results for the 10th percentile threshold, and Table A8 in Appendix 2 gives the results for the median threshold. The subsample approach confirms the signs of the variables explaining the optimum capital and risk levels. For the 10th percentile threshold, the small number of observations renders the coefficients for the subsample of banks with low capital buffers insignificant though. However, *LLOSS* is also insignificant for the median threshold.

Table 4:
Pooled 3SLS Estimates for Two Subsamples, 1993–2004

a) Capital Equation

	Banks with low capital buffers			Banks with high capital buffers		
	Coefficient	95% conf. interval		Coefficient	95% conf. interval	
Dep. variable	ΔCAP			ΔCAP		
ROA	–0.0035 (0.09)	–0.0800	0.0731	0.2267*** (5.71)	0.1490	0.3045
SIZE	–0.0001 (0.22)	–0.0009	0.0007	–0.0000 (0.08)	–0.0001	0.0001
$\Delta RISK$	–0.1888*** (4.09)	–0.2793	–0.0983	0.0151 (0.46)	–0.0489	0.0791
CAP_{t-1}	–0.1019*** (2.67)	–0.1768	–0.0271	–0.0305*** (3.77)	–0.0464	–0.0146
dyMERGER	–0.0001 (0.08)	–0.0028	0.0026	0.0001 (0.37)	–0.0006	0.0009
Constant	0.0094 (1.14)	–0.0068	0.0256	0.0044*** (2.63)	0.0011	0.0076
Year dummies	yes			yes		
# Observations	318			5,591		

Notes: The capital equation (Panel a) and the risk equation (Panel b, below) are estimated simultaneously using the three-stage least squares procedure. The dependent variable is $\Delta CAP_{i,t}$, which is defined as total regulatory capital over total assets. The threshold value for being classified as a bank with a low capital buffer is the 10th percentile of the standardized capital buffer in the pooled sample. *ROA* is the return on assets. *SIZE* is defined as the natural log of total assets. *RISK* is defined as total risk-weighted assets over total assets. *dyMERGER* is a dummy variable, which is unity in the year a bank takes over another bank and zero otherwise. Δ indicates the first difference. The absolute *t*-values are given in parentheses. ***, **, and * indicate statistical significance at the 1, 5, and 10 percent level, respectively, in a two-tailed *t*-test.

Table 4 continued

b) Risk equation

	Banks with low capital buffers			Banks with high capital buffers		
	Coefficient	95% conf. interval		Coefficient	95% conf. interval	
Dep. variable	$\Delta RISK$			$\Delta RISK$		
LLOSS	0.0274 (0.23)	−0.2038	0.2586	0.0535 (0.73)	−0.0892	0.1961
SIZE	−0.0007 (0.39)	−0.0044	0.0029	−0.0013*** (4.10)	−0.0019	−0.0007
ΔCAP	−4.2883*** (3.91)	−6.4380	−2.1385	3.5868*** (6.16)	2.4452	4.7283
$RISK_{t-1}$	−0.0421*** (3.02)	−0.0694	−0.0148	−0.0152*** (5.13)	−0.0210	−0.0094
dyMERGER	−0.0004 (0.05)	−0.0135	0.0128	0.0066*** (3.49)	0.0029	0.0104
Constant	0.0517 (1.38)	−0.0219	0.1253	0.0249*** (3.51)	0.0110	0.0387
Year dummies	yes			yes		
# Observations	318			5,591		

Notes: The capital equation (Panel a) and the risk equation (Panel b) are estimated simultaneously using the three-stage least squares procedure. The dependent variable is $\Delta RISK_{i,t}$, which is defined as total risk-weighted assets over total assets. The threshold value for being classified as a bank with a low capital buffer is the 10th percentile of the standardized capital buffer in the pooled sample. *LLOSS* is defined as new provisions over total assets. *SIZE* is defined as the natural log of total assets. *CAP* is defined as total regulatory capital over total assets. *dyMERGER* is a dummy variable, which is unity in the year a bank takes over another bank and zero otherwise. Δ indicates the first difference. The absolute *t*-values are given in parentheses. ***, **, and * indicate statistical significance at the 1, 5, and 10 percent level, respectively, in a two-tailed *t*-test.

With regard to the impact of banks' capital buffers on the speeds of capital and risk adjustment, the estimated speeds of capital and risk adjustment are higher for banks with low capital buffers. However, the 95 percent confidence intervals for banks with high and low capital buffers overlap. Even with the median threshold, the confidence intervals for lagged *RISK* still overlap. In contrast, the confidence intervals for lagged *CAP* do not overlap and, hence, my rule of thumb indicates a speed of capital adjustment that is more than four times higher for banks with low capital buffers. Yet, in sum, my rule of thumb provides only weak evidence in favor of H_3, and no evidence in favor of H_4.

With regard to the impact of banks' capital buffer on the coordination of capital and risk adjustments, the subsample approach confirms the findings of the dummy approach in the pooled regression. Banks with low capital buffers show a negative coordination. In contrast, banks with high capital buffers show a positive coordination, which is one-way, running from capital to risk and not vice versa. When using the median threshold, the results again are in line with the negative coordination for banks with low capital buffers and with the positive coordination for banks with high capital buffers. However, both modes of coordination are one-way. This different result is likely to be due to the fact that, when using the 10th percentile threshold, the subsample of banks with low capital buffers captures banks that are closer to the 8 percent regulatory minimum. These banks try harder to increase their capital buffer and, hence, coordinate capital and risk adjustments to a greater extent.

3.4.3 Rolling Window Approach

Classifying banks into two categories—banks with low capital buffers and banks with high capital buffers—according to a certain threshold, as done by both the dummy approach and the subsample approach, requires a rather restrictive assumption. This assumption is that banks behave differently when passing a certain threshold capitalization, which I arbitrarily set equal to the capital buffer of the 10th percentile bank or the median (25th percentile) bank as a robustness check. However, the occurrence of a regime shift at a certain threshold capital buffer is not supported by economic theory. Instead, a continuous change in behavior seems more plausible. Hence, I complement the dummy approach with a rolling window approach.

For the rolling window approach, I rank the banks according to their capital buffers. The observation with the lowest capital buffer (measured in standard deviations above the 8 percent regulatory minimum) is ranked highest, while the observation with the highest capital buffer is ranked lowest. I then estimate (21) and (22) for different subsamples. The first regression includes observations 1 to n, which contain the observations with the n lowest capital buffers. I repeat the same estimation for the observations 2 to $n+1$ etc., subsequently rolling through the whole sample. Finally, I plot the estimated coefficients and the 95 percent confidence interval against the corresponding number of iterations.

The advantage of the rolling window approach is that it is not necessary to model the impact of banks' capital buffer explicitly. The impact on banks' behavior is implicitly reflected in changing coefficient estimates. According to my hypotheses, the impact is expected to be primarily reflected in the speed of adjustment and in the coordination of capital and risk adjustments.

Figure 3 shows the results for a rolling window of 750 observations over the pooled sample. To a large degree, the results confirm the results of the dummy and subsample approach. I find that the estimated coefficients of the return on assets, *ROA*, are significant and positive for most iterations. The coefficients of loan loss provisions, *LLOSS*, are negative for banks with low capital buffers and positive for banks with high capital buffers, but insignificant for most of the iterations. The coefficients of bank size, *SIZE*, are negative, but also insignificant for most of the iterations. Only in the risk equation are they significant for banks with low capital buffers in several iterations. These banks seem to drive the significance in the dummy and subsample approach.

With respect to the speed of adjustment, the estimated coefficients of lagged capital and risk are significant and have the expected negative sign. Only for banks with high capital buffers do the coefficients become insignificant. With respect to capital, the estimated speed of adjustment is relatively stable for banks with low capital buffers and decreases slightly for banks with medium-sized capital buffers until it becomes insignificant for banks with high capital buffers. Here again, I use my rule of thumb to determine whether the decrease is significant: if the confidence intervals do not overlap, changes are significant. However, as the lower bound of the confidence interval for banks with medium-sized capital buffers is lower than the upper bound of the confidence interval for banks with low capital buffers, the decrease in the speed of adjustment is not significant.

With respect to the speed of risk adjustment, the coefficient of lagged risk is significant and negative for banks with low and medium-sized capital buffers and insignificant for banks with high capital buffers. In contrast to the speed of capital adjustment, the speed of risk adjustment does not move monotonically over the iterations: first, the speed of risk adjustment increases, before it decreases again. However, according to my rule of thumb, the change is not significant. Hence, I do not find evidence of either a higher speed of capital adjustment or a higher speed of risk adjustment for banks with low capital buffers. Further, the results of the rolling window approach confirm that banks adjust capital faster than risk. However, the speed of capital and risk adjustment is again found to be rather slow.

Figure 3:
Estimated Coefficients for a Rolling Window of 750 Banks, 1993–2004

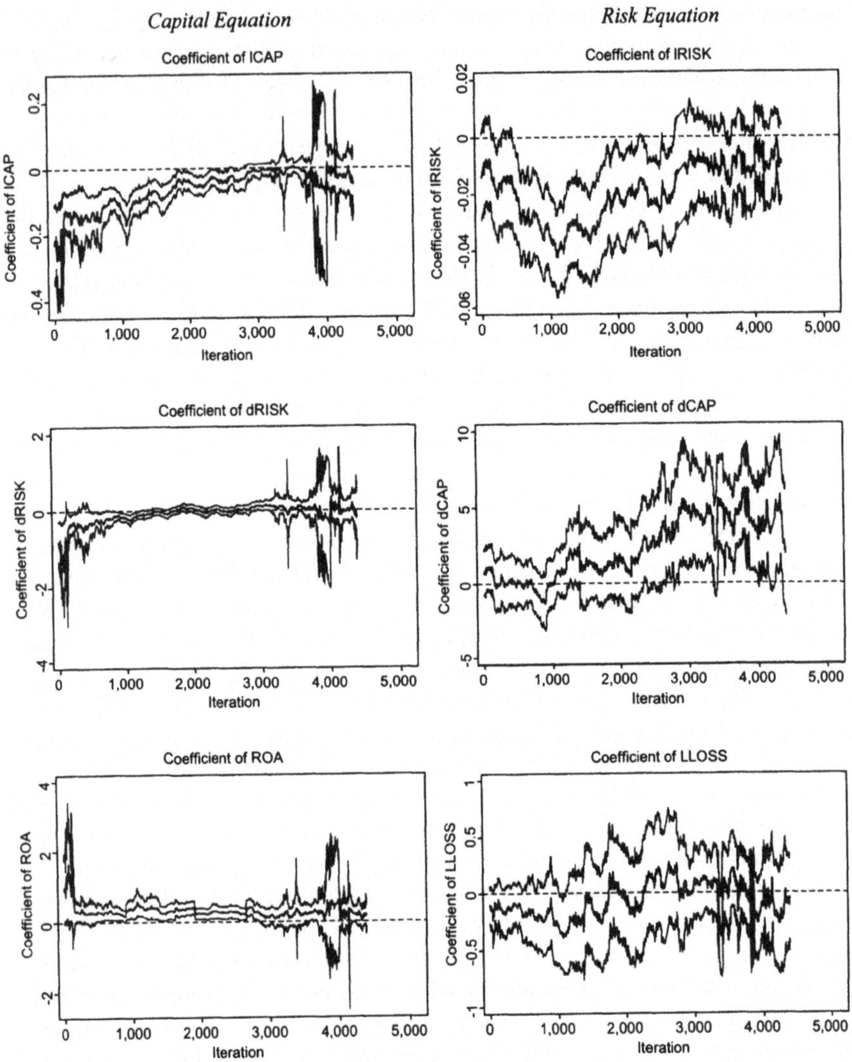

Figure 3 continued

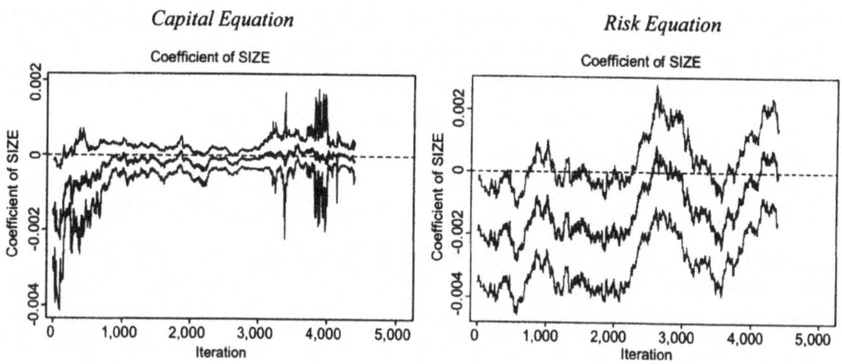

Notes: The figure gives the estimated coefficients as well as the upper and lower bound of the 95 percent confidence interval. The estimated coefficients of the dummy variables and the constant are not displayed. The coefficient is significant at the 5 percent level if zero is not included in the interval. The estimated coefficients with the 100 widest confidence bands are not displayed.

With respect to the coordination of capital and risk adjustments, the rolling window approach shows that, for banks with low capital buffers, the estimated coefficient of $\Delta RISK$ is negative and significant, while the estimated coefficient of ΔCAP is insignificant. In contrast, for banks with high capital buffers, the estimated coefficient of $\Delta RISK$ is insignificant, while the estimated coefficient of ΔCAP is positive and significant. These results are in line with a negative coordination of capital and risk adjustments for banks with low capital buffers and a positive coordination for banks with high capital buffers. Yet, the coordination is one-way, running from risk to capital for banks with low capital buffers and from capital to risk for banks with high capital buffers.

Figure 3 also shows that the confidence bands widen strongly for banks with high capital buffers, particularly in the capital equation. As these observations largely correspond to the years 2002–2004, I rerun the rolling window approach on the subperiod 1993–2001. The results are displayed in Figure A1 in Appendix 2. The results are qualitatively the same.

3.4.4 Dummy Variable Approach in a Dynamic Panel Regression

In Sections 4.1–4.3, the data are pooled over time and the 3SLS estimator is used, as is done in the literature (Shrieves and Dahl 1992; Jacques and Nigro

1997; Aggarwal and Jacques 2001; Rime 2001). Yet, this procedure does not account for possible bank-specific effects and, hence, the estimates may be biased if the assumption of nonexistent bank-specific effects is not correct. Therefore, I additionally use dynamic panel estimators as a robustness check.

When using dynamic panel estimators, the Hansen test is a crucial indicator of the validity of the instruments used. Unfortunately, the Hansen test is very sensitive to coefficients not being stable over time. Yet, the rolling-window approach indicates parameter instability for banks with high capital buffers, which correspond to later time periods in the sample, as capital buffers increase over the sample period. Indeed, when using the full sample, the Hansen test always indicates invalid instruments. In contrast, as soon as I leave out the years 2002–2004, the Hansen test indicates the instruments are valid. The results of estimating the simultaneous system of (19) and (20) based on this shortened time series are presented in Table 5. The Hansen test and the condition for consistency of the GMM estimator, i.e., the (lack of) evidence for first-order (second-order) serial correlation in the first-differenced residuals, are also presented.

The results show that the variables explaining the optimum capital and risk levels have the same sign as in the pooled regressions, but returns on assets, *ROA*, lose most of their significance. The capitalization dummy, *dyREG*, in the risk equation also looses some of its significance compared to the pooled 3SLS regressions and now even shows the expected negative sign in Specification 2.

With respect to the lagged endogenous variables, the panel regressions yield less significant speeds of capital adjustment. The coefficients of $RISK_{t-1}$ are even insignificant. In Specification 2, I allow banks with low capital buffers to differ in their speeds of adjustment. The coefficients of $dyREG*CAP_{t-1}$ and $dyREG*RISK_{t-1}$ are found to be significant and positive. Hence, for banks with low capital buffers, the estimated speeds fall out of the $[0;-1]$ interval and imply an explosive process.

With respect to the coordination of capital and risk adjustments, Specification 3 confirms the findings of the pooled 3SLS regressions: while banks with low capital buffers show a two-way negative coordination of capital and risk adjustment, banks with high capital buffers show a positive coordination, which is, however, only one-way, running from capital to risk. Although the counter-intuitive coefficients of $dyREG*CAP_{t-1}$ and $dyREG*RISK_{t-1}$ become insignificant, I also run the same specification without allowing for a different speed of capital adjustment for banks with low capital buffers. Specification 4 shows the results. The finding with respect to the coordination of capital and risk adjustments is confirmed. Yet, the coefficient of $RISK_{t-1}$ is insignificant, indicating a problem with the partial adjustment framework.

When using the 25th percentile threshold to distinguish between banks with high capital buffers and banks with low capital buffers, the results are qualita-

Table 5:
Blundell–Bond Two-Step GMM Estimates for Specifications with Regulatory Dummy and Interaction Terms, 1995–2001

a) Capital Equation

	1	2	3	4
Dep. variable	ΔCAP	ΔCAP	ΔCAP	ΔCAP
dyREG	–0.0038***	–0.0413***	–0.0139	0.0010
	(9.20)	(2.82)	(1.32)	(0.35)
ROA	0.0915	0.2161*	0.1462	0.1455
	(1.21)	(1.68)	(1.40)	(1.59)
SIZE	–0.0000	–0.0003*	–0.0001	–0.0001
	(0.42)	(1.91)	(1.27)	(0.87)
$\Delta RISK$	0.0339	–0.1046*	–0.0145	–0.0011
	(0.95)	(1.75)	(0.36)	(0.02)
$dyREG{*}\Delta RISK$			–0.4182***	–0.3692*
			(3.25)	(1.80)
CAP_{t-1}	–0.0172	–0.0696*	–0.0673**	–0.0574*
	(0.57)	(1.75)	(2.02)	(1.92)
$dyREG{*}CAP_{t-1}$		0.8566***	0.3511	
		(2.66)	(1.50)	
dyMERGER	0.0004	0.0022*	0.0013	0.0008
	(0.43)	(1.75)	(1.22)	(0.76)
Constant	0.0031	0.0124***	0.0085***	0.0070**
	(1.26)	(3.27)	(2.94)	(2.24)
Year dummies	yes	yes	yes	yes
# Observations	2,715	2,715	2,715	2,715
# Banks	391	391	391	391
Hansen test	0.039	0.675	0.729	0.134
AR(1) test	0.000	0.000	0.000	0.000
AR(2) test	0.723	0.191	0.394	0.514

Notes: The dependent variable is $CAP_{i,t}$, which is defined as total regulatory capital over total assets. *dyREG* is a dummy variable that is unity if the bank has a standardized capital buffer equal to or less than the 10th percentile and zero otherwise. *ROA* is the return on assets. *SIZE* is defined as the natural log of total assets. *RISK* is defined as total risk-weighted assets over total assets *dyMERGER* is a dummy variable that is unity in the year a bank has taken over another bank and zero otherwise. Lagged differences of CAP_i are used as instruments for equations in levels, in addition to lagged levels of CAP_i that are used as instruments for equations in first differences. In addition, I use $LLOSS_i$ and GMM-type instruments of $RISK_{i,t}$ as instruments for $\Delta RISK_{i,t}$ in order to account for the simultaneity of capital and risk adjustments. In the specifications where I include $dyREG_{i,t}{*}CAP_{i,t-1}$ and $dyREG_{i,t}{*}\Delta RISK_{i,t}$ among the regressors, I also use instrumental variables for these interaction terms. Δ indicates the first difference. ***, **, and * indicate statistical significance at the 1, 5, and 10 percent level, respectively, in a two-tailed *t*-test. Hansen test refers to the test of overidentifying restrictions. AR(1) and AR(2) test refer to the test for the null of no first-order and second-order autocorrelation in the first-differenced residuals.

Table 5 continued

b) Risk Equation

	1	2	3	4
Dep. variable	$\Delta RISK$	$\Delta RISK$	$\Delta RISK$	$\Delta RISK$
dyREG	0.0186***	–0.1256*	–0.0734	0.0268***
	(3.14)	(1.84)	(1.08)	(3.43)
LLOSS	–0.3625***	–0.2516	–0.3423**	–0.3204**
	(2.62)	(1.35)	(2.34)	(2.34)
SIZE	–0.0016***	–0.0028***	–0.0017***	–0.0014**
	(2.62)	(4.01)	(2.97)	(2.43)
ΔCAP	2.8370*	–2.1333*	1.7977*	2.9406***
	(1.86)	(1.95)	(1.84)	(2.69)
dyREGΔCAP*			–18.4149***	–18.1409**
			(3.12)	(2.42)
$RISK_{t-1}$	0.0142	0.0360	–0.0114	–0.0151
	(0.54)	(1.29)	(0.44)	(0.56)
dyREG$RISK_{t-1}$*		0.2477*	0.1934	
		(1.88)	(1.47)	
dyMERGER	0.0022	0.0098	0.0056	0.0023
	(0.51)	(1.63)	(1.14)	(0.50)
Constant	0.0264**	0.0463***	0.0444***	0.0375***
	(2.32)	(3.14)	(3.58)	(3.12)
Year dummies	yes	yes	yes	yes
# Observations	2,715	2,715	2,715	2,715
# Banks	391	391	391	391
Hansen test	0.489	0.292	0.492	0.834
AR(1) test	0.000	0.000	0.000	0.000
AR(2) test	0.900	0.280	0.698	0.970

Notes: The dependent variable is $RISK_{i,t}$, which is defined as total risk-weighted assets over total assets. *dyREG* is a dummy variable that is unity if the bank has a standardized capital buffer equal to or less than the 10th percentile and zero otherwise. *LLOSS* is defined as new provisions over total assets. *SIZE* is defined as the natural log of total assets. *CAP* is defined as total regulatory capital over total assets. *dyMERGER* is a dummy variable that is unity in the year a bank takes over another bank and zero otherwise. Lagged differences of $RISK_i$ are used as instruments for equations in levels, in addition to lagged levels of $RISK_i$ that are used as instruments for equations in first differences. In addition, I use $ROA_{i,t}$ and GMM-type instruments of CAP_i as instruments for $\Delta CAP_{i,t}$ in order to account for the simultaneity of capital and risk adjustments. In the specifications where I include $REG_{i,t}*RISK_{i,t-1}$ and $REG_{i,t}*\Delta CAP_{i,t}$ among the regressors, I also use instrumental variables for these interaction terms. Δ indicates the first difference. ***, **, and * indicate statistical significance at the 1, 5, and 10 percent level, respectively, in a two-tailed *t*-test. Hansen test refers to the test of overidentifying restrictions. AR(1) and AR(2) test refer to the test for the null of no first-order and second-order autocorrelation in the first-differenced residuals.

tively the same (Table A9 in Appendix 2). Only the negative coordination of capital and risk adjustments for banks with low capital buffers is now also only one-way, running from capital to risk.

In sum, with respect to the impact of banks' capital buffers, the results of the dynamic panel regressions confirm the results of the pooled regression only partly. While the results support a negative (positive) coordination of capital and risk adjustments for banks with low (high) capital buffers, the results do not support a higher speed of capital and risk adjustment for banks with low capital buffers. Besides, in contrast to the results of the pooled 3SLS estimations, the results of the dynamic panel estimations suggest that banks may not adjust asset risk towards a target level. This difference in the findings is likely to be due to the trend in the data. When taking first differences of *CAP* and *RISK*, as done in the next chapter, I find a speed of asset risk adjustment that is well within the required interval of $[0;1]$.

3.5 Conclusion

Minimum capital requirements play a prominent role in modern banking regulation. A growing branch of the banking literature has dealt with the question of how banks take capital regulation into consideration in their capital and risk decisions. This chapter has tested the predictions of the capital buffer theory (Marcus 1984; Milne and Whalley 2001) with respect to banks' behavior after an increase in minimum capital requirements.

I find that banks' capital buffer has an impact on capital and risk adjustments in several interesting respects. In line with the literature, I find evidence that banks adjust capital faster than risk. Further, I find some evidence that banks with low capital buffers adjust capital and risk faster than banks with high capital buffers. With respect to the coordination of capital and risk, I find evidence that, for banks with low capital buffers, adjustments in capital and risk are negatively related. In contrast, for banks with high capital buffers, adjustments in capital and risk are positively related. Contrary to expectations, the coordination is, however, found to be one-way for banks with high capital buffers, running from capital to risk. In summary, my findings are in line with the hypotheses derived from the buffer theory.

3.6 Appendix 1: Descriptive Statistics

Table A1:
Definition of the Bank-Specific (Control) Variables

Variable	Definition
CAP	Regulatory capital to total assets ratio
RISK	Risk-weighted assets to total assets ratio
SIZE	Natural log of total assets
ROA	Annual net profit over total assets
LLOSS	New net provisions over total assets
Absolute capital buffer	Basel capital-to-risk-weighted-assets ratio minus 0.08
Standardized capital buffer	Basel capital-to-risk-weighted-assets ratio minus 0.08 divided by the bank-specific standard deviation of the capital buffer over the observation period
dyMERGER	Unity for the acquirer in the year of the merger, and zero otherwise.
dyREG	Unity if bank is among the 10, 25, or 50 percent banks with the lowest standardized capital buffers, and zero otherwise (depending on the respective specification).

Note: All variables come from a confidential supervisory database kindly provided by Deutsche Bundesbank.

Table A2:
Descriptive Statistics for the Pooled Sample

	Mean	Minimum	5th percentile	Median	95th percentile	Maximum	Standard deviation
CAP	0.0579	0.0196	0.0343	0.0584	0.0785	0.1153	0.0128
RISK	0.5435	0.1796	0.3256	0.5625	0.6855	0.8369	0.1060
ΔCAP	0.0023	–0.0068	–0.0029	0.0021	0.0083	0.0130	0.0033
ΔRISK	0.0067	–0.0548	–0.0282	0.0060	0.0450	0.0729	0.0217
ROA	0.0024	–0.0310	0.0004	0.0023	0.0048	0.0212	0.0018
SIZE	20.6452	17.3704	19.1088	20.6526	22.2680	23.9673	0.9368
LLOSS	0.0037	–0.0213	–0.0003	0.0031	0.0101	0.0768	0.0039
Abs. capital buffer	0.0277	–0.0112	0.0046	0.0235	0.0647	0.1825	0.0196
Std. capital buffer	2.4766	–1.6014	0.4280	2.4372	4.6149	49.8166	1.7118
dyMERGER	0.0251	0.0000	0.0000	0.0000	0.0000	1.0000	0.1565

Notes: The absolute capital buffer is measured as the Basel capital ratio minus the 8 percent regulatory minimum. The standardized capital buffer is measured in standard deviations above the regulatory minimum.

Table A3:
Variable Means for Each Year of the Observation Period

	1993	1994	1995	1996	1997	1998	1999	2000	2001	2002	2003	2004
CAP	0.0441	0.0477	0.0512	0.0551	0.0573	0.0590	0.0607	0.0620	0.0635	0.0660	0.0682	0.0714
RISK	0.4924	0.5081	0.5251	0.5308	0.5280	0.5386	0.5494	0.5707	0.5762	0.5804	0.5825	0.5808
ΔCAP	.	0.0029	0.0026	0.0034	0.0024	0.0017	0.0016	0.0016	0.0015	0.0026	0.0018	0.0030
ΔRISK	.	0.0064	0.0087	–0.0007	0.0034	0.0117	0.0101	0.0229	0.0055	0.0042	0.0043	–0.0042
ROA	0.0029	0.0027	0.0030	0.0028	0.0025	0.0024	0.0023	0.0022	0.0020	0.0013	0.0016	0.0018
SIZE	20.1655	20.3406	20.4663	20.5644	20.6299	20.6593	20.7368	20.7929	20.8571	20.9106	20.9673	21.0041
LLOSS2	0.0030	0.0031	0.0045	0.0044	0.0041	0.0036	0.0013	0.0035	0.0036	0.0051	0.0048	0.0044
Abs. capital buffer	0.0106	0.0144	0.0183	0.0248	0.0303	0.0314	0.0324	0.0305	0.0319	0.0358	0.0392	0.0453
Std. capital buffer	1.2370	1.6757	1.9397	2.4401	2.7377	2.7467	2.7546	2.5423	2.6320	2.9160	3.1417	3.6566
dyMERGER	0.0330	0.0397	0.0305	0.0139	0.0139	0.0053	0.0250	0.0210	0.0237	0.0304	0.0513	0.0198
# Banks	698	629	590	575	577	571	560	523	507	493	468	454

Notes: The absolute capital buffer is measured as the Basel capital ratio minus the 8 percent regulatory minimum. The standardized capital buffer is measured in standard deviations above the regulatory minimum.

Table A4:
Correlations between Variables

	CAP	RISK	ΔCAP	ΔRISK	ROA	SIZE	LLOSS	Abs. cap. buf.	Std. cap. buf.
CAP	1								
RISK	0.6909***	1							
	(0.000)								
ΔCAP	0.1768***	–0.0163	1						
	(0.000)	(0.211)							
ΔRISK	–0.0502***	0.0773***	0.1595***	1					
	(0.000)	(0.000)	(0.000)						
ROA	0.0098	0.0390***	0.1237***	0.0534***	1				
	(0.425)	(0.002)	(0.000)	(0.000)					
SIZE	0.2039***	0.1596***	–0.0285**	–0.0645***	–0.0709***	1			
	(0.000)	(0.000)	(0.028)	(0.000)	(0.000)				
LLOSS	–0.0246**	0.0426***	0.004	–0.0318**	–0.4240***	0.0606***	1		
	(0.047)	(0.001)	(0.760)	(0.015)	(0.000)	(0.000)			
Abs. cap. buffer	0.4746***	–0.2842***	0.2333***	–0.1410***	–0.0298**	0.0848***	–0.0695***	1	
	(0.000)	(0.000)	(0.000)	(0.000)	(0.015)	(0.000)	(0.000)		
Std. cap. buffer	0.3116***	0.0195	0.0710***	–0.0889***	–0.0436***	0.0445***	–0.0467***	0.3861***	1
	(0.000)	(0.114)	(0.000)	(0.000)	(0.000)	(0.000)	(0.000)	(0.000)	
dyMERGER	–0.0505***	–0.0429***	–0.0007	0.0479***	–0.0601***	0.1088***	0.0543***	–0.0243**	–0.0195
	(0.000)	(0.001)	(0.955)	(0.000)	(0.000)	(0.000)	(0.000)	(0.047)	(0.114)

Notes: The absolute capital buffer is measured as the Basel capital ratio minus the 8 percent regulatory minimum. The standardized capital buffer is measured in standard deviations above the regulatory minimum. ***, **, and * indicate statistical significance at the 1, 5, and 10 percent level, respectively, in a two-tailed t-test.

Table A5:
Variable Means for Banks with Low and High Capital Buffers

a) 10th Percentile Threshold

	Banks with low capital buffer		Banks with high capital buffer	
	Mean	Standard deviation	Mean	Standard deviation
CAP	0.0440	0.0090	0.0595	0.0123
RISK	0.5122	0.1071	0.5469	0.1054
dCAP	0.0007	0.0028	0.0024	0.0033
dRISK	0.0110	0.0226	0.0065	0.0216
ROA	0.0026	0.0019	0.0023	0.0018
SIZE	20.4255	0.8648	20.6692	0.9413
LLOSS	0.0042	0.0047	0.0037	0.0038
Abs. capital buffer	0.0061	0.0050	0.0300	0.0192
Std. capital buffer	0.3873	0.2423	2.7064	1.6471
dyMERGER	0.0491	0.2162	0.0226	0.1485
# Observations	320		5,603	

Notes: Banks with capital buffers lower (higher) than 0.7472 standard deviations, i.e., the 10th percentile, above the 8 percent regulatory minimum are classified as having low (high) capital buffers.

b) Median Threshold

	Banks with low capital buffer		Banks with high capital buffer	
	Mean	Standard deviation	Mean	Standard deviation
CAP	0.0528	0.0111	0.0630	0.0124
RISK	0.5385	0.1062	0.5483	0.1057
dCAP	0.0020	0.0034	0.0025	0.0033
dRISK	0.0096	0.0218	0.0043	0.0213
ROA	0.0025	0.0019	0.0022	0.0018
SIZE	20.5797	0.9061	20.7091	0.9616
LLOSS	0.0039	0.0042	0.0036	0.0035
Abs. capital buffer	0.0187	0.0142	0.0365	0.0202
Std. capital buffer	1.4083	0.6806	3.5358	1.7672
dyMERGER	0.0275	0.1635	0.0229	0.1496
# Observations	2,700		3,223	

Notes: Banks with capital buffers lower (higher) than 2.5072 standard deviations, i.e., the median, above the 8 percent regulatory minimum are classified as having low (high) capital buffers.

3.7 Appendix 2: Robustness Checks

Table A6:
Pooled 3SLS Estimates for Specifications with Regulatory Dummy and Interactions Terms (definition of *dyREG* based on the 25th percentile capital buffer), 1993–2004

a) Capital Equation

	1	2	3
Dependent variable	ΔCAP	ΔCAP	ΔCAP
dyREG	–0.0013***	0.0010	0.0008
	(6.74)	(1.30)	(1.00)
ROA	0.2754***	0.3093***	0.2788***
	(7.63)	(7.40)	(7.28)
SIZE	–0.0001	–0.0003***	–0.0001*
	(1.39)	(3.47)	(1.73)
$\Delta RISK$	–0.0573**	–0.1686***	–0.0366
	(2.04)	(5.95)	(1.11)
*dyREG**$\Delta RISK$			–0.1331***
			(4.12)
CAP_{t-1}	–0.0506***	–0.0638***	–0.0510***
	(6.79)	(8.16)	(6.45)
*dyREG**CAP_{t-1}		–0.0343**	–0.0134
		(2.44)	(1.04)
dyMERGER	0.0005	0.0013***	0.0007*
	(1.38)	(2.98)	(1.87)
Constant	0.0075***	0.0117***	0.0078***
	(4.71)	(6.74)	(4.70)
Year dummies	yes	yes	yes
# Observations	5,909	5,909	5,909

Notes: The capital equation (Panel a) and the risk equation (Panel b, below) are estimated simultaneously using the three-stage least squares procedure. The dependent variable is $\Delta CAP_{i,t}$. *CAP* is defined as total regulatory capital over total assets. *dyREG* is a dummy variable that is unity if the bank has a standardized capital buffer equal to or less than the 25th percentile and zero otherwise. *ROA* is the return on assets. *SIZE* is defined as the natural log of total assets. *RISK* is defined as total risk-weighted assets over total assets. *dyMERGER* is a dummy variable, which is unity in the year a bank has taken over another bank and zero otherwise. Δ indicates the first difference. ***, **, and * indicate statistical significance at the 1, 5, and 10 percent level, respectively, in a two-tailed t-test.

Table A6 continued

b) Risk Equation

	1	2	3
Dependent variable	$\Delta RISK$	$\Delta RISK$	$\Delta RISK$
dyREG	0.0083***	0.0145***	0.0221***
	(8.08)	(4.21)	(4.94)
LLOSS	–0.0504	–0.1261**	–0.0811
	(0.73)	(2.09)	(1.14)
SIZE	–0.0014***	–0.0014***	–0.0013***
	(4.82)	(4.92)	(4.21)
ΔCAP	2.1716***	0.5314	2.7831***
	(4.26)	(1.22)	(4.70)
$dyREG*\Delta CAP$			-3.8348***
			(4.84)
$RISK_{t-1}$	–0.0208***	–0.0172***	–0.0175***
	(7.71)	(5.99)	(5.46)
$dyREG*RISK_{t-1}$		–0.0157***	–0.0130*
		(2.61)	(1.94)
dyMERGER	0.0070***	0.0068***	0.0062***
	(4.09)	(4.02)	(3.48)
Constant	0.0338***	0.0385***	0.0287***
	(5.20)	(5.98)	(4.12)
Year dummies	yes	yes	yes
# Observations	5,909	5,909	5,909

Notes The capital equation (Panel a) and the risk equation (Panel b) are estimated simultaneously using the three-stage least squares procedure. The dependent variable is $\Delta RISK_{i,t}$. *RISK* is defined as total risk-weighted assets over total assets. *dyREG* is a dummy variable that is unity if the bank has a standardized capital buffer equal to or less than the 25th percentile and zero otherwise. *LLOSS* is defined as new provisions over total assets. *SIZE* is defined as the natural log of total assets. *CAP* is defined as total regulatory capital over total assets. *dyMERGER* is a dummy variable, which is unity in the year a bank has taken over another bank and zero otherwise. Δ indicates the first difference. ***, **, and * indicate statistical significance at the 1, 5, and 10 percent level, respectively, in a two-tailed *t*-test.

Table A7:
Pooled 3SLS Estimates for Specifications with Regulatory Dummy and Interactions Terms (definition of *dyREG* based on the median capital buffer), 1993–2004

a) Capital Equation

	1	2	3
Dependent variable	ΔCAP	ΔCAP	ΔCAP
dyREG	–0.0007***	0.0013**	0.0019***
	(4.76)	(2.30)	(2.69)
ROA	0.2819***	0.2981***	0.2964***
	(7.95)	(7.75)	(7.84)
SIZE	–0.0001*	–0.0002***	–0.0001**
	(1.69)	(2.58)	(2.00)
$\Delta RISK$	–0.0644**	–0.1121***	–0.0231
	(2.42)	(4.06)	(0.64)
*dyREG**$\Delta RISK$			–0.1098***
			(3.02)
CAP_{t-1}	–0.0509***	–0.0469***	–0.0429***
	(7.13)	(5.84)	(5.10)
*dyREG**CAP_{t-1}		–0.0321***	–0.0292***
		(3.43)	(3.00)
dyMERGER	0.0005	0.0008**	0.0007*
	(1.37)	(1.97)	(1.66)
Constant	0.0077***	0.0088***	0.0073***
	(4.99)	(5.35)	(4.36)
Year dummies	yes	yes	yes
# Observations	5,909	5,909	5,909

Notes: The capital equation (Panel a) and the risk equation (Panel b, below) are estimated simultaneously using the three-stage least squares procedure. The dependent variable is $\Delta CAP_{i,t}$. *CAP* is defined as total regulatory capital over total assets. *dyREG* is a dummy variable that is unity if the bank has a standardized capital buffer equal to or less than the median and zero otherwise. *ROA* is the return on assets. *SIZE* is defined as the natural log of total assets. *RISK* is defined as total risk-weighted assets over total assets. *dyMERGER* is a dummy variable, which is unity in the year a bank has taken over another bank and zero otherwise. Δ indicates the first difference. ***, **, and * indicate statistical significance at the 1, 5, and 10 percent level, respectively, in a two-tailed *t*-test.

Table A7 continued

b) Risk Equation

	1	2	3
Dependent variable	$\Delta RISK$	$\Delta RISK$	$\Delta RISK$
dyREG	0.0064***	0.0103***	0.0186***
	(8.94)	(3.79)	(4.04)
LLOSS	–0.0755	–0.1177*	–0.0730
	(1.10)	(1.83)	(1.04)
SIZE	–0.0014***	–0.0014***	–0.0012***
	(4.78)	(4.84)	(3.89)
ΔCAP	1.9114***	1.0415**	3.6412***
	(3.79)	(2.30)	(4.14)
$dyREG*\Delta CAP$			–3.1231***
			(3.14)
$RISK_{t-1}$	–0.0219***	–0.0185***	–0.0168***
	(8.21)	(5.33)	(4.23)
$dyREG*RISK_{t-1}$		–0.0086*	–0.0097*
		(1.78)	(1.72)
dyMERGER	0.0074***	0.0072***	0.0064***
	(4.34)	(4.21)	(3.58)
Constant	0.0347***	0.0363***	0.0241***
	(5.39)	(5.59)	(3.07)
Year dummies	yes	yes	yes
# Observations	5,909	5,909	5,909

Notes: The capital equation (Panel a) and the risk equation (Panel b) are estimated simultaneously using the three-stage least squares procedure. The dependent variable is $\Delta RISK_{i,t}$. *RISK* is defined as total risk-weighted assets over total assets. *dyREG* is a dummy variable that is unity if the bank has a standardized capital buffer equal to or less than the median and zero otherwise. *LLOSS* is defined as new provisions over total assets. *SIZE* is defined as the natural log of total assets. *CAP* is defined as total regulatory capital over total assets. *dyMERGER* is a dummy variable, which is unity in the year a bank has taken over another bank and zero otherwise. Δ indicates the first difference. ***, **, and * indicate statistical significance at the 1, 5, and 10 percent level, respectively, in a two-tailed *t*-test.

Table A8:
Pooled 3SLS Estimates for Two Subsamples, 1993–2004

a) Capital Equation

	Banks with low capital buffers			Banks with high capital buffers		
	Coefficient	95% conf. interval		Coefficient	95% conf. interval	
Dep. variable	ΔCAP			ΔCAP		
ROA	0.3297***	0.2012	0.4582	0.2445***	0.1508	0.3382
	(5.03)			(5.11)		
SIZE	–0.0003**	–0.0006	–0.0000	–0.0001	–0.0002	0.0000
	(2.15)			(1.39)		
ΔRISK	–0.2194***	–0.3136	–0.1252	0.0066	–0.0602	0.0735
	(4.57)			(0.19)		
CAP_{t-1}	–0.1116***	–0.1418	–0.0813	–0.0267***	–0.0418	–0.0116
	(7.23)			(3.47)		
dyMERGER	0.0011	–0.0004	0.0027	0.0007	–0.0002	0.0015
	(1.48)			(1.50)		
Constant	0.0147***	0.0080	0.0214	0.0065***	0.0033	0.0097
	(4.30)			(3.95)		
Year dummies	yes			yes		
# Obs.	2,690			3,219		

Notes: The capital equation (Panel a) and the risk equation (Panel b, below) are estimated simultaneously using the three-stage least squares procedure. The dependent variable Δ*CAP*. *CAP* is defined as total capital over total assets. The threshold value for being classified as bank with a low capital buffer is the median of the standardized capital buffer in the pooled sample. *ROA* is the return on assets. *SIZE* is defined as the natural log of total assets. *RISK* is defined as total risk-weighted assets over total assets. *dyMERGER* is a dummy variable, which is unity in the year a bank takes over another bank and zero otherwise. Δ indicates the first difference. The absolute *t*-values are given in parentheses. ***, **, and * indicate statistical significance at the 1, 5, and 10 percent level, respectively, in a two-tailed *t*-test.

Table A8 continued

b) Risk Equation

	Banks with low capital buffers			Banks with high capital buffers		
	Coefficient	95% conf. interval		Coefficient	95% conf. interval	
Dep. variable	ΔRISK			ΔRISK		
LLOSS	–0.1192 (1.51)	–0.2737	0.0352	–0.0456 (0.44)	–0.2468	0.1556
SIZE	–0.0017*** (3.78)	–0.0026	–0.0008	–0.0008** (2.04)	–0.0016	–0.0000
ΔCAP	0.6845 (1.26)	–0.3785	1.7474	2.8309*** (3.57)	1.2770	4.3848
$RISK_{t-1}$	–0.0273*** (7.12)	–0.0349	–0.0198	–0.0171*** (4.59)	–0.0244	–0.0098
dyMERGER	0.0082*** (3.20)	0.0032	0.0132	0.0049** (2.06)	0.0002	0.0095
Constant	0.0544*** (5.87)	0.0362	0.0725	0.0143 (1.48)	–0.0047	0.0333
Year dummies	yes			yes		
# Observations	2,690			3,219		

Notes: The capital equation (Panel a) and the risk equation (Panel b) are estimated simultaneously using the three-stage least squares procedure. The dependent variable is Δ*RISK*. *RISK* is defined as total risk-weighted assets over total assets. The threshold value for being classified as bank with a low capital buffer is the median of the standardized capital buffer in the pooled sample. *LLOSS* is defined as new provisions over total assets. *SIZE* is defined as the natural log of total assets. *CAP* is defined as total regulatory capital over total assets. *dyMERGER* is a dummy variable, which is unity in the year a bank takes over another bank and zero otherwise. Δ indicates the first difference. The absolute *t*-values are given in parentheses. ***, **, and * indicate statistical significance at the 1, 5, and 10 percent level, respectively, in a two-tailed *t*-test.

Table A9:
Blundell–Bond Two-Step GMM Estimates for Specifications with Regulatory Dummy and Interaction Terms, 1995–2001

a) Capital Equation

	1	2	3	4
Dependent variable	ΔCAP	ΔCAP	ΔCAP	ΔCAP
dyREG	–0.0025***	–0.0101**	–0.0094**	–0.0024**
	(7.62)	(2.26)	(2.11)	(2.50)
ROA	0.1311	0.1653	0.1730	0.1333
	(1.64)	(1.46)	(1.59)	(1.49)
SIZE	0.0001	–0.0002	–0.0002	0.0000
	(0.57)	(1.44)	(1.48)	(0.27)
$\Delta RISK$	0.0431	–0.0824*	–0.0464	0.0265
	(1.16)	(1.79)	(1.03)	(0.47)
$dyREG*\Delta RISK$			–0.1193	–0.0091
			(1.51)	(0.10)
CAP_{t-1}	–0.0529	–0.0671	–0.0804**	–0.0532
	(1.59)	(1.54)	(2.13)	(1.60)
$dyREG*CAP_{t-1}$		0.1683*	0.1774**	
		(1.89)	(1.99)	
dyMERGER	0.0001	0.0008	0.0010	0.0004
	(0.15)	(0.78)	(1.09)	(0.40)
Constant	0.0031	0.0100***	0.0102***	0.0038
	(1.26)	(2.95)	(3.31)	(1.19)
Year dummies	yes	yes	yes	yes
# Observations	2,715	2,715	2,715	2,715
# Banks	391	391	391	391
Hansen test	0.011	0.121	0.510	0.102
AR(1) test	0.000	0.000	0.000	0.000
AR(2) test	0.850	0.216	0.209	0.693

Notes: The dependent variable is $CAP_{i,t}$, which is defined as total regulatory capital over total assets. *dyREG* is a dummy variable that is unity if the bank has a standardized capital buffer equal to or less than the 25th percentile and zero otherwise. *ROA* is the return on assets. *SIZE* is defined as the natural log of total assets. *RISK* is defined as total risk-weighted assets over total assets. *dyMERGER* is a dummy variable that is unity in the year a bank has taken over another bank and zero otherwise. Lagged differences of CAP_i are used as instruments for equations in levels, in addition to lagged levels of CAP_i, which are used as instruments for equations in first differences. In addition, I use $LLOSS_i$ and GMM-type instruments of $RISK_i$ as instruments for $\Delta RISK_{i,t}$ in order to account for the simultaneity of capital and risk adjustments. In the specifications where I include $dyREG_{i,t}*CAP_{i,t-1}$ and $dyREG_{i,t}*\Delta RISK_{i,t}$ among the regressors, I also use instrumental variables for these interaction terms. Δ indicates the first difference. ***, **, and * indicate statistical significance at the 1, 5, and 10 percent level, respectively, in a two-tailed *t*-test. Hansen test refers to the test of overidentifying restrictions. AR(1) and AR(2) test refer to the test for the null of no first-order and second-order autocorrelation in the first-differenced residuals.

Table A9 continued

b) Risk Equation

	1	2	3	4
Dependent variable	Δ*RISK*	Δ*RISK*	Δ*RISK*	Δ*RISK*
dyREG	0.0128***	–0.0478*	0.0453	0.0239***
	(4.07)	(1.80)	(1.23)	(3.52)
LLOSS	–0.3334**	–0.2357	–0.4915***	–0.3999***
	(2.49)	(1.44)	(3.00)	(2.67)
SIZE	–0.0016**	–0.0023***	–0.0012*	–0.0013*
	(2.45)	(3.62)	(1.79)	(1.79)
Δ*CAP*	2.9188**	–1.0024	3.3024***	2.9509**
	(2.11)	(0.87)	(2.60)	(2.36)
*dyREG**Δ*CAP*			–10.7815***	–9.1989**
			(3.40)	(2.27)
$RISK_{t-1}$	–0.0146	–0.0111	–0.0472*	–0.0465
	(0.49)	(0.46)	(1.86)	(1.32)
$dyREG*RISK_{t-1}$		0.0977**	–0.0335	
		(2.06)	(0.55)	
dyMERGER	0.0027	0.0053	–0.0012	–0.0006
	(0.63)	(0.98)	(0.23)	(0.12)
Constant	0.0419***	0.0593***	0.0518***	0.0529***
	(3.25)	(4.49)	(3.71)	(3.50)
Year dummies	yes	yes	yes	yes
# Observations	2,715	2,715	2,715	2,715
# Banks	391	391	391	391
Hansen test	0.612	0.067	0.612	0.946
AR(1) test	0.000	0.000	0.000	0.000
AR(2) test	0.798	0.347	0.680	0.648

Notes: The dependent variable is $RISK_{i,t}$, which is defined as total risk-weighted assets over total assets. *dyREG* is a dummy variable that is unity if the bank has a standardized capital buffer equal to or less than the 25th percentile and zero otherwise. *LLOSS* is defined as new provisions over total assets. *SIZE* is defined as the natural log of total assets. *CAP* is defined as total regulatory capital over total assets. *dyMERGER* is a dummy variable that is unity in the year a bank takes over another bank and zero otherwise. Lagged differences of $RISK_i$ are used as instruments for equations in levels, in addition to lagged levels of $RISK_i$, which are used as instruments for equations in first differences. In addition, I use $ROA_{i,t}$ and GMM-type instruments of CAP_i as instruments for $\Delta CAP_{i,t}$ in order to account for the simultaneity of capital and risk adjustments. In the specifications where I include $REG_{i,t}*RISK_{i,t-1}$ and $REG_{i,t}*\Delta CAP_{i,t}$ among the regressors, I also use instrumental variables for these interaction terms. Δ indicates the first difference. ***, **, and * indicate statistical significance at the 1, 5, and 10 percent level, respectively, in a two-tailed *t*-test. Hansen test refers to the test of overidentifying restrictions. AR(1) and AR(2) test refer to the test for the null of no first-order and second-order autocorrelation in the first-differenced residuals.

Figure A1:
Estimated Coefficients for a Rolling Window of 750 Banks, 1993–2001

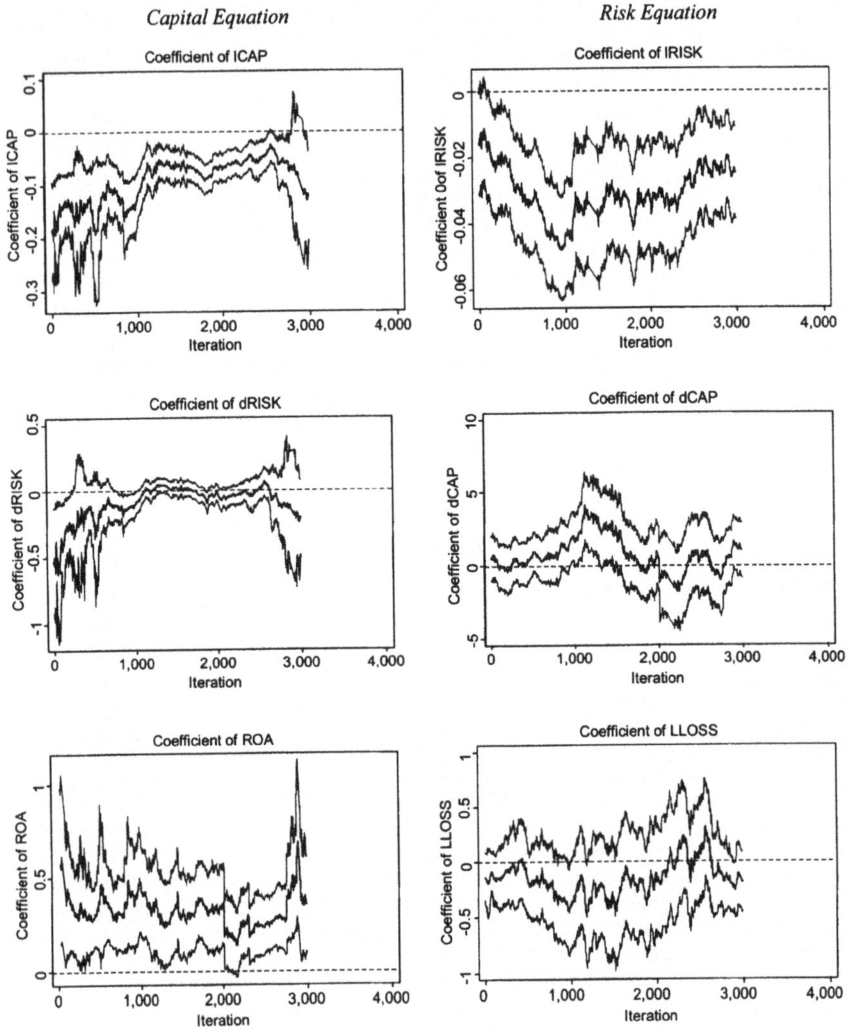

Figure A1 continued

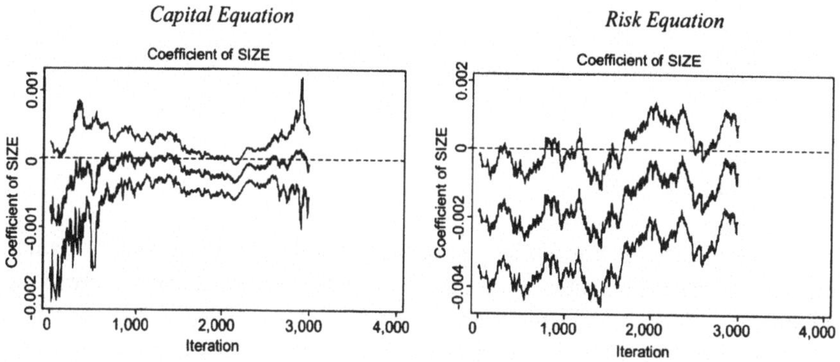

Notes: The figure gives the estimated coefficients as well as the upper and lower bound of the 95 percent confidence interval. The estimated coefficients of the dummy variables and the constant are not displayed. The coefficient is significant at the 5 percent level if zero is not included in the interval. The estimated coefficients with the 100 widest confidence bands are not displayed.

4 Capital and Risk Adjustments over the Business Cycle

4.1 Introduction

The role of banks in transmitting monetary shocks and the effect of banks' capitalization in this transmission process have been discussed extensively in the literature (e.g., Kishan and Opiela 2000; Van den Heuvel 2003). In contrast, their role in transmitting GDP shocks has received only minor attention, although poorly capitalized banks have the potential to amplify business cycles. Poorly capitalized banks facing materializing credit risk in a business cycle downturn have basically two options to avert falling below the minimum capital requirement. First, they could raise capital. However, this may be hard in a downturn, as external capital sources are scarce and expensive, while retaining earnings may not be an option due to low returns. And second, banks can increase their capital buffer by reducing risk-weighted assets. However, bank-specific assets are often not marketable and/or prices are depressed during a business cycle downturn to an extent that a sale implies prohibitive losses. Consequently, a decrease in risk-weighted assets occurs through a cut in lending. If this cut in lending is stronger than indicated by decreasing loan demand, the business cycle downturn is further amplified.

The empirical literature has taken two different microeconometric approaches in testing this hypothesis. The first approach is to analyze the effect of banks' capitalization on the transmission of business cycle fluctuations to lending. Studies following this approach indeed find evidence that low-capitalized banks are forced to cut their loan supply in a business cycle downturn (Peek and Rosengren 1995; Gambacorta and Mistrulli 2004).

The second approach is to analyze the effect of business cycle fluctuations on banks' capital buffers. Studies following this approach indeed find that capital buffers fluctuate countercyclically over the business cycle (Ayuso et al. 2004; Lindquist 2004). Given a countercyclical materialization of credit risk, a countercyclical effect of the capital buffer may be evidence for banks' shortsightedness (Borio et al. 2001; Ayuso et al. 2004): banks expand their loan portfolio in a business cycle upturn without building up their capital buffers accordingly. Hence, when the business cycle downturn sets in, banks' capital buffers cannot absorb the materializing credit risks. Then, banks have to increase their capital buffers by reducing lending.

Both approaches have their shortcomings. The first approach does not consider the effect of business cycle fluctuations on banks' capital buffers. In contrast, the second approach explicitly models banks' capital buffers. However, regressing banks' capital buffer on the business cycle cannot distinguish between banks' deliberate capital buffer decisions, i.e., supply-side effects, and demand-side effects working through loan demand. As loan demand is known to fluctuate procyclically[24] over the business cycle, demand-side effects may also lead to the countercyclical behavior of capital buffers through their effect on risk-weighted assets. However, this countercyclical behavior of capital buffers does not mean banks are shortsighted. Further, the second approach does not consider the effect of business cycle fluctuations on banks' loan supply.

This chapter uses the second approach, but tries to circumvent these conceptual problems. First, if one could demonstrate that banks' capitalization affects the behavior of capital buffers, this would indicate the existence of supply-side effects.[25] Hence, this chapter tests for asymmetries with respect to the capitalization of banks. And second, beyond analyzing the effect of business cycle fluctuations on capital buffers, this chapter analyzes the drivers of the detected negative effect. In order to do so, the capital buffer is decomposed into capital and risk-weighted assets, and the effect of business cycle fluctuations on both of these components is analyzed. As changes in risk-weighted assets are highly correlated with lending, changes in risk-weighted assets indicate changes in lending.

In addition, this chapter studies a banking market in which a potential retreat from lending in order to build up capital buffers may be particularly harmful. In Germany, bank lending constitutes 96 percent of outside funding for non-financial firms.[26] This number reflects the fact that the German economy is dominated by small- and medium-sized enterprises (the "Mittelstand"), which have limited access to external capital markets. As the small- and medium-sized enterprises borrow mainly from local savings and cooperative banks, this chapter focuses on the behavior of these two banking groups.

---

[24] To be clear, I use the term *procyclical* (*countercyclical*) to mean a variable that is co-moving with (moving in the opposite direction of) the business cycle. I do *not* use the term *procyclical* to mean a variable that amplifies business cycle fluctuations.

[25] While the business cycle may affect banks' capital buffers both through credit risk (supply-side effect) and through loan demand (demand-side effect), the effect of capitalization on the reaction of capital buffers to business cycles is clearly a supply-side effect (at least if the empirical methodology accounts for the endogeneity of capitalization).

[26] See Bank for International Settlements (2003). For comparison, in the United States, bank lending constituted only 45 percent of outside funding for nonfinancial firms in 2001.

Further, using one business cycle indicator for the economy as a whole may be too crude if the macroeconomic situation differs between regions. This is particularly a problem with savings and cooperative banks, which conduct their activities primarily within a limited regional area. Hence, this chapter also uses business cycle indicators that are available on a state level.

This chapter is organized as follows. Section 4.2 outlines the empirical model. Section 4.3 is concerned with the data. Section 4.4 presents the results and several robustness checks. Section 4.5 concludes.

4.2 The Empirical Model

As stated in the introduction, the aim of this chapter is to estimate the effect of business cycle fluctuations on banks' capital buffers. This section describes the empirical model and the estimation strategy used here. First, it derives the empirical model, states the hypotheses to be tested, and describes the methodology used. Second, it defines the measures of the variables of interest, i.e., banks' capital buffer, regulatory capital, risk-weighted assets, and the business cycle. Third, it defines the measures and the impact of the bank-specific control variables.

4.2.1 A Partial Adjustment Model

The banking literature shows that banks have an incentive to hold a capital buffer as an insurance against violation of the regulatory minimum capital requirement (Marcus 1984; Milne and Whalley 2001; Milne 2004). This incentive derives from two assumptions. First, banks cannot adjust capital and risk instantaneously; otherwise, they would not need to hold capital buffers.[27] And second, a violation of the regulatory minimum capital requirements triggers costly supervisory actions, possibly even leading to a bank's closure. Hence, banks stand to lose (part of) their charter value if they violate the regulatory minimum. However, raising capital is relatively costly compared to raising insured deposits. The trade-off between the cost of holding capital and the cost of failure (i.e., the charter value) determines the optimum capital buffer (Milne and Whalley 2001).

---

27 Banks may not be able to instantaneously adjust capital or risk when they face adjustment costs or illiquid markets. Furthermore, under asymmetric information, capital issues could be interpreted as a negative signal with regard to the bank's value (Myers and Majluf 1984), rendering banks unable or reluctant to react to negative capital shocks instantaneously.

Apart from this, the optimum capital buffer depends on the probability that the regulatory minimum will be violated and, hence, on the volatility of the capital ratio, which is mainly determined by banks' asset risks. For traditional banks, the main determinant of asset risk is credit risk. Thus, banks with higher credit risk have higher optimum capital buffers.

The materialization of credit risk fluctuates procyclically over the business cycle (e.g., Altman et al. 2005). During economic upturns, loans are less likely to default than during economic downturns. However, banks are likely to take credit risks during economic upturns when expanding their loan portfolios. Hence, forward-looking banks are expected to build up their capital buffers during economic upturns to be able to accommodate materializing credit risk during economic downturns. In contrast, shortsighted banks are expected to fail to provide for credit risk during economic upturns, but to be forced to increase their capital buffers during economic downturns (Borio et al. 2001; Ayuso et al. 2004).

These hypotheses are tested here using a partial adjustment framework, where banks aim at holding their respective optimum capital buffer. Hence, the specification becomes

(23) $$\Delta BUF_{i,t} = \alpha(BUF^{*}_{i,t} - BUF_{i,t-1}) + u_{i,t},$$

where $BUF_{i,t}$ ($BUF^{*}_{i,t}$) is the (optimum) capital buffer of bank i at time t, α is the speed of adjustment, and $u_{i,t}$ is the error term.

The optimum capital buffer is not readily observable, but it depends on the business cycle due to its effect on credit risk and bank-specific variables, as suggested by the banking literature. In order to obtain the standard form of an endogenous lag model, I have to transform (23) by adding $BUF_{i,t-1}$ to both sides of (23). Hence, the empirical model is specified as follows:[28]

(24) $$BUF_{i,t} = \alpha_0 + \alpha_1 BUF_{i,t-1} + \alpha_2 CYCLE_{j,t} + X_{i,t}\alpha + u_{i,t},$$

where $CYCLE_{j,t}$ is a measure of the business cycle in region j at time t, $X_{i,t}$ is a vector of bank-specific control variables for bank i at time t, and $\alpha_1 = 1 - \alpha$. Using the same representation as used in the literature simplifies comparisons of the results. Besides, using the standard form of an endogenous lag model has the advantage that my model can be estimated both with DPD for Ox (Doornik et al. 2002) and the Stata xtabond2 command (Roodman 2005).

---

28 Ayuso et al. (2004) use a similar specification. However, they derive their specification from a theoretical model in which banks minimize the costs of holding and adjusting capital. Estrella (2004) presents a theoretical model very similar to the one in Ayuso et al. (2004).

When I estimate (24) directly, α_1 is close to unity, indicating a unit-root problem within the data series of *BUF*. This is not surprising, as banks try to build up their capital buffer over the observation period (Figure 4 of Section 3). This was also seen in Chapter 3, where the speeds of capital and risk adjustments were close to zero due to the positive trends in capital and risk. The reason for this trend is likely to be the implementation of the Basel Capital Accord in Germany in 1993, which represented a negative shock to banks' capital buffers, as it raised capital requirement for most banks. Hence, in the aftermath of the implementation, banks tried to rebuild adequate capital buffers. By the end of the 1990s, the discussions on Basel II may have led to the prolongation of this positive trend.

As has been seen in Chapter 3, the Levin–Lin–Chu (2002) panel unit-root test cannot reject the null hypothesis of nonstationarity for *BUF*, but rejects it for ΔBUF. I address this unit-root problem by taking first differences of the capital buffer, the business cycle, and the bank-specific variables, thereby first-differencing the model.[29] Hence, the model I estimate is the following:

$$(25) \qquad \Delta BUF_{i,t} = \alpha_0 + \alpha_1 \Delta BUF_{i,t-1} + \alpha_2 \Delta CYCLE_{j,t} + \Delta X_{i,t}\alpha + \omega_{i,t},$$

where the error term, $\omega_{i,t}$, is assumed to consist of a bank-specific component, μ_i, and white noise, $\varepsilon_{i,t}$. Hence, $\omega_{i,t} = \mu_i + \varepsilon_{i,t}$ where $\mu_i \sim IID(0,\sigma_\mu^2)$, and $\varepsilon_i \sim IID(0,\sigma_\varepsilon^2)$, independent of each other and among themselves.

In contrast to the specification in levels, a negative α_2 does not mean that the capital buffer actually *de*creases in business cycle upturns and *in*creases in business cycle downturns. A negative α_2, rather, means that the increase in capital buffers, given by the positive trend in the data series, is dampened in business cycle upturns and boosted in business cycle downturns. Hence, the idea behind this specification is that the effect of business cycle fluctuations superimposes on the build-up of capital buffers.

Beyond analyzing the effect of business cycle fluctuations on capital buffers, I also analyze the driving forces of this effect. In order to be able to do so, I decompose the capital buffer into capital and risk-weighted assets and analyze the effect of business cycle fluctuations on both of these components. Hence, I estimate the following two equations:[30]

---

29 I additionally scale the first difference of real GDP using lagged real GDP. I do so to obtain GDP growth rates in order to make the results comparable to the findings in the literature, which also uses GDP growth rates. Further, I do not take differences of the dummy variables, as they are meant to capture differences in the *change* of the capital buffer.

30 Although *CAP* and *RISK* do not show unit roots, I still first-difference them analogously to *BUF*. This allows me to argue that observed changes in ΔBUF are due

(26) $$\Delta CAP_{i,t} = \beta_0 + \beta_1 \Delta CAP_{i,t-1} + \beta_2 \Delta CYCLE_{j,t} + \Delta X_{i,t}\beta + v_{i,t}$$

(27) $$\Delta RISK_{i,t} = \gamma_0 + \gamma_1 \Delta RISK_{i,t-1} + \gamma_2 \Delta CYCLE_{j,t} + \Delta X_{i,t}\gamma + w_{i,t}$$

where $CAP_{i,t}$ and $RISK_{i,t}$ are the regulatory capital and risk-weighted assets of bank i at time t. The error terms, $v_{i,t}$, and, $w_{i,t}$, are again assumed to consist of a bank-specific component and white noise, with the same assumptions as for (25).

4.2.2 Hypotheses

Taking as the null hypothesis that business cycle fluctuations do not have an impact on the change in banks' capital buffers, I can state my hypotheses in terms of the coefficient α_2 as follows:

H_5: $\alpha_2 > 0$. The capital buffer fluctuates procyclically over the business cycle. During business cycle upturns, when banks expand lending, potential risks tend to rise and banks increase their capital buffers by more than on average in order to account for these increasing risks. In business cycle downturns, when risks materialize, banks can then draw on these higher capital buffers.

H_6: $\alpha_2 < 0$. The capital buffer fluctuates countercyclically over the business cycle. The negative sign can be evidence for two competing arguments. It may indicate that banks actively increase their capital buffers during business cycle downturns, implying shortsightedness, i.e., that banks build up their capital buffers during business cycle upturns by less than on average, not accounting for the increasing risks. Alternatively, a negative sign may also indicate demand-side effects because increasing (decreasing) loan demand dampens (boosts) the increase in capital buffers in business cycle upturns (downturns).

If H_6 cannot be rejected, I cannot directly distinguish whether demand-side effects alone are behind the negative α_2 or whether supply-side effects also drive this result. However, evidence that banks with low capital buffers increase their risk-weighted assets in a business cycle downturn by less than banks with higher capital buffers would lend support to the existence of supply-side effects. In a business cycle downturn, banks with low capital buffers may be forced to increase their capital buffers relative to banks with high capital buffers by

---

to observed changes in ΔCAP and $\Delta RISK$. Further, in contrast to Chapter 3, I am only interested in the ultimate effect of $\Delta CYCLE$ on ΔCAP and $\Delta RISK$ and not in the interaction between ΔCAP and $\Delta RISK$. Hence, I use reduced form estimations here instead of specifying a structural model as used in Chapter 3.

decreasing risk-weighted assets. Taking as the null hypothesis that banks with low capital buffers decrease their risk-weighted assets in a business cycle downturn by the same amount as banks with higher capital buffers, I can state my hypotheses in terms of the coefficient γ_2 as follows:

H_7: $\gamma_2|_{downturn, low\ capital\ buffer} > \gamma_2|_{downturn, higher\ capital\ buffer}$. *During business cycle downturns, banks with low capital buffers increase their risk-weighted assets by less than banks with higher capital buffers. This asymmetry lends support to the claim that there are supply-side effects and, hence, that banks are shortsighted.*

H_8: $\gamma_2|_{downturn, low\ capital\ buffer} < \gamma_2|_{downturn, higher\ capital\ buffer}$. *During business cycle downturns, banks with low capital buffers increase their risk-weighted assets by more than banks with higher capital buffers. This asymmetry does not lend support to the claim that banks are shortsighted. However, it still lends support to the claim that there are supply-side effects, yet in an unexpected way. It indicates that banks may face some restrictions on adjusting their loan portfolio, which may also be behind their low capitalization.*

4.2.3 Methodology

Given the model in (25)–(27), I employ dynamic panel data techniques that control for the bank-specific component of the error term. The within estimator is known to produce biased estimates when the lagged dependent variable appears as a regressor. The bias in such estimates (the "Nickell bias") is of $O(1/T)$. Hence, its consistency depends on T being large (Nickell 1981). As T is about 10, in my case, I cannot argue that the Nickell bias approaches zero. To avoid the Nickell bias, I opt for an instrumental variable approach. In the following, I describe the estimation procedure by using (25) as an example. (26) and (27) are estimated using an analogous procedure.

I take the first difference of the model specified in (25) in order to eliminate the bank-specific effect, μ_i, and I try to find suitable instruments for $\Delta BUF_{i,t-1} - \Delta BUF_{i,t-2}$. Arellano and Bond (1991) suggest a generalized method of moments (GMM) estimator that uses the entire set of lagged values of $\Delta BUF_{i,t}$ as instruments. Blundell and Bond (1998) derive additional moment conditions that increase the asymptotic efficiency of the GMM estimator. Hence, I use the so-called system GMM estimator suggested by Blundell and Bond (1998), which uses lagged differences of $BUF_{i,t}$ as instruments for equations in levels in addition to the Arellano–Bond instruments.

In models with endogenous regressors, using too many instruments could result in seriously biased estimates. Hence, I only use a subsample of the whole history of the series as instruments in the later cross-section. To determine the optimal lag length of the instruments, I use the procedure suggested by Andrews and Lu (2001), as done in Chapter 3. To further reduce the problem of biased estimates, I again add together the columns of the optimal instrument matrix and, hence, use only one instrument for each variable and lag distance, rather than one for each time period, variable, and lag distance (Roodman 2005).

As, for my sample, the one- and two-step Blundell–Bond system GMM estimators produce quite similar estimates, I present only the (asymptotically) more efficient two-step estimates. However, the two-step estimates of the standard errors tend to be severely downward biased (Arellano and Bond 1991; Blundell and Bond 1998). To address this issue, I use the finite-sample correction to the two-step covariance matrix derived by Windmeijer (2005).

4.2.4 Measures of the Capital Buffer, Regulatory Capital, Risk-Weighted Assets, and Business Cycle Fluctuations

Banks' capital buffers are given by the capital they hold in excess of the regulatory minimum capital requirement. Hence, I define banks' capital buffer, *BUF*, as the Basel capital-to-risk-weighted-assets ratio minus the 8 percent regulatory minimum.

In order to estimate (26) and (27), I decompose the capital buffer into regulatory capital and risk-weighted assets. In order to scale capital and risk-weighted assets, I define my capital variable, *CAP*, as total regulatory capital over total assets and my risk-weighted-assets variable, *RISK*, as total risk-weighted assets over total assets.

With respect to business cycle fluctuations, *CYCLE*, I use the real output gap, *GAP*, which isolates the business cycle from the economic trend. I calculate the output gap by subtracting a nonlinear trend from real GDP using the Hoddrick–Prescott filter. As a robustness check, I also use the real GDP growth rate, *GDP*, as done by the literature (Ayuso et al. 2004; Lindquist 2004). Since savings and cooperative banks operate mainly in their own region and economic situations may differ between regions, I also calculate the real GDP growth rate, *SGDP*, for each German state separately.[31] The regional variations in the business cycle also help me generalize my results, as I have only one full business cycle in my data. The variable definitions are also given in Table A10 in Appendix 1.

I have also experimented with other business cycle indicators such as unemployment rates, the Ifo business climate index, state-level insolvency rates, etc.

31 Table A14 in Appendix 1 shows that *GDP* and *SGDP* have a correlation coefficient of 0.75.

Yet, these indicators showed time patterns that were very different from the ones observed for *GAP*, *GDP*, and *SGDP*. Hence, it was not surprising that the regression results were not conclusive and, hence, they are not presented in the following.

4.2.5 Bank-Specific Control Variables

In order to estimate the effect of business cycle fluctuations on changes in banks' capital buffers, I have to control for the effect of bank-specific variables on changes in the optimum capital buffer. In the following, I present the proxy variables suggested by the banking literature and their expected impact on changes in the optimum capital buffer. The variable definitions are also given in Table A1 in Appendix 1 of Chapter 3.

As raising capital through the capital markets is costly, retained *earnings* are frequently used to increase capital buffers. This implies that changes in profits have a positive impact on changes in the optimum capital buffer. But a negative impact may also be conceivable: high profits may reflect high charter values and, hence, the ability to permanently generate high profits and to increase capital buffers through retained earnings. Thus, high-profit banks need to hold lower capital buffers as an insurance against a probable violation of the regulatory minimum (Milne and Whalley 2001), which translates into changes in profits having a negative impact on changes in the optimum capital buffer. Hence, I include the banks' return on assets, *ROA*, with an ambiguous expected sign.

Changes in *asset risk* may have a positive as well as a negative impact on changes in the capital buffer. Banks may have reacted to the implementation of the Basel Capital Accord in 1993 by *increasing* asset risk and, hence, profitability in order to compensate for having to hold more expensive capital (Koehn and Santomero 1980). This moral hazard behavior would be reflected in changes in portfolio risk having a positive effect on changes in banks' capital buffers. In contrast, banks may have reacted to the implementation of the Basel Capital Accord by *decreasing* asset risk, as higher capital levels reduce incentives for risk-taking and higher levels of risk reduce the incentive for decreasing capital (Furlong and Keeley 1989). This behavior would be reflected in changes in asset risk having a negative effect on changes in banks' capital buffers. As banks make loan loss provisions against expected losses of their portfolio, I use new net provisions over total assets, *LLOSS*, as a proxy for risk and include *LLOSS* with an ambiguous expectation regarding the estimated sign.[32]

---

32 As the banking theory suggests that capital and risk may be simultaneously determined, I model risk as an endogenous variable to check robustness (see Section 4.4).

Furthermore, banks' *size* may affect the capital buffer through several channels. First, unexpected losses are in part due to asymmetric information between banks and their borrowers. Screening and monitoring reduce the asymmetry, but are costly and, thus, banks could balance the cost and gains from these activities against holding excess capital. If there are economies of scale in screening and monitoring, large banks should hold relatively less capital and instead undertake more monitoring and screening. Second, larger banks may have better investment and diversification opportunities.[33] Thus, they are subject to a lower probability of a large negative shock to their capital and only need to hold a lower capital buffer as insurance against such a shock. Third, there is a higher probability that larger banks in financial distress will be bailed out by the government, because of potential systemic effects ("too big to fail"). Fourth, the size of a bank may be an indicator of the bank's access to capital. Savings banks as publicly owned entities and cooperative banks, which are organized as credit cooperatives, are not allowed to raise Tier 1 capital via equity markets. Hence, they depend on retained earnings and capital injections by their public owners and cooperative members, respectively. However, big savings and cooperative banks may use subordinated debt issues to raise Tier 2 capital. Hence, I include the natural log of total assets, *SIZE*, to capture size effects with an expected negative sign.

Further, banks which hold *liquid assets* need less insurance against a possible violation of the minimum capital requirements. Further, liquid assets have, on average, a nonzero risk weight. Hence, banks can increase their capital buffer by liquidating these assets and, thus, banks with more liquid assets have a lower optimum capital buffer. I use bond holdings plus share holdings plus interbank assets over total assets, *LIQUID*, as a proxy for liquidity and include *LIQUID* with the expected negative sign.

I also include a dummy variable to capture *mergers*, *dyMERGER*. The reason for including this variable is the ongoing merger wave within the savings and particularly the cooperative bank sector (Deutsche Bundesbank 2003). The dummy variable is unity for the acquirer in the year of the merger and zero otherwise. The expected sign of the variable is negative given that acquiring banks are typically better capitalized before a merger.

Finally, I include a dummy variable in order to capture differences between *savings and cooperative banks*. *dySB* is unity if the bank is a savings bank and zero otherwise (cooperative bank).

---

33 In principle, the argument can also run the other way around, as small and specialized banks may be in a better position to assess the quality of loans (Acharya et al. 2006). However, savings and cooperative banks are more universal than specialized banks.

4.3 Data Description

As my results may have important implications for banks' loan supply, this chapter focuses on savings and cooperative banks, which have traditionally played a dominant role in lending to small- and medium-sized enterprises (SMEs) in Germany. SMEs form the backbone of the German economy and, in contrast to larger firms, rely heavily on bank loans.[34] Although not directly comparable with SME lending, for which data are not available, the share of savings and cooperative banks in lending to nonfinancial firms highlights the significance of the two banking groups: At the end of 2003, the share of the savings bank sector was 39 percent, the share of cooperative bank sector was 13 percent, and the share of the commercial bank sector, including the four large banks, was 44 percent.

My sample consists of all local savings and cooperative banks in west Germany. I exclude the central giro institutions from the sample, as their portfolios are very different from those of local savings and cooperative banks. I also exclude the seven private savings banks (so-called independent savings banks), as they are not subject to regional investment restrictions and have, hence, more degrees of freedom in deciding upon their loan portfolio. I also exclude east German banks from the sample, as east Germany had a very different business cycle up to 2000, because the east German economy had to catch up with the west German economy in the years following reunification and because east German savings and cooperative banks financed a substantial part of this catching-up process.

Further, my dataset includes 288 observations with negative capital buffers. These banks may undergo transitional adjustments in accordance with the supervisory authority. Alternatively, they may be distressed and, hence, may be under the control of the supervisory authority. In this case, they could not take deliberate investment and funding decisions. As I lack the data to discriminate between these two cases, I exclude these observations from the sample.[35] Finally, there are ten observations for capital buffers with values above 40 percentage points. All ten observations come from the cooperative sector and bias my respective coefficient estimates significantly. For this reason, these observations are also excluded. Hence, the sample consists of an unbalanced panel of 492 German

---

34 As regards the importance of the SMEs for employment and output in Germany, see Hauser (2000).

35 However, as removing randomly distributed observations from the sample is problematic, I run two robustness checks. First, I exclude the whole time series for a bank with one or more negative observations from the sample. And second, I leave all negative observations in the sample. Yet, the regression results are qualitatively the same for the different approaches.

savings and 2,159 cooperative banks in west Germany over the period 1993 to 2003. 1993 is the earliest date for which data on risk-weighted assets are available. 2004 is the latest date for which GDP data are available. However, the Hoddrick–Prescott filter, which I use to construct the output gap, is known to have a bad fit for the first and the last observation. To prevent the bad fit for the first observation, I construct my filtered GDP time series on the basis of a longer GDP time series back into the past. This leaves me with the bad fit for the last observation, which I, thus, drop from the sample.

The data were obtained from two different sources. The balance sheet data were kindly provided by Deutsche Bundesbank, which, in its prudential function, collects bank-level data. The macroeconomic data were obtained from the German Federal Statistical Office.

Tables A12 and A13a–b in Appendix 1 provide descriptive statistics for the business cycle indicators and the bank-specific variables. Table A13a provides the descriptive statistics for the subsamples for savings and cooperative banks. It also contains a Wilcoxon rank-sum test, which tests whether the subsamples come from the same population.[36] The test reveals that significant differences between the banks in each sector do indeed exist. Savings banks, on average, hold lower capital buffers, *BUF*, hold lower average risk-weighted assets, *RISK*, are larger, *SIZE*, and realize a lower return on assets, *ROA*, than their competitors in the cooperative sector. Hence, while savings and cooperative banks are both specialized in SME lending and compete with each other in their respective region, they exhibit several interesting differences with respect to their balance sheet structure and profitability. I account for this heterogeneity across banking sectors by running regressions separately for the two subsamples.

Table A13b provides the descriptive statistics for the subsamples for banks with high capital buffers and banks with low capital buffers.[37] The Wilcoxon rank-sum test shows that, on average, banks with low capital buffers take higher risks, as given by higher risk-weighted assets, *RISK*, and have higher loan loss reserves, *LLOSS*, as well as a higher standard deviation of the returns on assets, *ROA*. However, they are not rewarded by higher returns on assets, *ROA*. These findings point to a possible inefficiency of banks with low capital buffers.

Table A14 gives the correlation matrix. It shows that the four business cycle indicators that are used in this chapter are highly positively correlated with each

---

36 Given that I primarily test financial ratios, which are typically not normally distributed, I use the Wilcoxon rank-sum test, which does not depend on the normality assumption.

37 A bank is defined to have a low capital buffer if it is among the 5 percent least capitalized banks in its banking group for a respective year. Otherwise, it is defined as a bank with a high capital buffer.

other.[38] It also shows that two out of the three indicators suggest that capital buffers behave procyclically and that the third indicator suggests that capital buffers behave countercyclically. As will be seen below, controlling for bank-specific variables gives a more consistent picture.

Figure 4a shows the evolution of banks' capital buffers and the real output gap over the 11-year period from 1993 to 2003, while Figure 4b shows the evolution of *changes* in banks' capital buffers and *changes* in the real output gap. First of all, Figure 4a shows that savings and cooperative banks have been building up their capital buffers since the first Basel Capital Accord was enforced in Germany in 1993. This trend in capital buffers causes unit-root problems in the estimation. Hence, I take first differences of the capital buffers and explain changes in capital buffers as being the result of changes in the real output gap (as described in Section 2.1). Further, Figure 4a shows that an increase in the real output gap tends to dampen the increase in capital buffers for both well- and low-capitalized banks. This is even more clearly shown by Figure 4b. Changes in the capital buffer are negatively related to changes in the output gap. The only exception is changes in the capital buffers of low-capitalized cooperative banks, which are seemingly unrelated to changes in the output gap. Hence, figures 4a and 4b provide further evidence that capital buffers behave countercyclically over the business cycle. Additionally, Figure 4a shows that, while both banking sectors have built up capital buffers, well-capitalized cooperative banks have consistently maintained capital buffers larger than those of well-capitalized savings banks. This gap also widened over the observation period. Finally, Figure 4a shows that the gap between well- and low-capitalized banks also widened.

4.4 Regression Analysis

In the following subsections, I present the results of estimating (25)–(27). First, I show the baseline results for (25) for the full sample, using all four main business cycle indicators, and for savings and cooperative banks separately. Second, I test for asymmetries in the behavior of capital buffers with respect to economic upturns and downturns as well as with respect to the capitalization of banks. Third, I decompose the capital buffer into capital and risk-weighted assets and show the effect of the business cycle on these two components, corresponding to estimating (26) and (27). Fourth and finally, I show further robustness checks.

[38] Further, most variables are significantly correlated with each other. Most probably, this correlation stems from fixed effects, which the simple correlations do not take into account. The multivariate regression techniques, which I employ, do however account for such bank-specific fixed effects.

Figure 4:
Capital Buffers of German Savings and Cooperative Banks over the Business Cycle, 1993–2003

a. In Levels

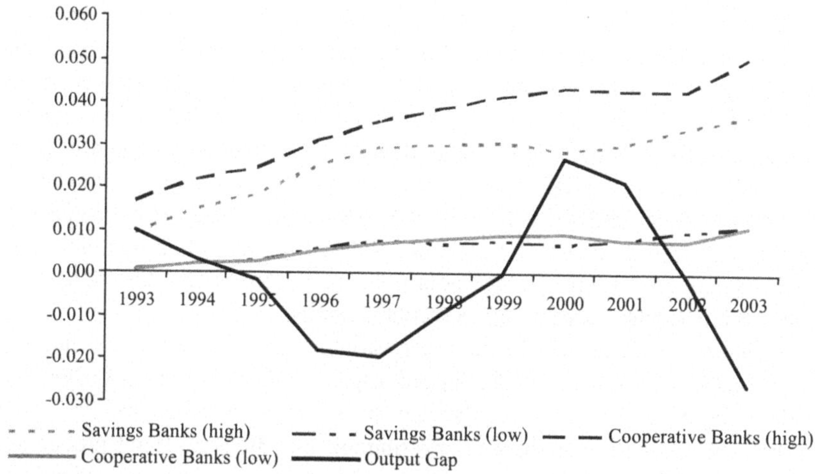

b. In Changes

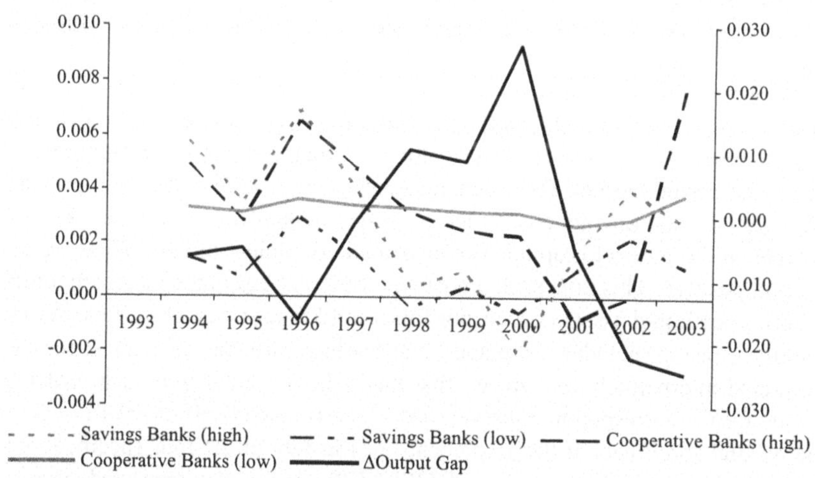

Notes: The capital buffer is defined as the Basel capital ratio minus 0.08. The output gap in this figure is defined as the real output gap in billions of chained (1970) euros. Low indicates banks that are among the 5 percent least capitalized banks in their banking group for a respective year. High refers to all remaining banks. In the lower part of this figure, the change in the output gap is given on the right-hand scale.

Source: Federal Statistical Office, own calculations using data provided by the Deutsche Bundesbank.

4.4.1 Adjustments in the Capital Buffer

Specifications 1–3 in Table 6 present the baseline results of estimating (25) for the full sample using my three main business cycle indicators, the Hansen test, and the tests of serial correlation in the first-differenced residuals. With respect to *CYCLE*, I find a highly significant and negative coefficient for all of my three business cycle indicators, i.e., the real output gap at the federal level, *GAP*, the real GDP growth at the federal level, *GDP*, and the real GDP growth at the state level, *SGDP*. This consistent picture indicates that capital buffers behave countercyclically and, thus, lends support to H_6. The implied effects are, however, small: when real GDP growth increases by 1.0 percentage point, the increase in the capital buffer decreases by 0.06 percentage points. This small effect is in line with the literature. Ayuso et al. (2004) find that when nominal GDP growth increases by 1.0 percentage point, the capital buffer (not the increase in the capital buffer) decreases by 0.3 percentage points.

The findings with respect to the other variables are also worth mentioning. The estimated coefficients of the lagged capital buffer confirm my dynamic specification at the 5 percent significance level across all indicators. As I take first differences of the variables before running the Blundell–Bond procedure, the estimated coefficient of the lagged capital buffer gives the speed of adjustment of the *change* in the capital buffer, which is rather fast: the estimated speeds imply that shocks to the change in the capital buffer are halved within 0.4 years.

The estimated coefficient of the return on assets, *ROA*, is significant and negative, implying that high-profit banks hold lower capital buffers as insurance against a probable violation of the regulatory minimum, as they can retain earnings to increase capital buffers. The estimated coefficient of *SIZE* is highly significant and negative, pointing to economies of scale, diversification effects, and advantages in the access to capital. The estimated coefficient of *LIQUID* is significant and positive. This unexpected positive effect implies that banks with a high proportion of liquid assets in their portfolios hold higher capital buffers. As my liquidity measure includes share and bond holdings, this positive effect may be interpreted alternatively to indicate that banks hold capital buffers in order to provide for the corresponding market risk. The estimated coefficient of *LLOSS* is positive and significant at the 10 percent level in two of the four specifications. My control variable for mergers (*dyMERGER*) yields an unexpected positive sign, implying that acquirers have lower capital buffers. The positive coefficient may simply be due to the fact that the statistics indicate the larger bank as the acquirer and that larger banks have, on average, lower capital buffers (see correlation matrix).

Table 6:
Blundell–Bond Two-Step System GMM Estimates for the Capital Buffer—All Banks, Savings Banks, and Cooperative Banks, 1995–2003

	1	2	3	4	5
	All banks	All banks	All banks	Sav. banks	Coop. banks
Dep. variable: ΔBUF_t	Real output gap (*GAP*)	Real GDP growth (*GDP*)	State-level real GDP growth (*SGDP*)	Real output gap (*GAP*)	Real output gap (*GAP*)
ΔBUF_{t-1}	0.0347**	0.0376**	0.0381**	0.0395*	0.0309*
	(2.21)	(2.38)	(2.40)	(1.77)	(1.73)
$\Delta CYCLE$	–0.0446***	–0.0625***	–0.0220***	–0.1293***	–0.0188***
	(8.95)	(6.99)	(3.58)	(15.67)	(3.22)
ΔROA	–0.4012***	–0.3994***	–0.4023***	–0.5425***	–0.3867***
	(3.99)	(4.02)	(3.98)	(4.41)	(3.72)
$\Delta SIZE$	–0.0193***	–0.0190***	–0.0192***	–0.0118***	–0.0192***
	(11.96)	(11.89)	(11.90)	(4.26)	(10.89)
$\Delta LIQUID$	0.0462***	0.0465***	0.0487***	0.0126**	0.0510***
	(15.11)	(15.09)	(16.15)	(2.07)	(15.32)
$\Delta LLOSS$	0.0378*	0.0364*	0.0322	0.0021	0.0454*
	(1.71)	(1.66)	(1.47)	(0.06)	(1.86)
dySB	–0.0010***	–0.0010***	–0.0010***		
	(9.31)	(9.53)	(9.48)		
dyMERGER	0.0070***	0.0069***	0.0069***	0.0028*	0.0070***
	(11.03)	(10.91)	(10.91)	(1.91)	(10.20)
Constant	0.0039***	0.0048***	0.0043***	0.0022***	0.0040***
	(34.85)	(30.86)	(30.11)	(13.62)	(33.67)
# Obs.	19,560	19,560	19,560	4,085	15,475
# Banks	2,651	2,651	2,651	492	2,159
Hansen test	0.204	0.240	0.164	0.001	0.306
AR(1) test	0.000	0.000	0.000	0.000	0.000
AR(2) test	0.476	0.524	0.624	0.127	0.349

Notes: The dependent variable is $\Delta BUF_{i,t}$. *BUF* is defined as the Basel capital ratio minus 0.08. *CYCLE* is defined differently for the various specifications. The respective definition is given in the respective column. *ROA* is defined as the return on assets ratio. *SIZE* is defined as the natural log of total assets. *LIQUID* is defined as bond plus share holdings plus interbank assets over total assets. *LLOSS* is defined as new net loan loss provisions over total assets. *dyMERGER* is unity for an acquiring bank in the year of the merger and zero otherwise. *dySB* is unity if the bank is a savings bank and zero otherwise (cooperative bank). In order to account for the unit root of *BUF*, all variables are first-differenced before applying the Blundell–Bond procedure. The only exceptions are the dummy variables. Real GDP is additionally scaled by lagged real GDP in order to obtain growth rates as used in the literature. Lagged differences of ΔBUF_i are used as instruments for equations in levels, in addition to lagged levels of ΔBUF_i, which are used as instruments for equations in first differences. Δ indicates the first difference. The absolute *t*-values are given in parentheses. ***, **, and * indicate statistical significance at the 1, 5, and 10 percent level, respectively, in a two-tailed *t*-test. Hansen test refers to the test of overidentifying restrictions. AR(1) and AR(2) test refer to the test for the null of no first-order and second-order autocorrelation in the first-differenced residuals.

The highly significant and negative coefficient for *dySB* indicates that savings banks and cooperative banks differ with regard to changes in their capital buffers. Given the evidence in Figure 4a, the negative dummy variable reflects the fact that the gap between the capital buffers of cooperative and savings banks widens over the observation period.

Including dummy variables is the simplest way to take the heterogeneity between savings and cooperative banks into account. But, given the evidence presented in Table A13a in Appendix 1, this heterogeneity is likely to be also contained in the slope coefficients. Hence, in specifications 4 and 5 in Table 6, I split the sample into savings and cooperative banks and run regressions on each of these subsamples separately. As the results for the other business cycle indicators are qualitatively the same, I only present the results for the real output gap at the federal level, *GAP*.

With respect to *CYCLE*, differentiating between savings and cooperative banks reveals an interesting difference in the behavior of the capital buffer: while the capital buffers of both savings and cooperative banks behave countercyclically over the business cycle, the capital buffers of savings banks react more than six times stronger to the business cycle than the capital buffers of cooperative banks. The standardized beta coefficients indicate an even more pronounced reaction of savings banks relative to cooperative banks: a one-standard-deviation increase in ΔGAP translates into a decrease in ΔBUF of 0.96 (0.09) standard deviations for savings banks (cooperative banks). As shown later in this chapter, the stronger reaction of changes in the capital buffer of savings banks is due to a countercyclical reaction of capital and a procyclical reaction of risk-weighted assets that is four times stronger than for cooperative banks.

The findings with respect to the other variables are also worth mentioning. With respect to the lagged dependent variable, the results again confirm my dynamic specification at the 10 percent significance level for both savings banks and cooperative banks. With respect to the other bank-specific variables, *ROA*, *SIZE*, *LIQUID*, and *LLOSS* have the same qualitative effect on capital buffers for both savings and cooperative banks. However, *LLOSS* is found to be significant at the 10 percent level for cooperative banks only. The merger dummy variable *dyMERGER* is significant and positive, yet more significant for cooperative banks, for which I could observe a merger wave in the period under study.

4.4.2 Asymmetries

In this subsection, I test for two asymmetries in the reaction of capital buffers to business cycle fluctuations. First, I test whether capital buffers react differently in business cycle upturns and downturns. To do so, I define a dummy variable, *dyUP*, which is unity during an economic upturn, i.e., $\Delta GAP > 0$, and zero otherwise. Then, I interact the dummy variable with the output gap and one minus the dummy variable with the output gap and include both interaction terms in the regression. Thus, the two coefficients correspond to business cycle upturns and downturns, respectively, which I then compare by means of a Wald test.

Specifications 1 and 2 in Table 7 show the results. For savings banks, I again find that capital buffers behave countercyclically, as the increase in capital buffers decreases in business cycle upturns and increases in downturns. For cooperative banks, business cycle downturns boost the increase in capital buffers, but business cycle upturns also boost the increase in capital buffers. However, the boost during a business cycle upturn is only half as strong as in a downturn, this difference being statistically significant, as confirmed by a Wald test. The result points to an interesting asymmetry for cooperative banks, since both business cycle upturns and downturns seem to boost the increase in capital buffers, the boost being stronger in a downturn.

Second, I test whether banks with low capital buffers react differently to business cycle fluctuations than banks with high capital buffers. To do so, I define a dummy variable, *dyLOW*, which is unity if a bank is among the 5 percent least capitalized banks in its banking group for a respective year and zero otherwise.[39] The idea behind this definition is that if a bank is badly capitalized compared to its peers, i.e., banks in the same banking group, this may signal problems within the bank. Principally, differing risk attitudes could also be behind differing capitalizations. However, I control for banks' risk-taking by including *LLOSS* in the regression. Further, risk attitudes are likely to differ only to a minor extent within the savings bank sector and the cooperative bank sector. Once I have defined the capitalization dummy variable, *dyLOW*, I interact it with the interaction terms defined in the last paragraph, as capitalization may matter more in a business cycle downturn.

Specifications 3 and 4 in Table 7 show that the results for banks with high capital buffers are in line with my previous results. For savings banks with high capital buffers, the increase in capital buffers decreases in a business cycle upturn and increases in a business cycle downturn. For cooperative banks with high capital buffers, the increase in capital buffers increases both in a business cycle upturn and downturn. On the contrary, both for savings banks with low capital buffers and for cooperative banks with low capital buffers, the increase in

---

39 As a robustness check, I also use other thresholds to distinguish between banks with low and high capital buffers. The results are consistent for different thresholds. However, the higher the threshold, the more banks with moderate capital buffers are classified as banks with low capital buffers. Hence, the difference in the effects for the two groups declines as the threshold rises.

Table 7:
Blundell–Bond Two-Step System GMM Estimates for the Capital Buffer—Savings Banks and Cooperative Banks, 1995–2003

	1	2	3	4
	Savings banks	Cooperative banks	Savings banks	Cooperative banks
Dependent variable: ΔBUF_t	Real output gap (*GAP*)	Real output gap (*GAP*)	Real output gap (*GAP*)	Real output gap (*GAP*)
ΔBUF_{t-1}	0.0390*	0.0430**	0.0372*	0.0416**
	(1.76)	(2.35)	(1.67)	(2.29)
$\Delta CYCLE*dyUP$	–0.1530***	0.0693***		
	(8.28)	(5.68)		
$\Delta CYCLE*(1-dyUP)$	–0.1067***	–0.1168***		
	(6.89)	(10.17)		
$\Delta CYCLE*dyUP*dyLOW$			–0.3065***	–0.2092***
			(7.42)	(7.02)
$\Delta CYCLE*(1-dyUP)*dyLOW$			0.1901***	0.3295***
			(6.19)	(8.55)
$\Delta CYCLE*dyUP*(1-dyLOW)$			–0.1426***	0.0842***
			(7.45)	(6.81)
$\Delta CYCLE*(1-dyUP)*(1-dyLOW)$			–0.1259***	–0.1407***
			(7.97)	(12.15)
ΔROA	–0.5366***	–0.3806***	–0.5416***	–0.3617***
	(4.46)	(3.78)	(4.73)	(3.52)
$\Delta SIZE$	–0.0127***	–0.0173***	–0.0115***	–0.0169***
	(4.35)	(9.74)	(4.07)	(9.63)
$\Delta LIQUID$	0.0128**	0.0534***	0.0131**	0.0520***
	(2.11)	(16.02)	(2.20)	(15.73)
$\Delta LLOSS$	0.0133	0.0435*	0.0138	0.0447*
	(0.34)	(1.79)	(0.36)	(1.85)
dyMERGER	0.0033**	0.0063***	0.0027*	0.0060***
	(2.13)	(9.09)	(1.76)	(8.78)
Constant	0.0026***	0.0027***	0.0025***	0.0027***
	(9.53)	(14.15)	(9.51)	(14.29)
# Observations	4,085	15,475	4,085	15,475
# Banks	492	2,159	492	2,159
Hansen test	0.001	0.274	0.001	0.307
AR(1) test	0.000	0.000	0.000	0.000
AR(2) test	0.144	0.813	0.170	0.826

Notes: The dependent variable is $\Delta BUF_{i,t}$. *BUF* is defined as the Basel capital ratio minus 0.08. *CYCLE* is defined as the real output gap. *dyUP* is unity during an economic upturn, i.e., $\Delta GAP>0$, and zero otherwise. *dyLOW* is unity if the bank is among the 5 percent least capitalized banks in its banking group for the respective year and zero otherwise. *ROA* is defined as the return on assets ratio. *SIZE* is defined as the natural log of total assets. *LLOSS* is defined new net loan loss provisions over total assets. *LIQUID* is defined as bond plus share holdings plus interbank assets over total assets. *dyMERGER* is unity for an acquiring bank in the year before the merger and zero otherwise. In order to account for the unit root of *BUF*, all variables are first-differenced before applying the Blundell–Bond procedure. The only exception is the merger dummy variable. Lagged differences of ΔBUF_i are used as instruments for equations in levels, in addition to lagged levels of ΔBUF_i, which are used as instruments for equations in first differences. Δ indicates the first difference. The absolute *t*-values are given in parentheses. ***, **, and * indicate statistical significance at the 1, 5, and 10 percent level, respectively, in a two-tailed *t*-test. Hansen test refers to the test of overidentifying restrictions. AR(1) and AR(2) test refer to the test for the null of no first-order and second-order autocorrelation in the first-differenced residuals.

capital buffers decreases both in a business cycle upturn and downturn. Hence, the 5 percent of banks with the lowest capital buffers lag further and further behind their peers over the observation period.

The results are also interesting with respect to the questions whether changes in the capital buffer over the business cycle simply reflect changes in loan demand. The finding that banks with low capital buffers increase their capital buffers by less than their peers in a business cycle downturn indicates that supply-side effects also play a role in the behavior of banks' capital buffers: if capital buffers were determined by loan demand only, the capital buffers of low-capitalized banks and the capital buffers of their well-capitalized peers should both behave similarly. I test this hypothesis more directly in the next subsection by running regressions on the two components of the capital buffer, i.e., capital and risk-weighted assets. The effect of loan demand is then expected to show in the regression for risk-weighted assets.

4.4.3 Adjustments in Regulatory Capital and Risk-Weighted Assets

In this subsection, I decompose the capital buffer into its numerator, i.e., regulatory capital, and its denominator, i.e., risk-weighted assets. Regressing capital and risk-weighted assets on business cycle fluctuations allows direct observation of where the adjustment in the capital buffer over the business cycle comes from.

Specifications 1 and 2 in tables 8 and 9 show the results for capital and risk-weighted assets. Capital fluctuates countercyclically for savings banks. For cooperative banks, the *CYCLE* is insignificant though. As will be seen below, this insignificance is due to the contrary effects for cooperative banks with high and low capital buffers that balance in the aggregate. Further, risk-weighted assets fluctuate procyclically over the business cycle both for savings banks and for cooperative banks, the fluctuation, however, being four times stronger for savings banks. As risk-weighted assets are highly correlated with lending, my findings suggest that the lending of savings banks fluctuates more strongly over the business cycle than the lending of cooperative banks. Yet, Buch et al. (2006) find that the sectoral lending of German cooperative banks fluctuates more strongly over the business cycle than the lending of German savings banks. Though these results seem to be at odds at first, they can easily be married. The endogenous variable in this chapter is risk-weighted assets scaled by total assets. As total assets of savings banks fluctuate less procyclically over the business cycle than total assets of cooperative banks, it is plausible that lending fluctuates *less* procyclically for savings banks than for cooperative banks, while, at the same time, risk-weighted assets scaled by total assets fluctuate *more* procyclically for savings banks than for cooperative banks. Further, the differences in the findings

Table 8:
Blundell–Bond Two-Step System GMM Estimates for Capital Savings—Banks and Cooperative Banks, 1995–2003

	1	2	3	4
	Savings banks	Cooperative banks	Savings banks	Cooperative banks
Dependent variable: ΔCAP_t	Real output gap (*GAP*)	Real output gap (*GAP*)	Real output gap (*GAP*)	Real output gap (*GAP*)
ΔCAP_{t-1}	0.0315	–0.0111	0.0331	–0.0042
	(1.21)	(0.44)	(1.28)	(0.17)
$\Delta CYCLE$	–0.0382***	0.0043		
	(8.38)	(1.24)		
$\Delta CYCLE*dyUP*dyLOW$			–0.1428***	–0.1071***
			(6.64)	(6.24)
$\Delta CYCLE*(1-dyUP)*dyLOW$			0.0923***	0.1839***
			(4.18)	(8.53)
$\Delta CYCLE*dyUP*(1-dyLOW)$			–0.0293***	0.0646***
			(3.05)	(9.74)
$\Delta CYCLE*(1-dyUP)*(1-dyLOW)$			–0.0532***	–0.0632***
			(6.27)	(10.39)
ΔROA	–0.2479***	–0.2665***	–0.2452***	–0.2500***
	(3.36)	(5.87)	(3.61)	(5.59)
$\Delta SIZE$	–0.0082***	–0.0134***	–0.0079***	–0.0123***
	(5.53)	(11.36)	(4.94)	(10.52)
$\Delta LIQUID$	–0.0418***	–0.0353***	–0.0421***	–0.0344***
	(11.70)	(18.74)	(11.78)	(18.67)
$\Delta LLOSS$	0.0390*	0.0788***	0.0393*	0.0832***
	(1.80)	(4.00)	(1.80)	(4.29)
dyMERGER	0.0022**	0.0046***	0.0021**	0.0041***
	(2.53)	(10.03)	(2.31)	(8.92)
Constant	0.0020***	0.0027***	0.0020***	0.0020***
	(20.03)	(31.27)	(13.46)	(16.73)
# Observations	4,085	15,475	4,085	15,475
# Banks	492	2,159	492	2,159
Hansen test	0.000	0.492	0.000	0.073
AR(1) test	0.000	0.000	0.000	0.000
AR(2) test	0.002	0.192	0.005	0.433

Notes: The dependent variable is $\Delta CAP_{i,t}$. *CAP* is defined as regulatory capital over total assets. *CYCLE* is defined as the real output gap. *dyUP* is unity during an economic upturn, i.e., $\Delta GAP > 0$, and zero otherwise. *dyLOW* is unity if the bank is among the 5 percent least capitalized banks in its banking group for the respective year and zero otherwise. *ROA* is defined as the return on assets ratio. *SIZE* is defined as the natural log of total assets. *LLOSS* is defined new net loan loss provisions over total assets. *LIQUID* is defined as bond plus share holdings plus interbank assets over total assets. *dyMERGER* is unity for an acquiring bank in the year before the merger and zero otherwise. All variables are first-differenced before applying the Blundell–Bond procedure. The only exception is the merger dummy variable. Lagged differences of ΔCAP_i are used as instruments for equations in levels, in addition to lagged levels of ΔCAP_i, which are used as instruments for equations in first differences. Δ indicates the first difference. The absolute *t*-values are given in parentheses. ***, **, and * indicate statistical significance at the 1, 5, and 10 percent level, respectively, in a two-tailed *t*-test. Hansen test refers to the test of overidentifying restrictions. AR(1) and AR(2) test refer to the test for the null of no first-order and second-order autocorrelation in the first-differenced residuals.

Table 9:

Blundell–Bond Two-Step System GMM Estimates for Risk-Weighted Assets—Savings Banks and Cooperative Banks, 1995–2003

	1	2	3	4
	Savings banks	Cooperative banks	Savings banks	Cooperative banks
Dependent variable: $\Delta RISK_t$	Real output gap (*GAP*)	Real output gap (*GAP*)	Real output gap (*GAP*)	Real output gap (*GAP*)
$\Delta RISK_{t-1}$	–0.0534***	–0.0484***	–0.0361*	–0.0484***
	(2.76)	(2.96)	(1.91)	(2.94)
$\Delta CYCLE$	0.3641***	0.0920***		
	(13.49)	(4.99)		
$\Delta CYCLE*dyUP*dyLOW$			0.6782***	0.5832***
			(3.25)	(5.36)
$\Delta CYCLE*(1-dyUP)*dyLOW$			–0.2174	–0.3850***
			(1.59)	(3.94)
$\Delta CYCLE*dyUP*(1-dyLOW)$			0.5452***	0.0441
			(9.78)	(1.16)
$\Delta CYCLE*(1-dyUP)*(1-dyLOW)$			0.1621***	0.1405***
			(3.65)	(4.34)
$\Delta LLOSS$	0.4364	–0.1626	0.3888	–0.1948
	(1.54)	(0.78)	(1.37)	(0.92)
ΔROA	–0.0390***	–0.0142**	–0.0344***	–0.0153***
	(3.30)	(2.45)	(2.87)	(2.63)
$\Delta SIZE$	–0.4412***	–0.5614***	–0.4425***	–0.5600***
	(20.06)	(37.96)	(20.02)	(37.58)
$\Delta LIQUID$	0.2974***	0.2127**	0.2081*	0.2130**
	(2.61)	(2.57)	(1.79)	(2.56)
dyMERGER	0.0131***	0.0008	0.0117***	0.0014
	(3.44)	(0.33)	(2.98)	(0.60)
Constant	0.0094***	0.0022***	0.0063***	0.0025***
	(14.76)	(6.27)	(7.02)	(4.90)
# Observations	4,085	15,475	4,085	15,475
# Banks	492	2,159	492	2,159
Hansen test	0.897	0.005	0.563	0.008
AR(1) test	0.000	0.000	0.000	0.000
AR(2) test	0.972	0.204	0.828	0.203

Notes: The dependent variable is $\Delta RISK_{i,t}$. *RISK* is defined as risk-weighted assets over total assets. *CYCLE* is defined as the real output gap. *dyUP* is unity during an economic upturn, i.e., $\Delta GAP > 0$, and zero otherwise. *dyLOW* is unity if the bank is among the 5 percent least capitalized banks in its banking group for the respective year and zero otherwise. *ROA* is defined as the return on assets ratio. *SIZE* is defined as the natural log of total assets. *LLOSS* is defined new net loan loss provisions over total assets. *LIQUID* is defined as bond plus share holdings plus interbank assets over total assets. *dyMERGER* is unity for an acquiring bank in the year before the merger and zero otherwise. All variables are first-differenced before applying the Blundell–Bond procedure. The only exception is the merger dummy variable. Lagged differences of $\Delta RISK_i$ are used as instruments for equations in levels, in addition to lagged levels of $\Delta RISK_i$, which are used as instruments for equations in first differences. Δ indicates the first difference. The absolute *t*-values are given in parentheses. ***, **, and * indicate statistical significance at the 1, 5, and 10 percent level, respectively, in a two-tailed *t*-test. Hansen test refers to the test of overidentifying restrictions. AR(1) and AR(2) test refer to the test for the null of no first-order and second-order autocorrelation in the first-differenced residuals.

may also be explained to some extent by the fact that both studies use slightly different databases and that Buch et al. (2005) use sectoral business cycles, while I use aggregate and regional business cycles.

The effect of the business cycle on capital and risk-weighted assets taken together explains why the effect of the business cycle on banks' capital buffer is higher for savings banks than for cooperative banks. The countercyclical behavior of the capital buffer for cooperative banks stems from the procyclical fluctuation of risk-weighted assets. For savings banks, the countercyclical fluctuation of capital and the procyclical fluctuation of risk-weighted assets jointly drive the countercyclical fluctuation of the capital buffer, leading to a six times stronger fluctuation of the capital buffer for savings banks than for cooperative banks.

In addition, decomposing the capital buffer into capital and risk-weighted assets allows testing whether changes in the capital buffer over the business cycle simply reflect changes in the loan demand or whether changes in the capital buffer are also driven by supply-side effects. To do so, I again interact the business cycle with my dummy variables for economic upturns and downturns and for banks with low capital buffers and banks with high capital buffers and include the four interaction terms in the regression. Specifications 3 and 4 in tables 8 and 9 show the results for capital and risk-weighed assets, respectively.

Cooperative banks with high capital buffers boost the increase in capital, irrespective of the business cycle. Similarly, savings banks with high capital buffers boost the increase in capital in a business cycle downturn, but they dampen the increase in capital in a business cycle upturn. With respect to risk-weighted assets, both savings and cooperative banks with high capital buffers dampen the increase in risk-weighted assets in a business cycle downturn, but only savings banks boost it in a business cycle upturn. Consequently, the buildup of the capital buffer of well-capitalized cooperative banks during business cycle upturns has its roots in an increase in capital without an increase in risk-weighted assets.

A possible explanation why, for savings banks, risk-weighted assets behave more strongly procyclically over the business cycle is likely to lie in different types of borrowers. While savings banks lend mostly to the trades and crafts sector, cooperative banks lend mainly to the agricultural sector. And the trades and crafts sector is likely to be more cyclical than the agriculture sector, which follows its own cycles.

With regard to banks with low capital buffers, the finding that these banks fall further behind their well-capitalized peers over the observation period, irrespective of the economic situation, is driven by both a lower increase in capital and a higher increase in risk-weighted assets. Both savings and cooperative banks dampen the increase in capital buffers in business cycle upturns and downturns. At the same time, they boost the increase in risk-weighted assets. However, for savings banks, the coefficient of $\Delta CYCLE * (1 - dyUP) * dyLOW$ in the *RISK* equation is slightly insignificant (*t*-value: 1.59).

The results in this section can be summed up as two points. First, changes in capital fluctuate countercyclically for savings banks and are independent of the business cycle for cooperative banks, while changes in risk-weighted assets move in tandem with the business cycle for both sectors. Second, the effect is asymmetric with regard to the capitalization of banks: banks with low capital buffers dampen the increase in capital in both business cycle upturns and downturns and boost the increase in risk-weighted assets in business cycle upturns. In addition, cooperative banks with low capital buffers boost the increase in risk-weighted assets even in business cycle downturns.

The results also shed some light on the question whether the countercyclical behavior of capital buffers reflects the fact that banks are shortsighted. According to the argumentation of Ayuso et al. (2004), banks that do not build up capital sufficiently in upturns to provide for their higher exposure to credit risk will be forced to increase buffers during downturns. My findings show that, while low-capitalized savings banks indeed increase their exposure to credit risk by boosting the increase in risk-weighted assets in an upturn, they fail to boost the increase in capital correspondingly. In a business cycle downturn, however, low-capitalized savings banks do not manage to increase capital either. Further, they do not dampen the increase in risk-weighted assets as their well-capitalized peers do. Hence, they fail to boost the increase in capital buffers in a downturn. This lends support to H_8, i.e., savings banks with low capital buffers may face barriers to adjustments. Even more, cooperative banks with low capital buffers *boost* the increase in risk-weighted assets in a downturn.

Thus, my results support the view that fluctuations in banks' capital buffers are not exclusively driven by fluctuations in loan demand over the business cycle, but also by the deliberate decisions of banks, i.e., supply-side effects. My results, however, do not support the widely held concern that banks with low capital buffers retreat from lending in order to increase their capital buffers in a business cycle downturn, thereby further aggravating the downturn. Instead, the supply-side effects show up in the unexpected behavior of low-capitalized banks, which dampen the increase in capital buffers in a downturn.

Finally, based on Italian data, Gambacorta and Mistrulli (2005) find that the lending of banks with low capital buffers reacts more strongly to business cycle fluctuations than the lending of banks with high capital buffers. Yet, my results for risk-weighted assets indicate that this is neither true for German savings banks nor for cooperative banks.

4.4.4 Robustness Checks

For most of my specifications, the Hansen test indicates that I have used valid instruments. Yet, for a few specifications, it rejects the instruments at the 5 percent level. However, the Hansen test is well known for its tendency to overreject. Further, the test for second-order autocorrelation in the first-differenced residuals points to potential problems in some specifications. Hence, I additionally run pooled OLS and fixed effects (FE) estimations including the lagged buffer as a robustness check. The reason for doing so is that simulation studies show that the OLS estimator is typically biased upwards, while the FE estimator is biased downwards in bivariate dynamic specifications (Bond 2002). In multivariate dynamic specifications, as in my case, it is not necessarily true that the GMM estimates lie in between the OLS and FE estimates. But if both the OLS estimator and the FE estimator also give a significant and negative coefficient for *CYCLE*, this may nevertheless serve as an indicator of the robustness of my results. The results reported in Table A15 in Appendix 2 again lend support to the hypothesis that the capital buffers of both savings banks and cooperative banks behave countercyclically.

In addition, I also run OLS estimations for the *CAP* and *RISK* specifications as a robustness check. The results are given in Table A16 in Appendix 2. The results confirm the findings of the GMM estimations.

So far, I have treated the bank-specific control variables as exogenous. However, they may also be endogenous. Hence, I model the bank-specific control variables as endogenous to check robustness. To do so, I include GMM-style instruments also for *ROA*, *SIZE*, *LIQUID*, and *LLOSS* in addition to the GMM-style instruments for *BUF*, *CAP*, and *RISK*. The results are given in Table A17 in Appendix 2. Treating the bank-specific control variables as endogenous does not substantially change the results. In particular, the findings with respect to the interaction terms remain. But the Hansen test deteriorates. Against the background that the Hansen test of the original specification indicates that I have used valid instruments, I stick with treating *ROA*, *SIZE*, *LIQUID*, and *LLOSS* as exogenous.

Last but not least, including dummy variables for the capitalization of banks creates an endogeneity problem, as the endogenous variables *BUF*, *CAP*, and *RISK* determine the capitalization of banks. Thus, as a robustness check, I include GMM-style instruments for the interaction terms. The results are given in Table A18 in Appendix 2. The interaction terms keep their significance and sign. Only the coefficient of $\Delta CYCLE * dyUP * (1 - dyLOW)$ becomes significant and negative at the 5 percent level in the *RISK* equation for cooperative banks (Specification 6). However, the Hansen test indicates that I have used invalid instruments when controlling for the endogeneity problem. Hence, I am confident in my original specification, as the endogeneity problem may not be severe enough for the Hansen test to reject the overidentifying restrictions of the original specification.

4.5 Conclusion

This chapter has examined how the capital buffers of German savings and cooperative banks fluctuate over the business cycle. I find strong evidence that capital buffers behave countercyclically, the capital buffers of savings banks reacting more strongly to the business cycle than the capital buffers of cooperative banks. What drives the stronger reaction of savings banks is the stronger procyclical fluctuation of risk-weighted assets and the countercyclical fluctuation of capital for savings banks compared to the procyclical fluctuation of capital for cooperative banks.

Further, banks with low capital buffers react differently to the business cycle than banks with relatively higher capital buffers:

In business cycle downturns, low-capitalized banks dampen the increase in capital, while their well-capitalized peers boost the increase in capital. In addition, low capitalized banks dampen (savings banks) the increase in risk-weighted assets by less or even boost the increase in risk-weighted assets (cooperative banks).

In business cycle upturns, low-capitalized banks dampen the increase in capital by more (savings banks) or boost it by less (cooperative banks) than their well-capitalized peers. In addition, they boost the increase in risk-weighted assets considerably more.

These findings imply that low-capitalized banks do not catch up with their well-capitalized peers, but rather that they fall further behind over the observation period. The reasons may be manifold. One plausible explanation may be differing risk attitudes. A low capital buffer would then simply reflect banks' lower risk aversion. However, as I control for banks' risk-taking, this explanation is only valid if the proxy variable I use does not fully capture banks' risk attitude. An alternative explanation may be poor risk management of low-capitalized banks. However, my analysis does not allow for such conclusions. Hence, further research on this topic is clearly required.

While this issue may raise supervisory concerns, it also implies that low-capitalized banks do not retreat from lending, as low capitalized banks do not decrease risk-weighted assets in a downturn. Hence, the result does not lend support to the widely held concern that banks with low capital buffers retreat from lending in order to increase their capital buffers in a business cycle downturn, thereby further aggravating the downturn. However, this conclusion is subject to the caveat that I have not directly analyzed the impact of banks' capital buffer on lending, but rather on risk-weighted assets. Hence, future research will have to model the relationship between banks' capital buffer, the business cycle, and loan supply in more detail.

4.6 Appendix 1: Descriptive Statistics

Table A10:
Definition of the Business Cycle Indicators

Variable	Definition	Available for states ("Bundesländer")
GDP	Annual real GDP growth rate	No
SGDP	Annual real GDP growth rate	Yes
GAP	Annual real output gap in billions of chained (1970) euros	No
dyUP	Unity in a business cycle upturn, i.e., if $\Delta GAP > 0$	

Notes: All variables are from the German Federal Statistical Office.

Table A11:
Definition of the Bank-Specific (Control) Variables

Variable	Definition
BUF	Basel capital-to-risk-weighted-assets ratio minus 0.08
CAP	Regulatory capital-to-total-assets ratio
RISK	Risk-weighted assets to total assets ratio
SIZE	Natural log of total assets
ROA	Annual net profit over total assets
LLOSS	New net provisions over total assets
LIQUID	Bond holdings plus share holdings plus interbank assets over total assets
dyMERGER	Unity for the acquirer in the year of the merger and zero otherwise.
dySB	Unity if bank is a savings bank and zero otherwise (cooperative bank)
dyLOW	Unity if bank is among the 5 percent least capitalized banks in its banking group for a respective year and zero otherwise

Notes: All variables are from a confidential supervisory database kindly provided by the Deutsche Bundesbank.

Table A12:
Descriptive Statistics for the Business Cycle Indicators

Variable	Mean	Std. dev.	Minimum	Maximum
GDP	0.0128	0.0097	–0.0012	0.0286
SGDP	0.0122	0.0136	–0.0206	0.0503
GAP	–0.0030	0.0179	–0.0258	0.0269

Table A13:
Descriptive Statistics for the Bank-Specific (Control) Variables

a) By Banking Sector

	Savings banks			Cooperative banks			
Variable	Obs.	Mean	Std. dev.	Obs.	Mean	Std. dev.	Wilcoxon test
BUF	4,085	0.0277	0.0156	15,475	0.0360	0.0265	17.21***
RISK	4,085	0.5844	0.0702	15,475	0.6216	0.0983	26.22***
CAP	4,085	0.0626	0.0095	15,475	0.0711	0.0157	37.83***
ROA	4,085	0.0024	0.0019	15,475	0.0027	0.0028	14.15***
SIZE	4,085	20.7117	0.9621	15,475	18.6693	1.1018	–81.61***
LIQUID	4,085	0.3040	0.0734	15,475	0.3257	0.1053	–27.98***
LLOSS	4,085	0.0035	0.0037	15,475	0.0033	0.0049	–11.47***
dyMERGER	4,085	0.0228	0.1492	15,475	0.0605	0.2384	9.61***

Notes: H_0: Samples are from an identical population versus two-sided alternatives. ***, **, and * indicate statistical significance at the 1, 5 and 10 percent levels, respectively, in a two-tailed *t*-test.

b) By Capitalization

	95 percent highest capitalized banks (*dyLOW*= 0)			5 percent lowest capitalized banks (*dyLOW*= 1)			
Variable	Obs.	Mean	Std. dev.	Obs.	Mean	Std. dev.	Wilcoxon test
BUF	18,537	0.0358	0.0246	1,023	0.0072	0.0031	52.08***
RISK	18,537	0.6104	0.0935	1,023	0.6752	0.0888	27.33***
CAP	18,537	0.0699	0.0151	1,023	0.0589	0.0082	–21.49***
ROA	18,537	0.0027	0.0020	1,023	0.0022	0.0079	13.40***
SIZE	18,537	19.0816	1.3637	1,023	19.3547	1.2145	–7.09***
LIQUID	18,537	0.2105	0.0906	1,023	0.1652	0.0734	16.24***
LLOSS	18,537	0.0032	0.0046	1,023	0.0050	0.0055	–12.84***
dyMERGER	18,537	0.0537	0.2255	1,023	0.0323	0.1768	3.00***

Notes: H_0: Samples are from an identical population versus two-sided alternatives. ***, **, and * indicate statistical significance at the 1, 5 and 10 percent levels, respectively, in a two-tailed *t*-test.

Table A14:
Correlation Matrix

	BUF	*RISK*	*CAP*	*ROA*	*SIZE*	*LIQUID*	*dyMERGER*	*LLOSS*	*dySB*	*GDP*	*SGDP*
BUF	1.00										
RISK	–0.34***	1.00									
CAP	0.68***	0.43***	1.00								
ROA	0.12***	–0.01*	0.11***	1.00							
SIZE	–0.25***	–0.04***	–0.26***	–0.11***	1.00						
LIQUID	0.41***	–0.71***	–0.16***	0.06***	0.17***	1.00					
dyMERGER	–0.01	0.07***	0.04***	–0.05***	0.14***	–0.06***	1.00				
LLOSS	–0.14***	0.26***	0.07***	–0.22***	0.11***	–0.25***	0.06***	1.00			
dySB	–0.14***	–0.16***	–0.23***	–0.06***	0.61***	–0.09***	–0.07***	0.02**	1.00		
GDP	–0.05***	–0.02***	–0.07***	–0.01	–0.07**	–0.01	0.02***	–0.07***	–0.02**	1.00	
SGDP	0.01	0.05***	0.04***	–0.06***	–0.07***	–0.01	0.04***	–0.02**	–0.05***	0.75***	1.00
GAP	0.01	0.05***	0.05***	–0.05***	0.05***	–0.08***	0.07***	–0.02***	0.02***	0.55***	0.42***

Notes: ***, **, * indicate significance at the 1, 5, and 10 percent level, respectively.

4.7 Appendix 2: Robustness Checks

Table A15:

Fixed Effects and Pooled OLS Estimates for the Capital Buffer—Savings and Cooperative Banks, 1995–2003

Dependent variable: ΔBUF_t	1	2	3	4
	Savings banks		Cooperative banks	
	FE	POLS	FE	POLS
ΔBUF_{t-1}	–0.0583***	0.0064	–0.1028***	–0.0031
	(2.83)	(0.33)	(5.95)	(0.20)
$\Delta CYCLE$	–0.1177***	–0.1143***	–0.0241***	–0.0257***
	(16.21)	(16.20)	(4.15)	(4.59)
ΔROA	–0.4942***	–0.4074***	–0.3453***	–0.3144***
	(4.21)	(3.42)	(3.64)	(3.08)
$\Delta SIZE$	–0.0053**	–0.0092***	–0.0172***	–0.0175***
	(2.19)	(3.98)	(10.31)	(11.57)
$\Delta LIQUID$	0.0130**	0.0221***	0.0496***	0.0543***
	(2.15)	(4.00)	(14.17)	(15.84)
$\Delta LLOSS$	–0.0081	–0.0076	0.0484*	0.0501**
	(0.22)	(0.22)	(1.91)	(2.12)
dyMERGER	–0.0001	0.0014	0.0057***	0.0050***
	(0.04)	(1.18)	(8.42)	(8.70)
Constant	0.0023***	0.0023***	0.0044***	0.0041***
	(14.34)	(14.91)	(38.74)	(37.49)
# Observations	4,085	4,085	15,475	15,475
# Banks	492		2,159	
R-squared	0.09	0.08	0.06	0.06

Notes: The dependent variable is $\Delta BUF_{i,t}$. *BUF* is defined as the Basel capital ratio minus 0.08. *CYCLE* is defined as the real output gap. *ROA* is defined as the return on assets ratio. *SIZE* is defined as the natural log of total assets. *LLOSS* is defined new net loan loss provisions over total assets. *LIQUID* is defined as bond plus share holdings plus interbank assets over total assets. *dyMERGER* is unity for an acquiring bank in the year before the merger and zero otherwise. In order to account for the unit root of *BUF*, all variables are first first-differenced before applying the fixed effects and the OLS procedure. The only exception is *dyMERGER*. Δ indicates the first difference. The absolute *t*-values are given in parentheses. ***, **, and * indicate statistical significance at the 1, 5, and 10 percent level, respectively, in a two-tailed *t*-test.

Table A16:
Pooled OLS Estimates—Savings and Cooperative Banks, 1995–2003

	1	2	3	4	5	6
	Savings banks			Cooperative banks		
Dependent variable:	Δ*BUF*	Δ*CAP*	Δ*RISK*	Δ*BUF*	Δ*CAP*	Δ*RISK*
Δ*Dep. Variable*$_{t-1}$	–0.0138	–0.0209	–0.0618***	–0.0110	–0.0658**	–0.0451**
	(0.70)	(1.08)	(4.10)	(0.68)	(2.08)	(2.44)
Δ*CYCLE**dyUP* dyLOW*	–0.3258***	–0.1302***	0.7753***	–0.2692***	–0.1589***	0.4340***
	(9.75)	(7.28)	(4.68)	(10.97)	(10.00)	(4.57)
Δ*CYCLE**(1–*dyUP*)* *dyLOW*	0.2301***	0.1139***	–0.2590**	0.3755***	0.2148***	–0.4002***
	(10.25)	(7.56)	(2.19)	(12.66)	(11.51)	(4.83)
Δ*CYCLE**dyUP* (1–*dyLOW*)	–0.1961***	–0.0484***	0.5525***	0.0117	0.0129*	–0.0085
	(12.48)	(6.34)	(11.44)	(1.00)	(1.71)	(0.25)
Δ*CYCLE**(1–*dyUP*)* (1–*dyLOW*)	–0.0466***	–0.0196***	0.1139***	–0.0686***	–0.0287***	0.0687**
	(3.18)	(2.63)	(2.66)	(6.11)	(3.74)	(2.43)
Δ*ROA*	–0.4038***	–0.1863***	0.6615***	–0.2943***	–0.2200***	–0.2244
	(3.60)	(2.67)	(2.70)	(2.83)	(4.67)	(1.51)
Δ*SIZE*	–0.0114***	–0.0095***	–0.0225***	–0.0166***	–0.0118***	–0.0088*
	(4.40)	(6.07)	(2.64)	(10.73)	(11.45)	(1.86)
Δ*LIQUID*	0.0225***	–0.0380***	–0.4886***	0.0530***	–0.0362***	–0.5926***
	(4.06)	(13.61)	(27.36)	(15.49)	(15.67)	(58.18)
Δ*LLOSS*	0.0274	0.0535***	0.3028***	0.0502**	0.0601***	0.2495***
	(0.77)	(2.89)	(2.95)	(2.13)	(3.11)	(3.24)
dyMERGER	0.0022*	0.0024***	0.0075**	0.0045***	0.0033***	0.0007
	(1.72)	(3.42)	(2.34)	(7.74)	(8.42)	(0.39)
Constant	0.0036***	0.0025***	0.0055***	0.0039***	0.0027***	0.0018***
	(13.89)	(18.19)	(7.32)	(21.68)	(17.75)	(3.76)
# Observations	4,085	4,085	4,085	15,475	15,475	15,475
R-squared	0.11	0.14	0.31	0.08	0.12	0.35

Notes: The dependent variable is defined differently for the various specifications, as given at the top of the respective columns. *BUF* is defined as the Basel capital ratio minus 0.08. *CAP* is defined as regulatory capital over total assets. *RISK* is defined as risk-weighted assets over total assets. *CYCLE* is defined as the real output gap. *dyUP* is unity during an economic upturn, i.e., Δ*GAP*>0, and zero otherwise. *dyLOW* is unity if the bank is among the 5 percent least capitalized banks in its banking group for the respective year and zero otherwise. *ROA* is defined as the return on assets ratio. *SIZE* is defined as the natural log of total assets. *LLOSS* is defined new net loan loss provisions over total assets. *LIQUID* is defined as bond plus share holdings plus interbank assets over total assets. *dyMERGER* is unity for an acquiring bank in the year before the merger and zero otherwise. In order to account for the unit root of *BUF*, all variables are first first-differenced before applying the pooled OLS procedure. The only exception is *dyMERGER*. Δ indicates the first difference. The absolute *t*-values are given in parentheses. ***, **, and * indicate statistical significance at the 1, 5, and 10 percent level, respectively, in a two-tailed *t*-test.

Table A17:

Blundell–Bond Two-Step System GMM Estimates for the Capital Buffer (ROA, SIZE, LIQUID, and LLOSS Modeled as Endogenous Variables)—Savings Banks and Cooperative Banks, 1995–2003

	1	2	3	4	5	6
		Savings banks			Cooperative banks	
Dependent variable:	ΔBUF	ΔCAP	$\Delta RISK$	ΔBUF	ΔCAP	$\Delta RISK$
$\Delta Dep.\ Variable_{t-1}$	0.0180	0.0120	–0.0451**	0.0416**	–0.0042	–0.0484***
	(0.69)	(0.46)	(2.32)	(2.29)	(0.17)	(2.94)
$\Delta CYCLE*dyUP*dyLOW$	–0.3239***	–0.1354***	0.6076***	–0.2092***	–0.1071***	0.5832***
	(7.69)	(6.37)	(3.01)	(7.02)	(6.24)	(5.36)
$\Delta CYCLE*(1-dyUP)*dyLOW$	0.1868***	0.0939***	–0.2708*	0.3295***	0.1839***	–0.3850***
	(5.63)	(4.13)	(1.90)	(8.55)	(8.53)	(3.94)
$\Delta CYCLE*dyUP*(1-dyLOW)$	–0.1483***	–0.0303***	0.5107***	0.0842***	0.0646***	0.0441
	(7.20)	(3.06)	(8.96)	(6.81)	(9.74)	(1.16)
$\Delta CYCLE*(1-dyUP)*(1-dyLOW)$	–0.1142***	–0.0541***	0.1484***	–0.1407***	–0.0632***	0.1405***
	(6.82)	(6.31)	(3.27)	(12.15)	(10.39)	(4.34)
ΔROA	–0.6601***	–0.3754***	0.7939**	–0.3617***	–0.2500***	–0.1948
	(4.63)	(6.20)	(2.23)	(3.52)	(5.59)	(0.92)
$\Delta SIZE$	–0.0070***	–0.0066***	–0.0240**	–0.0169***	–0.0123***	–0.0153***
	(2.88)	(5.58)	(2.58)	(9.63)	(10.52)	(2.63)
$\Delta LIQUID$	0.0154**	–0.0418***	–0.4779***	0.0520***	–0.0344***	–0.5600***
	(2.29)	(10.58)	(18.43)	(15.73)	(18.67)	(37.58)
$\Delta LLOSS$	0.0140	0.0561**	0.3313***	0.0447*	0.0832***	0.2130**
	(0.30)	(2.39)	(2.72)	(1.85)	(4.29)	(2.56)
dyMERGER	0.0007	0.0012	0.0091**	0.0060***	0.0041***	0.0014
	(0.44)	(1.36)	(2.31)	(8.78)	(8.92)	(0.60)
Constant	0.0025***	0.0019***	0.0060***	0.0027***	0.0020***	0.0025***
	(9.26)	(14.10)	(7.17)	(14.29)	(16.73)	(4.90)
# Observations	4,085	4,085	4,085	15,475	15,475	15,475
# Banks	492	492	492	2,159	2,159	2,159
Hansen test	0.000	0.000	0.027	0.307	0.073	0.008
AR(1) test	0.000	0.000	0.000	0.000	0.000	0.000
AR(2) test	0.361	0.022	0.778	0.826	0.433	0.203

Notes: The dependent variable is defined differently for the various specifications, as given at the top of the respective columns. *BUF* is defined as the Basel capital ratio minus 0.08. *CAP* is defined as regulatory capital over total assets. *RISK* is defined as risk-weighted assets over total assets. *CYCLE* is defined as the real output gap. *dyUP* is unity during an economic upturn, i.e., $\Delta GAP>0$, and zero otherwise. *dyLOW* is unity if the bank is among the 5 percent least capitalized banks in its banking group for the respective year and zero otherwise. *ROA* is defined as the return on assets ratio. *SIZE* is defined as the natural log of total assets. *LLOSS* is defined new net loan loss provisions over total assets. *LIQUID* is defined as bond plus share holdings plus interbank assets over total assets. *dyMERGER* is unity for an acquiring bank in the year before the merger and zero otherwise. In order to account for the unit root of *BUF*, all variables are first first-differenced before applying the Blundell–Bond procedure. The only exception is *dyMERGER*. Δ indicates the first difference. Lagged differences of ΔBUF (specifications 1 and 4), ΔCAP (specifications 2 and 5), $\Delta RISK$ (specifications 3 and 6) are used as instruments for equations in levels, in addition to lagged levels of these variables, which are used as instruments for equations in first differences. In addition, GMM-style instruments for $\Delta LLOSS$, ΔROA, $\Delta SIZE$, and $\Delta LIQUID$ are included. The absolute *t*-values are given in parentheses. ***, **, and * indicate statistical significance at the 1, 5, and 10 percent level, respectively, in a two-tailed *t*-test.

Table A18:
Blundell–Bond Two-Step System GMM Estimates (Interaction Terms Modeled as Endogenous Variables)—Savings Banks and Cooperative Banks, 1995–2003

	1	2	3	4	5	6
		Savings banks			Cooperative banks	
Dependent variable:	Δ*BUF*	Δ*CAP*	Δ*RISK*	Δ*BUF*	Δ*CAP*	Δ*RISK*
Δ*Dep. Variable*$_{t-1}$	0.0265	0.0034	–0.0406**	0.0144	0.0170	–0.0529***
	(0.89)	(0.12)	(2.05)	(0.52)	(0.45)	(3.50)
Δ*CYCLE***dyUP** *dyLOW*	–0.5388***	–0.2452***	1.0693***	–0.3714***	–0.1884***	0.8236***
	(8.29)	(7.10)	(3.90)	(8.96)	(7.77)	(6.14)
Δ*CYCLE**(1–*dyUP*)* *dyLOW*	0.3337***	0.1438***	–0.3687**	0.4098***	0.2226***	–0.5374***
	(6.43)	(4.94)	(2.33)	(6.46)	(5.98)	(4.49)
Δ*CYCLE***dyUP** (1–*dyLOW*)	–0.1906***	–0.0315***	0.5383***	0.0616***	0.0443***	–0.0861**
	(8.76)	(3.09)	(10.33)	(3.86)	(5.22)	(2.26)
Δ*CYCLE**(1–*dyUP*)* (1–*dyLOW*)	–0.0495***	–0.0337***	0.1138**	–0.0798***	–0.0468***	0.1067***
	(2.79)	(3.79)	(2.57)	(6.02)	(6.12)	(3.46)
Δ*ROA*	–0.5310***	–0.2425***	0.3893	–0.5552***	–0.3338***	–0.3841
	(3.49)	(3.03)	(1.30)	(2.84)	(4.06)	(1.16)
Δ*SIZE*	–0.0071***	–0.0050***	–0.0381***	–0.0117***	–0.0084***	–0.0162***
	(2.86)	(3.68)	(3.24)	(5.44)	(6.17)	(2.71)
Δ*LIQUID*	0.0066	–0.0452***	–0.4270***	0.0485***	–0.0392***	–0.5722***
	(0.91)	(11.87)	(20.22)	(11.37)	(16.61)	(38.16)
Δ*LLOSS*	0.0536	0.0583**	0.2338*	0.0357	0.0262	0.3305***
	(1.06)	(2.31)	(1.92)	(1.07)	(1.08)	(2.84)
dyMERGER	0.0010	0.0011	0.0109***	0.0038***	0.0029***	0.0003
	(0.57)	(1.22)	(2.59)	(4.53)	(5.13)	(0.13)
Constant	0.0033***	0.0022***	0.0060***	0.0033***	0.0020***	0.0028***
	(12.00)	(14.76)	(6.50)	(13.78)	(12.84)	(5.30)
# Observations	4,085	4,085	4,085	15,475	15,475	15,475
# Banks	492	492	492	2,159	2,159	2,159
Hansen test	0.000	0.000	0.015	0.000	0.000	0.000
AR(1) test	0.000	0.000	0.000	0.000	0.000	0.000
AR(2) test	0.308	0.045	0.749	0.386	0.661	0.276

Notes: The dependent variable is defined differently for the various specifications, as given at the top of the respective columns. *BUF* is defined as the Basel capital ratio minus 0.08. *CAP* is defined as regulatory capital over total assets. *RISK* is defined as risk-weighted assets over total assets. *GDP* is defined as real GDP growth. *ROA* is defined as the return on assets ratio. *SIZE* is defined as the natural log of total assets. *LLOSS* is defined new net loan loss provisions over total assets. *LIQUID* is defined as bond plus share holdings plus interbank assets over total assets. *dyMERGER* is unity for an acquiring bank in the year before the merger and zero otherwise. In order to account for the unit root of *RISK*, all variables are first first-differenced before applying the Blundell–Bond procedure. The only exception is *dyMERGER*. Δ indicates the first difference. Lagged differences of Δ*BUF* (specifications 1 and 4), Δ*CAP* (specifications 2 and 5), Δ*RISK* (specifications 3 and 6) are used as instruments for equations in levels, in addition to lagged levels of these variables, which are used as instruments for equations in first differences. In addition, GMM-style instruments for the interaction terms are included. The absolute *t*-values are given in parentheses. ***, **, and * indicate statistical significance at the 1, 5, and 10 percent level, respectively, in a two-tailed *t*-test.

5 The Disciplining Effect of Charter Value on Risk-Taking

5.1 Introduction

The workhorse of the traditional banking literature is the model of moral hazard: As deposit rates are irresponsive to the risk-taking of banks due to the existence of deposit insurance, banks have an incentive to decrease capital-to-asset ratios and to increase asset risk, thereby increasing their probability of default and extracting wealth from the deposit insurance system.

However, the prediction of moral hazard theory that banks take extreme risks contrasts with the behavior of real banks. First, banks typically hold a substantial capital buffer in excess of the regulatory minimum capital requirements. For instance, in the United States, banks held a regulatory capital buffer of 4.04 percentage points at the end of the 1990s, compared to 3.3 in Germany and 3.81 in Japan (Barth et al. 2001). And second, the majority of banks seem to have such a low probability of default that they extract virtually no wealth from the deposit insurance system (Santomero and Vinso 1977; Marcus and Shaked 1984).

These empirical findings have inspired the literature to search for an incentive that could moderate the moral hazard behavior of banks. Such an incentive has been found in banks' charter value (Marcus 1984). The charter value is the net present value of future rents. This charter value would be lost in the case of bankruptcy and, hence, represents the bank's private cost of failure. The higher the bank's charter value, the higher the bank's private cost of asset risk and leverage is.

An increasing number of papers have tried to test the disciplining effect of charter value on banks' risk-taking, which is measured either as default risk, asset risk, or leverage risk. Keeley (1990) finds that US banks with higher charter value have a lower leverage risk (measured as capital to assets on a market-value basis) and a lower default risk, as reflected in lower risk premia on large, uninsured CDs. Demsetz et al. (1996) also find that US banks with higher charter value have a lower default risk, their measure of default risk being based on banks' stock return volatility. Gropp and Vesala (2004) find that EU banks with higher charter value have lower leverage risk (measured as the book value of liabilities over the market-value of total assets). Evidence for asset risk (measured as problem loans over total assets) and default risk (measured as the interday volatility of the banks' stock price corrected for market volatility) is, however, mixed. In sum, the microeconomic literature suggests that banks with higher charter values are less risky.

In addition to studying the link between charter value and risk-taking, the literature has also studied the effect of competition on charter value. Hellmann et al. (2000) present a theoretical model which shows that if competition erodes the bank's charter value, banks decrease capital-to-asset ratios and increase asset risk.

Keeley (1990) provides evidence supporting this hypothesis. He finds that the liberalization of branching and multibank holding company expansion laws in the United States had a negative effect on banks' charter value. From this, he concludes that increased competition eroded banks' charter value, thereby increasing bank failures in the United States during the 1980s. A more recent study by Furlong and Kwan (2005) confirms that banks' charter value had a disciplining effect on risk-taking in the United States.[40]

I contribute to the empirical literature in three ways. First, in addition to studying the disciplining effect of charter value on banks' risk-taking, I also study the determinants of charter value, placing a particular focus on competition. To do so, I use a two-step approach: In the first-step regressions, I regress banks' charter value on bank-specific variables and country-specific variables approximating the degree of competition. In the second-step regressions, I regress banks' risk-taking on banks' charter value. Hence, this approach models the link between competition and banks' charter value explicitly. Second, as the theoretical literature predicts the relationship between charter value and risk-taking to be nonlinear, I run robustness checks with respect to potential nonlinearities.

Third, while most papers provide evidence for US banks, I provide evidence for banks in EU member countries. The data is from the Fitch IBCA BankScope database. The reason I do not use German data, in contrast to Chapters 3 and 4, is twofold. First, in order to calculate my measure of banks' charter value, I need data on market values of banks' equity. Yet, in Germany, only a minority of commercial banks are listed on a stock exchange. And second, in order to measure the impact of competition on the charter value of listed commercial banks, a

---

40 There is also a related literature that uses macroeconomic data on the country level to study the existence of a competition-stability nexus. It does so by discussing the relative efficiency and risk in banking sectors of different countries with different degrees of competition. While Bordo et al. (1995) and Staikouras and Wood (2000) find no evidence for a trade-off between competition and stability, Hoggarth et al. (1998) find evidence for such a trade-off. In a further historical study for the United Kingdom, Capie (1995) shows that banking systems can be less competitive and at the same time quite stable. For a more comprehensive overview of this literature, see Carletti and Hartmann (2003).

measure of competition for Germany as a whole may be adequate, since commercial banks are not subject to a regional principle as savings banks and cooperative banks are. Yet, when using one measure of competition for Germany as a whole, competition varies only over time. Using a cross-country dataset instead increases variation in the measure of competition a lot.

This chapter is organized as follows. Section 5.2 describes the empirical model and the methodology used. It also gives the variable definitions and their expected effect on risk-taking. Section 5.3 describes the data. Section 5.4 shows the regression results. Section 5.5 concludes.

5.2 The Empirical Model

The aim of this chapter is twofold. First, this chapter aims at studying the effect of banks' charter value on banks' risk-taking. And second, it aims at studying the determinants of banks' charter value and, hence, the factors that ultimately drive banks' risk-taking. The empirical approach I use mirrors these two aims by employing two sets of regressions, the first-step regressions studying the determinants of charter value and the second-step regressions studying the impact of charter value on banks' risk-taking.

The first-step regressions also serve an econometrical purpose. As banks' charter value may not be independent of banks' risk-taking in the second-step regressions, the empirical strategy has to account for this potential endogeneity of banks' charter value. To do so, I have to find suitable instruments for banks' charter value in the second-step regressions. To be a suitable instrument, variables have to be highly correlated with banks' charter value. Yet, at the same time, they have to be exogenous and they should not have an impact on banks' risk-taking. However, for most bank-specific and macroeconomic variables, it is hard to argue that they affect only banks' charter value, but not banks' risk-taking. Hence, the natural instruments are lagged levels of banks' charter value. But they are only valid if charter value follows an autoregressive process. Hence, the first-step regression tests whether banks' charter value indeed follows an autoregressive process.

In the following, I first outline the empirical model. Then, I state the hypotheses to be tested and describe the methodology. Finally, I define my measures of charter value and risk and my measures of the bank-specific and macroeconomic control variables.

5.2.1 A Two-Step Dynamic Model

In the first-step regressions, I regress banks' charter value on a set of bank-specific and macroeconomic variables capturing banks' efficiency and rent-generation possibilities. As banks' charter value mirrors banks' market power, which banks build up over several periods, I use an endogenous lag model. Hence, I estimate the following model:

$$(28) \quad q_{i,t} = \alpha_0 + \alpha_1 q_{i,t-1} + X_{i,t}\alpha + u_{i,t} \, ,$$

where $q_{i,t}$ is the charter value of bank i at time t, and X is a vector of bank-specific and macroeconomic variables. The error term, $u_{i,t}$, is assumed to consist of a bank-specific component, μ_i, and white noise, $\varepsilon_{i,t}$. Hence, $u_{i,t} = \mu_i + \varepsilon_{i,t}$, where $\mu_i \sim IID(0,\sigma_\mu^2)$, and $\varepsilon_i \sim IID(0,\sigma_\varepsilon^2)$, independent of each other and among themselves.

In the second-step regressions, I regress banks' risk-taking on banks' charter value and a set of bank-specific and macroeconomic control variables. As banks may adjust risk over several periods, I estimate the following endogenous lag model:

$$(29) \quad RISKTAKING_{i,t} = \beta_0 + \beta_1 RISKTAKING_{i,t-1} + \beta_2 q_{i,t} + Y_{i,t}\beta + w_{i,t} \, ,$$

where $RISKTAKING_{i,t}$ is the risk-taking of bank i at time t, q is the charter value, and Y is a vector of bank-specific and macroeconomic control variables. The error term, w, is again assumed to consist of a bank-specific component, η_i, and white noise, $v_{i,t}$. Hence, $w_{i,t} = \eta_i + v_{i,t}$, where $\eta_i \sim IID(0,\sigma_\eta^2)$, and $v_i \sim IID(0,\sigma_v^2)$, independent of each other and among themselves.

5.2.2 Hypotheses

With respect to the first-step regression, I analyze the determinants of banks' charter value. Among other things, I test whether more efficient banks have higher charter values and whether banks generate rents in the deposit or loan market. Yet, the main hypothesis is that competition decreases banks' charter values. Hence, taking as the null hypothesis that competition does not have an effect on banks' charter value, I test the following hypothesis:

H_9: Competition has a negative effect on banks' charter value.

With respect to the second-step regression, I test whether charter value has a moderating effect on banks' risk-taking. The theoretical literature (Marcus 1984;

Hellman et al. 2000; Milne and Whalley 2001) shows that charter value gives banks the incentive to hold capital and to decrease asset risk. The model of Milne and Whalley (2001), however, predicts that the effect of charter value on risk-taking is nonlinear: for banks with high charter values, a decrease in the charter value increases banks' optimum capital buffers. The intuition is that banks with lower charter values also have lower expected returns. Hence, the possibility to cushion negative capital shocks through retained earnings decreases, as the charter value decreases. Thus, banks have to hold higher capital-to-asset ratios to protect their charter value. Only if the charter value falls close to the fixed cost of recapitalization is the relationship reversed, as the incentive for banks to protect their charter value is rapidly eroded.

In line with the empirical literature (Keeley 1990; Demsetz et al. 1996; Gropp and Vesala 2004), I first test whether banks with high charter values have a lower probability of default, as given by higher capital (buffers), and lower asset risk. Hence, taking as the null hypothesis that charter value does not have an effect on banks' capital and asset risk, I test the following alternative hypothesis:

H_{10}: Banks' charter value has a positive (negative) effect on capital (asset risk).

As a robustness check, I then test for two nonlinearities as predicted by Milne and Whalley (2001). First, as outlined in Section 2.6.3 of Chapter 2, Milne and Whalley (2001) predict that, for banks with high charter values, the optimum capital buffer increases, as the charter value decreases. Only if the charter value falls close to the fixed cost of recapitalization is the relationship reversed. Second, with respect to asset risk, Milne and Whalley (2001) predict that the effect of charter value on asset risk works through its effect on the impact of capital on asset risk: asset risk depends positively on capital, the positive effect being more pronounced the higher the charter value. Hence, I test whether the effect of banks' capital buffer on banks' asset risk depends on the size of banks' charter value.

5.2.3 Methodology

Given the empirical model in (28) and (29), I employ dynamic panel data techniques that control for the bank-specific effects μ_i and η_i. The within estimator is known to produce biased estimates when the lagged dependent variable appears as a regressor. The bias in such estimates (the "Nickell bias") approaches zero as T approaches infinity (Nickell 1981). However, in my case, T is relatively small compared to N. To avoid the Nickell bias, I use an instrumental variable approach.

I take the first difference of the model specified in (29) in order to eliminate the individual effect μ_i, and I try to find suitable instruments for $RISKTAKING_{i,t-1} - RISKTAKING_{i,t-2}$ (the procedure for (28) is analogous). Arellano and Bond (1991) suggest a generalized method of moments (GMM) estimator that uses the entire set of lagged values of $RISKTAKING_i$ as instruments. However, persistence in observed *RISKTAKING* adjustments may result in the problem of weak instruments and losses in asymptotic efficiency when using the Arellano and Bond GMM estimator (Blundell and Bond 1998). As my results indicate indeed a high persistence in observed *RISKTAKING* adjustments, I use the so-called system GMM estimator suggested by Blundell and Bond (1998), which uses lagged differences of $RISKTAKING_i$ as instruments for equations in levels in addition to the Arellano–Bond instruments. However, in models with endogenous regressors, using too many instruments could result in seriously biased estimates. Hence, I only use a subsample of the whole history of the series as instruments in the later cross-section. To determine the optimal lag length of the instruments, I use the procedure suggested by Andrews and Lu (2001). In addition, I create one instrument for each variable and lag distance, rather than one for each time period, variable, and lag distance.[41]

As, for my sample, the one- and two-step Blundell–Bond system GMM estimator produce quite similar estimates, I present only the (asymptotically) more efficient two-step estimates. However, the two-step estimates of the standard errors tend to be severely downward biased (Arellano and Bond 1991; Blundell and Bond 1998). To compensate, I use the finite-sample correction to the two-step covariance matrix derived by Windmeijer (2005).

Finally, as a bank's charter value, q_i, may be endogenous (see next subsection), I also use GMM-style instruments for q_i. The first-step regression results justify this procedure, as lagged q_i is found to be significant in the regressions for q_i. Hence, lagged levels of q_i indeed contain information on q_i and can serve as instruments for q_i.

5.2.4 Definitions of Charter Value and Risk-Taking

In the following two subsections, I define my measures of charter value, risk-taking, and the bank-specific and macroeconomic control variables. The definitions are also given in Table A19 in Appendix 1 of this chapter.

A bank's charter value is defined as the net present value of future rents that a bank earns when it stays in business. Hence, it equals the market value of a bank's assets minus its replacement costs. As the market value of assets is not

41 See the help file for Stata command xtabond2 ("collapse" suboption) for details (Roodman 2005).

readily available, I use the sum of the market value of the bank's equity capital and the book value of the bank's liabilities as a proxy. As the replacement costs of assets are not readily available, I use the book value of assets as a proxy. The bank's charter value is then defined as:

$$Charter\,Value_{i,t} = Equity\,Capital_{i,t}^{market\ value} + Liabilities_{i,t}^{book\ value} - Assets_{i,t}^{book\ value}$$

To scale the left hand side, the charter value is divided by the book value of assets. Finally, subtracting 1 and simplifying gives Tobin's q, by which I proxy the charter value in the following. Hence and in line with the empirical literature (Keeley 1990; Gropp and Vesala 2004; Demsetz et al. 1996), my measure for bank i's charter value at time t is defined as:

$$q_{i,t} = \frac{Charter\,Value_{i,t}}{Assets_{i,t}^{book\ value}} + 1 = \frac{Equity\,Capital_{i,t}^{market\ value} + Liabilities_{i,t}^{book\ value}}{Assets_{i,t}^{book\ value}},$$

where all measures are taken at the end of year t.

The assumption is that the charter value is capitalized into the market value of equity, but not into the book value of assets. Hence, a bank with a higher charter value should have a higher q. Tobin's q is an ideal measure of a bank's charter value, as greater market power both in the asset market and in the deposit market is reflected in a higher q. Banks without market power should have a Tobin's q of 1.

There are two shortcomings to using q as a proxy for charter value, which are due to probable measurement errors both in the numerator and the denominator. First, the book value of liabilities is a good proxy for the market value only if the liabilities consist mainly of short-term debt. This is true for banks with a large proportion of demand deposits. However, as banks rely increasingly on market sources of funding, the market value of liabilities is more sensitive to changes in interest rates, which are not reflected in the book value. Second, the book value of assets is measured at the historical costs, not the current replacement costs. Hence, when q is observed to differ from 1, this difference may be due to asset return realizations rather than to banks' market power.

A further shortcoming consists in the fact that the deposit insurance subsidy and, hence, the probability of a bank's failure may be capitalized into the market value of equity. As my measures of risk-taking try to capture the bank characteristics that are the main determinants of the probability of default, Tobin's q may be endogenous in the second-step regressions. The empirical analysis has to account for this by modeling q as an endogenous variable.

With respect to risk-taking, I use six measures that all capture different aspects of risk. First, I use banks' absolute capital buffer, *BUF*, which is defined as the Basel I capital ratio minus the 8 percent regulatory minimum. The idea is that *BUF* is a measure of banks' distance to default. As the Basel I capital ratio is defined as capital over risk-weighted assets, it is also a combined measure of both banks' capital, i.e., leverage risk, and asset risk. Second, I use banks' standardized capital buffer, *SBUF*. *SBUF* is defined as the absolute capital buffer divided by the bank-specific standard deviation of the Basel I capital ratio. The rationale for *SBUF* is as follows. If the risk-weighted assets do not fully account for banks' asset risk, two banks with different degrees of asset risk may have different distances to default despite their holding the same absolute capital buffer. Suppose Bank A and B hold a capital buffer of 2 percent. However, Bank A holds a higher asset risk than Bank B and, hence, Bank A's capital ratio is more volatile. Thus, Bank A needs a higher capital buffer than Bank B as insurance against a breach of the capital requirement. Measuring the capital buffer in absolute terms (2 percent) is, thus, misleading in the sense that Bank A is closer to a breach of the regulatory minimum than Bank B. The standardized capital buffer accounts for this.

In addition, I decompose the absolute capital buffer into capital and risk-weighted assets, as they measure two different aspects of banks' risk-taking. Hence, third, I use banks' ratio of capital to total assets to capture banks' leverage risk, *CAP*. And fourth, I use the ratio of risk-weighted assets to total assets to capture banks' asset risk, *RISK*. The rationale for this measure is that the allocation of bank assets among risk categories is the major determinant of banks' asset risk. Apart from allocation, banks' asset risk is also determined by the quality of loans. Hence, fifth, I use the ratio of impaired loans to gross loans to capture the quality of loans, *ILGL*. And sixth, I use the ratio of loan loss reserves to gross loans, *LLRGL*, as an additional quality indicator.

I would have liked to complement these risk measures based on accounting values with risk measures based on market values, such as banks' idiosyncratic risk or banks' z-score. However, BankScope does not include the necessary data to calculate these measures and complementing it with data from Datastream poses a problem, as the data sources are not compatible (see below).

5.2.5 Bank-Specific and Macroeconomic Control Variables

In the first-step regressions (see (28)), I regress banks' charter value on its determinants. As banks' charter value is the net present value of future rents, the determinants of charter value are found in the sources of banks' possibility to generate rents. Banks may generate rents if (i) they have market power in the deposit or the loan market; or (ii) they have access to a superior production technology; or (iii) they extract wealth from the deposit insurance system when premia are mispriced.

Hence, abstracting from the third case, the regressors in the first-step regression are to capture banks' competitive environment and banks' efficiency. To account for banks' *efficiency*, I include banks' cost-income ratio, *CIR*. As banks with higher efficiency are expected to earn higher rents, *CIR* is included with an expected negative sign.

To account for the competitive environment in the various EU countries, I use four country-specific, time-varying variables. First, I use the *concentration* ratio of the five biggest banks (in terms of total assets) in country *j*, *CR5*. The idea is that in countries with a higher degree of concentration, banks have a higher degree of monopoly power, which they use to extract higher rents. Thus, *CR5* is included with an expected positive effect on q. Second, I use the *average profitability* of banks in country *j*, $avROA_{j,t}$. *avROA* indirectly measures the degree of competition in country *j*, as, in countries with a higher degree of competition, the average profitability in the banking sector is expected to be lower (ceteris paribus). Hence, *avROA* is included with an expected positive sign. Third, I use the *spread between the lending rate and the deposit rate* in country *j*, *SPREAD*. *SPREAD* is also an indirect measure of the degree of competition in country *j*, as, in countries with a higher degree of competition, the spread between the lending rate and the deposit rate is expected to be lower. Hence, *SPREAD* is included with an expected positive sign. And fourth, I use a novel measure of *integration*, which I construct as follows:

$$INTEGR_{j,t} = 0.5\left[(lr_{j,t} - lr_{bench,t})^2 + (dr_{j,t} - dr_{bench,t})^2\right],$$

where $lr_{j,t}$ and $dr_{j,t}$ are the lending rate and deposit rate in country j at time t, respectively. $lr_{bench,t}$ and $dr_{bench,t}$ are the benchmark lending rate and deposit rate at time t, respectively. $lr_{bench,t}$ is equal to the lowest lending rate in any of the EU countries at time t, while $dr_{bench,t}$ is equal to the highest deposit rate in any of the EU countries at time t. Hence, *INTEGR* is a distance measure that measures competition relative to the countries with the highest degree of competition in the lending and deposit market. As banks' market power in the lending and deposit market are traditionally the two most important sources of banks' charter value, *INTEGR* is an ideal measure of competition as a determinant of charter value. Thus, *INTEGR* is included with an expected positive sign.

In addition, I use the growth in *market capitalization* of the stock exchange in the respective country *j*, *gMKTCAP*. The rationale for this variable is not to capture the competitive environment, but to control for the general market sentiment, which is expected to have a positive effect on the market value of bank i and, hence, also on q. In addition, I include the full set of year and country dummy variables. The country dummy variables are, among other things, to capture differences in the coverage of the deposit insurance.

As the banking systems in the different EU countries differ with respect to their institutional and supervisory structures, macroeconomic competition variables are unlikely to capture fully the competitive environment. Hence and in accordance with the literature, I additionally use bank-specific variables that capture the balance-sheet and income structure of banks. First, I include the ratio of customer loans to total assets, *CUSTLOANS*, and the ratio of customer deposits to total assets, *CUSTDEP*, to test whether banks earn rents in the *loan and deposit market*. And second, I include the share of noninterest revenue in total operating income, *NIC*, to test whether banks earn rents from providing financial services that generate *noninterest revenues*.

Finally, bank *size* may also affect charter value, as large banks may have greater market power than small banks. To capture this effect, I include the natural logarithm of total assets, *SIZE*, with an expected positive sign.

In the second-step regressions (see (29)), I regress banks' risk-taking on banks' charter value, bank-specific control variables, and GDP growth. In the following, I explain the impact of the bank-specific variables on my measure of risk-taking.

Apart from the indirect effect of expected profits on the capital buffer through its impact on the charter value, *realized profits* are expected to have a direct effect on banks' risk-taking: banks retain part of their earnings, thereby increasing their ratio of capital to total assets and their capital buffer. Hence, I include banks' return on assets, *ROA*, as a measure of profits with an expected positive sign.

Apart from the indirect effect of *size* on the capital buffer through its impact on the charter value, size may also have a direct effect on banks' risk-taking. First, unexpected losses are in part due to asymmetric information between banks and their borrowers. Screening and monitoring reduce the asymmetry, but are costly and, thus, banks will balance the cost and gains from these activities against holding excess capital. If there are economies of scale in screening and monitoring, large banks should hold relatively less capital and instead undertake more monitoring and screening. Second, larger banks may have better investment and diversification opportunities. Thus, their asset quality, as reflected in loan loss provisions and impaired loans, may be higher and, thus, they are subject to a lower probability of a large negative shock to their capital buffer and only need to hold a lower capital buffer as insurance against such a shock. This effect could also have the inverse effect if small and specialized banks have a lower probability of a negative capital shock. Third, larger banks have a higher probability of being bailed out by the government when they are suffering from financial distress due to potential systemic effects ("too big to fail"). Hence, I include the natural log of total assets, *SIZE*, to capture size effects with ambiguous expectations regarding the estimated sign.

Liquidity is expected to have a negative effect on banks' risk-taking. For instance, holding liquid assets reduces the need for insurance against a possible violation of the minimum capital requirements and, thus for banks' to hold a large capital buffer. I approximate liquidity, *LIQUID*, by the ratio of liquid assets to total assets and include *LIQUID* with an expected negative effect on banks' risk-taking.

Market discipline may have a moderating effect on banks' risk-taking, as uninsured debtors may force banks to have more capital, less risk-weighted assets, higher capital buffers, and a higher asset quality. I approximate market discipline using the ratio of subordinated debt to total assets, *SOD*.

Further, I control for the impact of *risk management skills*. The idea is that banks with higher charter values may have superior skills in risk management and can, thus, better control their probability of default. Hence, they can afford to have less capital, lower capital buffers, a lower asset quality, and more risk-weighted assets. I approximate banks' risk management skills using the ratio of off-balance-sheet items to total assets, $OBS_{i,t}$, with an expected positive effect on banks' risk-taking.

In addition, apart from its indirect effect through charter value, efficiency could also have a direct effect on risk-taking, as banks with a low degree of efficiency may also have a higher probability of default. Hence, I include banks' cost-income ratio, *CIR*, with an expected positive sign.

Finally, in addition to the bank-specific control variables, I also include GDP growth, $gGDP_{j,t}$, in order to capture *country-specific macroeconomic effects*. In addition, I include the full set of year and country dummy variables.

5.3 Data Description

The data used in this chapter are obtained from two sources. The balance sheet and income statement data is from the Fitch IBCA BankScope database (Update 164.2, March 2004). One specificity of BankScope is the fact that it lists banks several times if they file their annual report on a consolidated as well as an unconsolidated basis. In order to have an individual bank only once in the sample, I reduce the sample to EU banks with consolidated statements, EU banks with unconsolidated statements if they do not have a consolidated companion, and EU banks with aggregated statements if they do not have a companion. Further, as the closure policies may differ between the supervisory authorities in the different EU countries, I drop the 10 observations with negative capital buffers. Finally, as the measure of charter value that I use here, Tobin's q, requires the market value of equity, the available data set reduces to an unbalanced panel of 95 EU banks over the period 1997–2003. I supplement the bank-specific data with country-level data, which I obtain from Datastream, OECD, and the ECB.

I tried to increase the number of observations by complementing the BankScope data with market values of equity taken from Datastream. However, when I compared the data from Datastream with the data from BankScope, the market values of equity were not consistent. They even fluctuated countercyclically for the same bank. Hence, I decided to use only the data provided by BankScope.

The composition of the banks by EU member country is given in Table A20 in Appendix 1. Two details are worth mentioning. First, Belgian banks are lacking from the sample, as BankScope does not provide enough observations on market capitalizations for Belgian banks to include Belgian banks in the dynamic regressions. And second, Danish banks dominate the sample, as BankScope provides the highest number of market capitalizations for Danish banks. I run various robustness checks concerning this dominance, such as regressions on subsamples without Danish banks and regressions with Danish country dummies interacted with the explanatory variables. But the effect of the charter value on the capital buffer remain unchanged.

Appendix 1 also gives several descriptive statistics of the variables. Table A21 shows that banks' charter value ranges from 0.86 to 1.68, with an average of 1.02. Hence, the average bank seems to have a low degree of market power. Table A22 gives the variable means over time. The variable that shows the most striking development over time is the integration measure, *INTEGR*. It falls strongly over time, indicating that the lending and borrowing rate in the EU have converged strongly.

Table A23 gives the correlation for the variables of the first-step regressions. Banks' charter value, q, is most highly correlated with the share of noninterest income, *NIC*, and bank size, *SIZE*.

Table A24 gives the correlation for the variables of the second-step regressions. Banks' charter value, q, is negatively correlated with both the capital and the asset risk measures. As will be seen in Section 4.2, only the negative effect of charter value on capital remains when I control for other variables in the regression analysis.

5.4 Regression Analysis

This section shows the regression results. First, it shows the results of the first-step regressions, which study the determinants of banks' charter value. And second, it shows the results of the second-step regressions, which study the effect of banks' charter value on banks' risk-taking.

5.4.1 Charter Value

Table 10 gives the results of estimating (28) in addition to the Hansen test and the tests of serial correlation in the first-differenced residuals. As one of the reasons for running the first-step regressions is to see whether lagged levels of banks' charter value, q, are suitable instruments for q in the second-step regression, I first estimate a pure autoregressive model. Specification 1 shows that the estimated coefficient of q_{t-1} is highly significant and positive. A Wald test rejects the hypothesis that the coefficient is equal to one, indicating that banks' charter value does not follow a random walk. Hence, lagged levels of q seem to provide information on q and are, thus, suitable instruments for q.

Further, I additionally include bank-specific variables among the regressors. Specification 2 shows that banks' cost-income ratio, *CIR*, has a highly significant and negative effect, indicating that highly efficient banks have higher charter values. The share of noninterest revenue, *NIC*, is found to have a highly significant and positive effect on q, indicating that banks providing financial services that generate noninterest revenues have higher charter values. In contrast, the insignificance of the share of customer loans, *CUSTLOANS*, and customer deposits, *CUSTDEP*, indicates that banks seemingly do not earn rents in their traditional banking business. Bank size, *SIZE*, is found to be insignificant. Although *SIZE* is highly correlated with most of the other bank-specific variables, this result does not seem to be driven by multicollinearity: *SIZE* is still insignificant if all other bank-specific variables are dropped from the regression. This finding is in line with evidence for the United States provided by Keeley (1990), but in contrast to evidence for a large cross-country sample provided by De Nicolo (2000). The latter study finds, also based on BankScope data, that bigger banks have lower charter values. This different finding may be due to the fact that De Nicolo (2000) uses a set of more heterogeneous countries and another time period.

The inclusion of the bank-specific variables slightly deteriorates the results of the test of first-order autocorrelation in the first-differenced residuals. But the hypothesis of a white noise error term of the original model (see (28)), i.e., the model before taking first differences, still cannot be rejected at the 10 percent level. In addition, the test statistics of the test of second-order autocorrelation and of the Hansen test remain insignificant. Hence, I am still confident in the results of Specification 2 (and 3, for which the same arguments apply).

Table 10:
Blundell–Bond Two-Step System GMM Estimates for Charter Value, 1997–2003

Dep. variable: q	1	2	3	4
q_{t-1}	0.6618***	0.5852***	0.6498***	0.5865***
	(21.04)	(14.72)	(24.27)	(18.08)
gMKTCAP			0.0152	0.0084
			(0.77)	(0.43)
CR5			–0.1030	–0.1195
			(1.11)	(1.14)
avROA			0.3741	–0.6042
			(0.19)	(0.25)
INTEGR			0.0004	0.0001
			(0.29)	(0.09)
SPREAD			0.0292***	0.0264***
			(3.71)	(3.14)
CIR		–0.0842***		–0.0572**
		(3.31)		(2.45)
NIC		0.0878***		0.0946***
		(2.93)		(3.42)
CUSTDEP		–0.0238		0.0136
		(0.61)		(0.43)
CUSTLOANS		–0.0332		–0.0251
		(1.10)		(1.06)
SIZE		–0.0045		0.0010
		(1.19)		(0.44)
Constant	0.3882***	0.7244***	0.3169***	0.4716***
	(10.21)	(3.32)	(3.72)	(4.01)
Year and country dummies	yes	yes	yes	yes
# Observations	476	475	320	319
# Banks	93	93	90	90
Hansen test	0.676	0.727	0.955	0.983
AR(1) test	0.009	0.014	0.057	0.062
AR(2) test	0.713	0.667	0.337	0.252

Notes: The dependent variable is q, which is defined as the market value of equity plus the book value of liabilities over the book value of total assets. *CIR* is defined as the cost-income ratio. *NIC* is defined as the share of noninterest revenue in total revenues. *CUSTDEP* is defined as the share of customer deposits to total assets. *CUSTLOANS* is defined as the share of customer loans to total assets. *gMKTCAP* is defined as the growth of market capitalization of the stock market in country *j*. *CR5* is defined as the concentration ratio of the five biggest banks (in terms of total assets) in country *j*. *avROA* is defined as total bank profits divided by total bank assets in country *j*. *SPREAD* is defined as the lending rate minus deposit rate in country *j*. *INTEGR* is a distance measure, capturing the degree of integration. The exact definition is given in Section 2.5. Lagged differences of q are used as instruments for equations in levels, in addition to lagged levels of q, which are used as instruments for equations in first differences. The absolute *t*-values are given in parentheses. ***, **, and * indicate statistical significance at the 1, 5, and 10 percent level, respectively, in a two-tailed t-test. Hansen test refers to the test of overidentifying restrictions. AR(1) and AR(2) test refer to the test for the null of no first-order and second-order autocorrelation in the first-differenced residuals.

Finally, I include country-specific variables capturing the competitive environment. As I have data for the average return on assets only until 2001, the number of observations included in the regression decreases compared to Specification 2. Hence, in order to have a higher number of degrees of freedom, I first exclude the bank-specific variables from the regressors. Specification 3 shows the results. As expected, the spread between the lending and deposit rate, *SPREAD*, is found to have a significant and positive effect on q. But the concentration ratio, *CR5*, the average return on assets, *avROA*, and my measure of integration, *INTEGR*, are found to be insignificant. The insignificance of *INTEGR* is in line with earlier findings: while all legal barriers to the free flow of capital have been abolished in the EU and, hence, interest rates have been converging as indicated by *INTEGR*, the integration of cross-border banking activities has not picked up the same speed (Buch 2000, Sander and Kleimeier 2004).[42]

Though not reported here, I also experimented with government bond yields and money market rates in order to control for financial market conditions. However, these interest rates were also found to be insignificant. As, in addition, the test statistics deteriorated, I do not show the results.

In addition, I include the growth of market capitalization in order to control for the market sentiment. However, it is found to be insignificant. Only when year and country dummy variables are excluded is it found to have the expected significant and positive effect.

When I include both the bank-specific variables and the country-specific variables, the results remain qualitatively the same (Specification 4). Only the significance level declines due to a lower number of degrees of freedom. Hence, in sum, the first-step regressions identify banks' efficiency and noninterest revenues as significant determinants of charter value. With respect to the country-specific competition measures, only the spread between lending and deposit rates has a significant and positive effect on banks' charter value. Further, the first-step regressions show that lagged levels of q are suitable instruments for q in the second-step regressions.

5.4.2 Risk-Taking

In the second-step regression, I regress different measures of banks' risk-taking on banks' charter value and control variables. The results of estimating (29), in

42 The reason for this may lie in institutional differences across EU countries, which lead to a large home bias despite the single European currency (Buch 2002). But also information costs may play a role (Buch 2003). Further, the prevalence of universal banking in most EU countries, which gives banks a certain degree of monopoly power, is likely to be a barrier to market entry for foreign banks (Buch and Golder 2000).

addition to the Hansen test and the tests of serial correlation in the first-differenced residuals, are presented in tables 11 and 12.

In Table 11, the charter value, q, is modeled as an exogenous variable. The results show that q has a highly significant and negative effect on capital, *CAP*, and the absolute capital buffer, *BUF*, but no significant effect on the standardized capital buffer, *SBUF*, risk-weighted assets, *RISK*, loan loss reserves, *LLRGL*, and impaired loans, *ILGL*. As q does not have a significant effect on *RISK*, the negative effect of q on *BUF* seems to come through the negative effect of q on capital, and not on risk-weighted assets.

The effect of q on the absolute capital buffer, *BUF*, and on the capital-to-asset ratio, *CAP*, is significant not only in a *statistical* sense, but also in an *economic* sense. If q increases by one standard deviation, *BUF* decreases by 0.06 standard deviations (i.e., 0.24 percentage points) and *CAP* decreases by 0.1 standard deviations (i.e., 0.38 percentage points). Given that in some years in the observation period the average capital buffer in excess of the regulatory capital requirement was less than 4 percentage points, a quarter of a percentage point decrease does not pose a problem to banks, but it is also not negligible.

In order to control for the potential endogeneity of q, the charter value is modeled as an endogenous variable in Table 12. To do so, I use lagged levels of q as GMM-style instruments for q. The results show that the significant and negative effect of q on *CAP* and *BUF* remains. The negative effect is contrary both to usual expectations and to the findings of other papers that find a significant and negative effect of charter value on leverage risk for banks in the United States and in the European Union (Keeley 1990; Gropp and Vesala 2004). The negative effect is, however, in line with the predictions by Milne and Whalley (2001) for banks whose charter value is higher than their cost of recapitalization. Banks with high charter values have a higher expected cash flow, which allows them to cushion negative capital shocks without having to incur the cost of recapitalization. Hence, they need to hold only lower capital buffers to be insured against negative capital shocks and to protect their charter value.

The findings with respect to the control variables also give some interesting insights. The significance of the lagged endogenous variables supports the dynamic specification. When subtracting 1 and multiplying by –1, the coefficient estimates can be interpreted as the speeds of adjustment in the endogenous variable. For instance, the estimated speed of *BUF* is about 0.2 and a Wald test indicates that the estimated speed is highly significant. The estimated speed implies that shocks to the capital buffer are halved within three years.

The banks' return on assets, *ROA*, is found to have a significant and positive effect on *BUF* and *CAP*, indicating that banks rely heavily on retained earnings in order to increase capital. Further, *ROA* has a slightly significant and negative effect on impaired loans, *ILGL*. However, *ROA* becomes insignificant if modeled

Table 11:
Blundell–Bond Two-Step System GMM Estimates for Risk-Taking (Charter Value Modeled as Exogenous Variable), 1997–2003

	1	2	3	4	5	6
Dep. variable	*BUF*	*SBUF*	*CAP*	*RISK*	*ILGL*	*LLRGL*
Lagged dep. variable	0.8110*** (14.27)	0.4734*** (3.90)	0.4577*** (3.04)	0.5389*** (3.29)	0.8294*** (7.67)	0.7295*** (7.25)
q	–0.0375** (2.47)	–3.5228 (1.56)	–0.0588*** (3.66)	–0.1107 (1.26)	0.0358 (0.95)	0.0026 (0.29)
ROA	0.5235** (2.48)	30.8183 (1.65)	0.8699*** (3.34)	0.9355 (0.58)	–0.4900* (1.87)	–0.3083 (1.16)
SIZE	–0.0003 (0.55)	–0.0129 (0.16)	–0.0051*** (3.80)	–0.0273*** (3.43)	0.0005 (0.55)	–0.0009 (1.35)
LIQUID	0.0282*** (3.21)	1.4349 (1.25)	–0.0008 (0.04)	–0.2960** (2.04)	0.0080 (0.69)	0.0184 (1.64)
SOD	0.3608*** (4.07)	34.8820*** (3.94)	0.2876*** (5.27)	0.6708 (0.90)	–0.0661 (0.69)	–0.0275 (0.50)
OBS	0.0005 (0.21)	–0.0940 (0.76)	0.0057 (1.55)	0.0707* (1.70)	0.0033** (2.04)	0.0019** (2.16)
CIR	0.0010 (0.11)	0.3796 (0.38)	–0.0201 (1.58)	–0.0496 (0.80)	0.0067 (0.54)	–0.0082 (1.47)
gGDP	–0.1040** (2.40)	–7.4824*** (2.94)	0.0182 (0.42)	0.6967*** (2.81)	–0.0199 (0.38)	–0.0191 (0.93)
Constant	0.0250 (1.12)	4.5118* (1.73)	0.1942*** (4.05)	0.8276*** (3.86)	–0.0437 (0.72)	0.0388 (1.03)
Year and country dummies	yes	yes	yes	yes	yes	yes
# Obs.	491	491	394	387	301	365
# Banks	95	95	88	88	76	85
Hansen test	0.290	0.034	0.481	0.790	0.157	0.541
AR(1) test	0.000	0.000	0.000	0.001	0.046	0.007
AR(2) test	0.683	0.958	0.684	0.104	0.649	0.954

Notes: *BUF* is defined as the Basel capital ratio minus 0.08. *SBUF* is defined as *BUF* divided by the bank-specific standard deviation of *BUF*. *CAP* is defined as the ratio of capital to total assets. *RISK* is defined as the ratio of risk-weighted assets to total assets. *ILGL* is defined as the ratio of impaired loans to gross loans. *LLRGL* is defined as the ratio of loan loss reserves to gross loans. *q* is defined as the market value of equity plus the book value of liabilities over the book value of total assets. *ROA* is defined as the return on average assets. *SIZE* is defined as the natural log of total assets. *LIQUID* is defined as liquid assets over total assets. *SOD* is defined as subordinated debt over total assets. *OBS* is defined as off-balance-sheet items over total assets. *CIR* is defined as banks' cost-income ratio. *gGDP* is defined as nominal GDP growth. Lagged differences of the endogenous variable are used as instruments for equations in levels, in addition to lagged levels, which are used as instruments for equations in first differences. The absolute *t*-values are given in parentheses. ***, **, and * indicate statistical significance at the 1, 5, and 10 percent level, respectively, in a two-tailed *t*-test. Hansen test refers to the test of overidentifying restrictions. AR(1) and AR(2) test refer to the test for the null of no first-order and second-order autocorrelation in the first-differenced residuals.

Table 12:
Blundell–Bond Two-Step System GMM Estimates for Risk-Taking (Charter Value Modeled as Endogenous Variable), 1995–2003

	1	2	3	4	5	6
Dep. variable	*BUF*	*SBUF*	*CAP*	*RISK*	*ILGL*	*LLRGL*
Lagged dep. variable	0.7809***	0.4548***	0.4595***	0.6019**	0.7748***	0.6929***
	(13.12)	(3.79)	(3.04)	(2.36)	(9.79)	(8.15)
q	–0.0361***	–1.8458	–0.0501***	–0.1110	–0.0009	–0.0114
	(4.87)	(0.23)	(4.35)	(1.13)	(0.07)	(0.52)
ROA	0.5980**	26.7158*	0.8558***	0.6517	–0.5100*	–0.3671
	(2.30)	(1.90)	(3.30)	(0.29)	(1.76)	(1.39)
SIZE	–0.0001	–0.0293	–0.0051***	–0.0265**	–0.0003	–0.0010
	(0.21)	(0.41)	(3.80)	(2.18)	(0.65)	(1.42)
LIQUID	0.0290***	1.9954*	–0.0016	–0.4581**	0.0003	0.0109
	(3.23)	(1.78)	(0.08)	(2.22)	(0.03)	(1.46)
SOD	0.2823***	37.1807	0.2864***	0.4207	0.0766	–0.0273
	(3.20)	(1.54)	(5.22)	(0.41)	(1.53)	(0.49)
OBS	–0.0020	–0.2119	0.0055	0.0611	0.0022*	0.0025*
	(1.12)	(1.07)	(1.52)	(0.99)	(1.99)	(1.94)
CIR	–0.0023	0.4702	–0.0195	–0.0057	–0.0015	–0.0077
	(0.22)	(0.35)	(1.55)	(0.08)	(0.15)	(0.88)
gGDP	–0.0843**	–7.8466**	0.0155	0.4271*	–0.0226	–0.0148
	(2.13)	(2.21)	(0.37)	(1.87)	(0.39)	(0.70)
Constant	0.0272	3.2802	0.1851***	0.7801*	0.0235	0.0425
	(1.59)	(0.35)	(4.03)	(1.95)	(1.09)	(1.24)
Year and country dummies	yes	yes	yes	yes	yes	yes
# Obs.	491	491	394	387	301	365
# Banks	95	95	88	88	76	85
Hansen test	0.340	0.121	0.839	0.080	0.261	0.631
AR(1) test	0.000	0.000	0.000	0.015	0.045	0.006
AR(2) test	0.696	0.878	0.657	0.106	0.507	0.978

Notes: *BUF* is defined as the Basel capital ratio minus 0.08. *SBUF* is defined as *BUF* divided by the bank-specific standard deviation of *BUF*. *CAP* is defined as the ratio of capital to total assets. *RISK* is defined as the ratio of risk-weighted assets to total assets. *ILGL* is defined as the ratio of impaired loans to gross loans. *LLRGL* is defined as the ratio of loan loss reserves to gross loans. *q* is defined as the market value of equity plus the book value of liabilities over the book value of total assets. *ROA* is defined as the return on average assets. *SIZE* is defined as the natural log of total assets. *LIQUID* is defined as liquid assets over total assets. *SOD* is defined as subordinated debt over total assets. *OBS* is defined as off-balance-sheet items over total assets. *CIR* is defined as banks' cost-income ratio. *gGDP* is defined as nominal GDP growth. Lagged differences of the endogenous variable and *q* are used as instruments for equations in levels, in addition to lagged levels, which are used as instruments for equations in first differences. The absolute *t*-values are given in parentheses. ***, **, and * indicate statistical significance at the 1, 5, and 10 percent level, respectively, in a two-tailed *t*-test. Hansen test refers to the test of overidentifying restrictions. AR(1) and AR(2) test refer to the test for the null of no first-order and second-order autocorrelation in the first-differenced residuals.

as an endogenous variable. Hence, the negative effect may be driven by a reverse causality, as impaired loans reduce banks' revenues. Bank size, *SIZE*, is found to have a significant and negative impact on capital, *CAP*, and risk-weighted assets, *RISK*, which is in line with the empirical literature (Demsetz et al. 1996).

Liquidity, *LIQUID*, has a highly significant and positive effect on banks' capital buffer, *BUF*, through its significant and negative effect on risk-weighted assets, *RISK*. This positive effect is counterintuitive, as banks with high liquidity only need to hold lower capital buffers to be equally insured against a negative capital shock. However, as *LIQUID* does not have significant effects on the other risk measures, the negative effect on risk-weighted assets may be due to pure arithmetics: *LIQUID* comprises government bonds and share holdings, which have a relatively low risk weight.

Subordinated debt, *SOD*, is found to have a highly significant and positive effect on *BUF* and *CAP*. It has also a highly significant effect on *SBUF* when q is modeled as an exogenous variable. Hence, banks that face higher market discipline seem to hold higher capital-to-(risk-weighted)-asset ratios. Risk management skills, proxied by off-balance-sheet items, *OBS*, are found to have a slightly significant and positive effect on risk-weighted assets, *RISK*, impaired loans, *ILGL*, and loan loss reserves, *LLRGL*. This finding implies that banks more engaged in off-balance-sheet activities have a higher asset risk. Banks' cost-income ratio, *CIR*, is found to be insignificant for all risk measures. Hence, efficiency seems to have only an indirect effect on banks' risk-taking through its effect on banks' charter value.

GDP growth, *gGDP*, is found to have a negative effect on banks' absolute and standardized capital buffers through its significant and positive impact on risk-weighted assets. The negative effect on risk-weighted assets implies that procyclical fluctuations in loan demand may be behind this effect. Yet, the effect is rather weak: A one-percentage-point increase in GDP growth decreases absolute capital buffers, *BUF*, by 0.1 percentage points, standardized capital buffers, *SBUF*, by 0.07 standard deviations, and the average risk-weight, *RISK*, by 0.7 percentage points (compared to an average risk-weight of 76 percent).

Finally, the year and country dummy variables (the estimated coefficients of which I do not report here) are found to be mostly insignificant, but an F test rejects the joint insignificance.

5.4.3 Robustness Checks

I run various robustness checks. First, besides the charter value, the bank-specific control variables may also be endogenous. *ROA* could be endogenous, as banks' charter value determines banks' profitability. Adjustments in liquid asset holdings, *LIQUID*, and in the length of the balance sheet, *SIZE*, may be part of the banks' risk strategy. Hence, I model the bank-specific variables as endogenous variables by additionally including lagged levels as GMM-style instruments. The results are qualitatively the same and, hence, are not reported here. The only change occurs when *ROA* and *SOD* are modeled as an endogenous variable, as they become insignificant. Additionally, in the *CAP* regression, charter value, *q*, becomes insignificant if *ROA* is modeled as an endogenous variable. But in all other specifications, the significant and negative effect of *q* on *BUF* and *CAP* remains.

Second, as already mentioned above, I run various robustness checks concerning the dominance of Danish banks in the sample, such as regressions on subsamples and regressions with Danish country dummy variables interacted with the explanatory variables. However, the negative effect of *q* on the different risk measures remains stable over all regressions. Third, as the dataset for some countries contains only a low number of banks, I also run regressions in which I exclude these countries. Again, the significant and negative effect of *q* on *BUF* and *CAP* remains unchanged.

Fourth, the dataset contains various outliers, some of which are probably data mistakes. Hence, instead of excluding outliers in an arbitrary way, I exclude observations that lie outside four standard deviations around the variable mean.[43] Again, the negative effect of *q* on *BUF* and *CAP* remains.

Fifth, I run regressions on subsamples of periods. Again, the significant and negative effect of *q* on *BUF* and *CAP* is not affected. Even when I run pure cross-section regressions for each year within the observation period, the negative effect remains. However, it is mostly insignificant probably due to the low number of observations for single years. In order to use more than the information given by single years, while still staying within the cross-sectional regressions, I run *between* estimates, which are basically regressions on the variable means over time. The effect of *q* on *BUF* and *CAP* is again found to be significant and negative.

Sixth, as dynamic panel data estimators are known to produce sensitive results, I additionally run pooled ordinary least squares (OLS) regressions. The charter value, *q*, is again found to have a significant and negative effect on *BUF* and *CAP*, irrespectively of whether *q* is modeled as an exogenous variable or endogenous variable or whether observations are modeled as being independent observations across banks (countries), but not necessarily independent within banks (countries). With respect to the other variable estimates, the OLS estimates basically confirm the Blundell–Bond results.

---

43 This procedure is suggested by Demirgüç-Kunt et al. (2000).

Seventh and finally, I test two potential nonlinearities that the option-pricing model by Milne and Whalley (2001) predicts. The first nonlinearity concerns the effect of banks' charter value on banks' optimum capital buffer. As outlined in Section 2.6.3 of Chapter 2, as long as banks' charter value is higher than the cost of recapitalization, banks' optimum capital buffer is decreasing in banks' charter value, while it is increasing otherwise. The problem with testing this prediction is that banks' cost of recapitalization is not observable. Further, characteristics of banks that are highly correlated with the cost of recapitalization are hard to observe. Against this background of lacking alternatives, I test the effect of banks' charter value on banks' capital buffer without controlling for the cost of recapitalization. In addition, banks' optimum capital buffers are also not observable. However, the endogenous lag model I use can be interpreted as a partial adjustment model, in which banks adjust towards their optimum capital buffers and in which the optimum capital buffer depends on banks' charter value and other bank-specific variables.

To start with, I run regressions on subsamples for banks with high and low charter values, the results of which I do not report here. The relationship is always found to be negative, regardless of which cutoff value I use in order to distinguish between banks with high and low charter values. Further, I use a spline function approach, which allows the effect of banks' charter value to vary over the size of the charter value. In order to do so, I first create variables containing a linear spline of q, with the knots being placed at the percentiles of q. Second, I include these newly created variables instead of q in the Blundell–Bond regressions. Table A25 in Appendix 2 gives the results for *BUF* with two and four splines and q modeled as an exogenous and endogenous variable, respectively. Two splines mean that there is one knot at the median value of q. Four splines mean that there are knots at the 25th percentile, the median, and the 75th percentile of q. The results show that all estimates of the splines of q are negative, but only one estimate is significant in each specification.

Besides the spline function approach, I also experiment with quadratic forms of q. However, in these specifications, the coefficient of q^2 is found to be insignificant, while the coefficient of q is again found to be significant and negative.

In sum, the results do not support the hypothesis that the relationship between banks' charter value and capital buffer depends on the size of the charter value. It may, however, be worth mentioning that the finding of a negative relationship does not necessarily reject the prediction by Milne and Whalley (2001) of a nonlinear relationship if all banks in the sample have a charter value higher than their cost of recapitalization.

The second nonlinearity that I test concerns the effect of banks' charter value on banks' asset risk. As outlined in Section 2.6.3 of Chapter 2, the Milne and Whalley (2001) model predicts that asset risk depends positively on capital, the positive effect being more pronounced the higher the charter value. I test this prediction by including *CAP* in the equations for *RISK*, *ILGL*, and *LLRGL*. I additionally include a dummy variable for banks with low charter values and its interaction with *CAP*. I find that *CAP* has a highly significant and positive effect on *RISK*, *ILGL*, and *LLRGL*. However, as soon as I model *CAP* as an endogenous variable to account for the potential endogeneity of *CAP*, the effect becomes insignificant. Further, the interaction term is found to be insignificant in all specifications, irrespectively of the threshold charter value I use to distinguish between banks with high and low charter values. Hence, my findings support neither the first nor the second hypothesized nonlinearity.

5.5 Conclusion

This chapter has provided empirical evidence on the determinants of banks' charter value and the effect of banks' charter value on banks' risk-taking. In a first step, the charter value was explained by banks' competitive environment, banks' efficiency, and other bank-specific variables. In a second step, six measures of risk-taking were regressed on charter value. BankScope data on 95 EU stock-listed banks over the period 1997–2003 were used and dynamic panel data estimation techniques were employed.

The first-step regressions show that efficiency and noninterest revenue are important *bank-specific* determinants of charter value. With respect to the *country-specific* determinants that capture the competitive environment of banks, the market spread between lending and deposit rates is the only variable found to be significant. Hence, the link between competition and banks' charter value is found to be rather weak.

The second-step regressions show that banks' charter value has a negative effect on capital-to-(risk-weighted)-asset ratios. This negative effect is contrary to expectations and also contrary to findings for the United States. While a positive finding has always been interpreted as support for the disciplining effect of charter value on banks' risk-taking, a positive effect is not necessarily at odds with this disciplining effect. While charter value may give banks the incentive to hold a capital buffer, the desired magnitude of the capital buffer may still decrease in banks' charter value: banks with high charter values have higher expected earnings. These can be used to cushion negative capital shocks. Hence, banks with high charter values need to hold only lower capital buffers to protect their charter value.

In sum, while the literature argues that increasing competition decreases charter values, thereby increasing incentives for risk-taking, I do not find support for this hypothesis for the EU. According to my findings, the relationship between competition and charter value is only a weak one. Further, when banks' charter value decreases, banks increase their capital buffers and, hence, hold higher safety cushions above the regulatory minimum. Therefore, increasing competition does not seem to destabilize banks in the EU.

One plausible explanation for the weak link between competition and banks' charter value may be that the static effects of competition (negative effect on charter value) may partly be compensated for by the dynamic effects of competition (positive effect on charter value), working through increased efficiency. However, as I control for banks' efficiency, this argument is only valid if my measure of efficiency, i.e., the cost-income ratio, does not fully capture banks' efficiency. Further, the cost-income ratio does not show a negative trend over the observation period either. Hence, further research on the effect of competition on banks' charter value is clearly required.

Finally, another strand of the literature studies market discipline as an alternative mechanism to curb banks' moral hazard behavior. Based on a large cross-country panel data set, Nier and Baumann (2006) find that market discipline has a negative effect on banks' risk-taking. Yet, the interaction of market discipline, charter value, and risk-taking is largely unexplored. I leave this question to future research.

5.6 Appendix 1: Descriptive Statistics

Table A19:
Description of the Bank-Specific and Macroeconomic Variables

Variable	Definition
q	Market value of equity plus book value of liabilities divided by book value of total assets
BUF	Basel capital-to-risk-weighted-assets ratio minus 0.08
SBUF	Basel capital-to-risk-weighted-assets ratio minus 0.08 divided by the bank-specific standard deviation of the capital buffer over the observation period
CAP	Regulatory capital to total assets ratio
RISK	Risk-weighted assets to total assets ratio
CIR	Cost-income ratio
NIC	Total operating income minus net interest revenue divided by total operating income
CUSTLOANS	Customer loans divided by total assets
CUSTDEP	Customer deposits divided by total assets
ROA	Return on average assets / 100
SIZE	Natural log of total assets in euros
LIQUID	Liquid assets over total assets
SOD	Subordinated debt over total assets
OBS	Off-balance-sheet items over total assets
gGDP	Nominal GDP growth
gMKTCAP	Growth in market capitalization
CR5	Concentration ratio of the five biggest banks (in terms of total assets)
avROA	Total bank profits divided by total bank assets
INTEGR	Integration measure, for exact calculation see Section 2.3
SPREAD	Lending rate minus deposit rate

Notes: The macroeconomic variables *gGDP*, *gMKTCAP*, *CR5*, *avROA*, *INTEGR*, and *SPREAD* vary between countries and time periods and have been obtained from Datastream, the OECD, and the ECB. The bank-specific variables vary between banks and time periods and have been obtained from BankScope.

Table A20:
Composition of Observations and Banks by Country

	Number of Observations	Number of Banks		Number of Observations	Number of Banks
Austria	5	1	Italy	71	17
Denmark	227	36	Luxemburg	6	1
Finland	12	2	Netherlands	7	1
France	24	4	Portugal	19	3
Germany	25	5	Spain	46	11
Greece	21	5	Sweden	14	2
Ireland	23	4	United Kingdom	15	3
			Total	515	95

Table A21:
Descriptive Statistics

	# Obs.	Mean	Min.	5th percentile	Median	95th percentile	Max.	Std. dev.
q	515	1.0223	0.8620	0.9467	1.0118	1.1408	1.6792	0.0648
BUF	515	0.0473	0.0000	0.0099	0.0390	0.1108	0.3778	0.0412
SBUF	515	3.3546	0.0000	0.5499	3.0094	6.5550	21.9439	2.5084
CAP	430	0.0973	0.0138	0.0480	0.0882	0.1616	0.1930	0.0373
RISK	430	0.7590	0.1496	0.4531	0.7525	1.1324	1.3091	0.2164
ILGL	335	0.0304	0.0000	0.0033	0.0191	0.0870	0.2137	0.0334
LLRGL	386	0.0355	0.0000	0.0049	0.0315	0.0798	0.1291	0.0229
ROA	515	0.0094	–0.0154	0.0010	0.0087	0.0214	0.0342	0.0063
SIZE	515	15.3621	10.3634	11.3492	15.8677	19.7649	20.6374	2.7679
LIQUID	515	0.2187	0.0155	0.0580	0.2071	0.4490	0.6219	0.1205
SOD	501	0.0164	0.0000	0.0000	0.0159	0.0398	0.0660	0.0136
OBS	506	0.3178	0.0002	0.0474	0.2370	0.7233	3.9886	0.3705
CIR	514	65.4480	30.6700	44.8800	65.5200	84.2200	224.8900	0.1333
CUSTLOANS	515	0.5753	0.0759	0.3040	0.5906	0.7580	0.8690	0.1363
CUSTDEP	515	0.5757	0.0605	0.2397	0.5956	0.8124	0.8973	0.1804
NIC	515	0.3400	–0.1186	0.1448	0.3128	0.6244	0.9397	0.1480
CR5	483	53.5362	17.0000	23.0000	60.0000	71.0000	88.0000	18.3156
avROA	391	0.0099	0.0028	0.0055	0.0097	0.0137	0.0304	0.0029
SPREAD	455	4.4513	1.8100	2.0900	4.7000	6.2300	8.8100	1.1276
INTEGR	455	19.0408	2.9012	6.4649	13.6322	38.8081	62.7716	12.4167
gMKTCAP	510	0.0853	–0.4572	–0.3136	0.0546	0.6669	1.5529	0.2943
gGDP	515	0.0202	–0.1114	–0.0870	0.0066	0.2226	0.2789	0.0836

Table A22:
Variable Means for Each Year of the Observation Period

	1997	1998	1999	2000	2001	2002	2003
q	1.0213	1.0280	1.0248	1.0317	1.0157	1.0078	1.0389
BUF	0.0674	0.0533	0.0469	0.0438	0.0396	0.0395	0.0478
SBUF	3.7400	3.7237	3.3149	3.1022	3.0753	3.1912	3.7900
CAP	0.1023	0.1015	0.0979	0.0967	0.0938	0.0929	0.1005
RISK	0.7098	0.7359	0.7596	0.7804	0.7791	0.7653	0.7765
ILGL	0.0254	0.0358	0.0380	0.0289	0.0276	0.0304	0.0216
LLRGL	0.0279	0.0330	0.0322	0.0367	0.0381	0.0383	0.0360
ROA	0.0094	0.0095	0.0094	0.0106	0.0084	0.0073	0.0143
SIZE	14.6559	14.9176	15.2149	15.4397	15.6891	15.8363	15.6511
LIQUID	0.2500	0.2441	0.2198	0.2065	0.2140	0.2072	0.1768
SOD	0.0122	0.0127	0.0147	0.0162	0.0185	0.0204	0.0212
OBS	0.4222	0.2624	0.2904	0.3092	0.3016	0.3136	0.3935
CIR	0.6669	0.6470	0.6557	0.6477	0.6576	0.6621	0.6317
CUSTLOANS	0.5358	0.5697	0.5749	0.5912	0.5770	0.5860	0.5888
CUSTDEP	0.6255	0.6053	0.5814	0.5608	0.5553	0.5559	0.5500
NIC	0.3004	0.3249	0.3338	0.3688	0.3372	0.3345	0.4134
CR5	0.5619	0.5551	0.5473	0.4924	0.5325	0.5346	.
avROA	0.0096	0.0092	0.0092	0.0105	0.0108	.	.
INTEGR	29.4187	36.1970	25.9161	10.0436	8.3332	10.4421	5.4395
SPREAD	4.7347	4.4739	4.1817	4.6071	4.5863	4.2583	3.7114
gMKTCAP	0.2905	0.2799	0.2023	−0.0022	−0.2038	−0.1496	0.5695
gGDP	−0.0595	0.0378	0.0067	−0.0761	0.0126	0.0980	0.2303
# Observations	63	72	81	87	88	92	32

Notes: A dot indicates missing values.

Table A23:
Correlations between the Variables of the First-Step Regression

	Q	*CUSTLOANS*	*CUSTDEP*	*NIC*	*CIR*	*SIZE*	*CR5*	*avROA*	*SPREAD*	*INTEGR*
Q	1									
CUSTLOANS	–0.11**	1								
CUSTDEP	–0.16***	0.21***	1							
NIC	0.41***	–0.48***	–0.60***	1						
CIR	–0.21***	–0.27***	0.00	0.06	1					
SIZE	0.39***	–0.27***	–0.74***	0.59***	–0.04	1				
CR5	–0.34***	0.18***	0.50***	–0.43***	–0.09**	–0.56***	1			
avROA	0.10**	0.09*	0.25***	–0.08*	–0.17***	–0.09*	0.14***	1		
SPREAD	–0.21***	–0.09*	0.15***	–0.01	0.11**	–0.22***	0.04	0.30***	1	
INTEGR	0.21***	–0.06	0.07	0.03	–0.06	0.01	–0.04	–0.11**	–0.05	1
gMKTCAP	0.10*	–0.13***	–0.01	0.09*	–0.07	–0.01	0.02	–0.06	0.01	0.53***

Notes: ***, **, and * indicate statistical significance at the 1, 5, and 10 percent level, respectively.

Table A24:
Correlations between the Variables of the Second-Step Regression

	Q	*BUF*	*SBUF*	*CAP*	*RISK*	*ILGL*	*LLRGL*	*ROA*	*SIZE*	*LIQUID*	*SOD*	*OBS*	*CIR*
Q	1												
BUF	–0.15***	1											
SBUF	–0.11**	0.35***	1										
CAP	–0.35***	0.57***	0.27***	1									
RISK	–0.26***	–0.06	0.01	0.75***	1								
ILGL	–0.13**	–0.07	–0.12**	–0.18***	–0.17**	1							
LLRGL	–0.39***	0.29***	0.11**	0.55***	0.44***	0.37***	1						
ROA	0.15***	0.37***	0.10**	0.64***	0.46***	–0.38***	0.19***	1					
SIZE	0.39***	–0.43***	–0.23***	–0.81***	–0.66***	0.24***	–0.49***	–0.42***	1				
LIQUID	0.31***	–0.07	–0.09**	–0.45***	–0.55***	0.25***	–0.11***	–0.23***	0.40***	1			
SOD	0.04	–0.24***	0.09**	–0.10**	0.10**	0.08	–0.04	–0.17***	0.18***	–0.08**	1		
OBS	0.03	–0.06	–0.03	0.25***	0.35***	0.01	0.14***	0.19***	–0.07	0.04	–0.04	1	
CIR	–0.21***	–0.12***	0.03	–0.15***	–0.08*	0.26***	0.11**	–0.48***	–0.04	0.04	0.02	–0.04	1
gGDP	0.08*	–0.09**	0.00	–0.06	–0.01	–0.07	–0.06	0.06	0.14***	–0.02	0.13***	–0.01	–0.07*

Notes: ***, **, and * indicate statistical significance at the 1, 5, and 10 percent level, respectively.

5.7 Appendix 2: Robustness Checks

Table A25:
Blundell–Bond Two-Step System GMM Estimates for the Absolute Capital Buffer, 1997–2003

	1	2	3	4
Dependent variable: *BUF*	*q* exogenous	*q* endogenous	*q* exogenous	*q* endogenous
BUF_{t-1}	0.8119***	0.7699***	0.8088***	0.7640***
	(14.36)	(14.24)	(14.25)	(14.66)
q_1	–0.0427	–0.0554	–0.0117	–0.0693
	(0.80)	(0.32)	(0.18)	(0.35)
q_2	–0.0382**	–0.0341***	–0.0544	–0.2417
			(0.47)	(0.60)
q_3			–0.1811*	–0.1915
			(1.77)	(1.04)
q_4			–0.0212	–0.0354***
	(2.51)	(3.82)	(1.15)	(4.36)
ROA	0.5169**	0.5686**	0.5491**	0.8256***
	(2.44)	(2.00)	(2.56)	(2.91)
SIZE	–0.0002	–0.0004	–0.0003	–0.0001
	(0.48)	(0.60)	(0.54)	(0.08)
LIQUID	0.0283***	0.0325***	0.0304***	0.0355***
	(3.23)	(2.68)	(3.39)	(3.07)
SOD	0.3647***	0.2840***	0.3546***	0.3117***
	(3.99)	(2.63)	(3.88)	(2.95)
OBS	0.0005	–0.0023	0.0008	–0.0016
	(0.22)	(1.12)	(0.33)	(0.61)
CIR	0.0013	0.0004	0.0000	0.0014
	(0.13)	(0.04)	(0.00)	(0.13)
gGDP	–0.1052**	–0.1120***	–0.1081**	–0.1123***
	(2.42)	(3.11)	(2.45)	0.7640***
Constant	0.0297	0.0483	0.0022	0.0603
	(0.57)	(0.28)	(0.04)	(0.30)
Year and country dummies	yes	yes	yes	yes
# Observations	491	491	491	491
# Banks	95	95	95	95
Hansen test	0.286	0.264	0.260	0.893
AR(1) test	0.000	0.000	0.000	0.000
AR(2) test	0.675	0.667	0.675	0.556

Notes: The dependent variable is $BUF_{i,t}$, which is defined as the Basel capital ratio * 100 minus 0.08. *q* is defined as the market value of equity plus the book value of liabilities over the book value of total assets. q_1–q_4 refer to the linear splines of *q*. In specifications 1 and 2, the knot is placed at the median value of *q*. In specifications 3 and 4, the knots are placed at the 25th percentile, the median value, and the 75th percentiles of *q*. ROA is defined as the return on average assets. *SIZE* is defined as the natural log of total assets. *LIQUID* is defined as liquid assets over total assets. *SOD* is defined as subordinated debt over total assets. *OBS* is defined as off-balance-sheet items over total assets. *CIR* is defined as banks' cost-income ratio. *gGDP* is defined as nominal GDP growth. Lagged differences of BUF_i are used as instruments for equations in levels, in addition to lagged levels of BUF_i, which are used as instruments for equations in first differences. In addition, in specifications 2 and 4 I use lagged levels of *q*, in order to account for the potential endogeneity of *q*. The absolute *t*-values are given in parentheses. ***, **, and * indicate statistical significance at the 1, 5, and 10 percent level, respectively, in a two-tailed *t*-test. Hansen test refers to the test of overidentifying restrictions. AR(1) and AR(2) test refer to the test for the null of no first-order and second-order autocorrelation in the first-differenced residuals.

6 Final Remarks

The fact that the Basel Committee on Banking Supervision has been working on formulating the new capital standards called Basel II since 1999 (including four past quantitative impact studies (QIS) and a fifth upcoming one) clearly shows how much emphasis today's banking regulators put on minimum capital requirements. This study aims at contributing to the understanding of how banks behave in the light of capital requirements. In particular, the three empirical chapters of this study analyze the following three questions. How do banks adjust capital and asset risk after an increase in capital requirements (Chapter 3)? How do banks adjust their regulatory capital buffer over the business cycle (Chapter 4)? And, What is the impact of banks' charter value on the regulatory capital buffer (Chapter 5)?

Findings

Chapter 3 finds that banks' capital buffers have an impact on capital and asset risk adjustments in several interesting respects. In line with the literature, I find some evidence that banks with low capital buffers adjust capital and asset risk faster than banks with high capital buffers. With respect to the coordination of capital and asset risk, I find evidence that, for banks with low capital buffers, adjustments in capital and asset risk are negatively related. In contrast, for banks with high capital buffers, adjustments in capital and asset risk are positively related. Contrary to expectations, the coordination is, however, found to be one-way for banks with high capital buffers, running from capital to asset risk. In summary, my findings are in line with the hypotheses derived from the buffer theory (Marcus 1984; Milne and Whalley 2001).

Chapter 4 finds strong evidence that capital buffers of German savings banks and cooperative banks behave countercyclically, the capital buffers of savings banks reacting more strongly to the business cycle than the capital buffers of cooperative banks. What drives the stronger reaction of savings banks is the stronger procyclical fluctuation of risk-weighted assets and the countercyclical fluctuation of capital for savings banks, compared to a procyclical fluctuation of capital for cooperative banks. Further, I find that banks with low capital buffers do not decrease their risk-weighted assets more strongly in a business cycle downturn than banks with high capital buffers. Hence, this result does not lend support to the widely held concern that banks with low capital buffers retreat from lending in order to increase their capital buffers in a business cycle downturn, thereby further aggravating the downturn.

Chapter 5 provides empirical evidence on the determinants of banks' charter values and the effect of banks' charter values on banks' risk-taking in the EU. While the literature argues that increasing competition decreases charter values, thereby increasing incentives for risk-taking, I do not find support for this hypothesis for the EU. According to my findings, the relationship between competition and charter value is only weak. Further, when banks' charter values decrease, banks increase their capital buffers and, hence, hold higher safety cushions above the regulatory minimum. Therefore, increasing competition does not seem to destabilize banks in the EU.

Caveats

These findings are subject to several caveats. First, this study assumes that the observed behavior of banks is due to the fact that banks try to hold an optimum capital buffer above the regulatory minimum. Yet, another reason for their behavior may lie in the fact that they adjust their actual capital towards economic capital (i.e., the capital they need to cover their asset risk with a certain probability) and that they do not take regulatory capital into account as long as their economic capital is larger than the regulatory minimum. The problem with empirically testing this alternative hypothesis lies in the fact that the data to calculate banks' value at risk, the most commonly used measure of economic capital, are not available. However, the conflict between these two alternative hypotheses may not be so large, as banks that target economic capital also have to take into account the potential costs of violating the regulatory capital requirement.

Another caveat is due to the fact that the theoretical underpinnings, in particular with respect to Chapter 4, are rather weak. First, the theoretical effect of business cycles on banks' capital buffers and their loan supply is largely unexplored. Also, the feedback effects from banks' lending back into the macroeconomy are not well understood yet. But these are crucial in determining the ultimate economic significance of bank lending effects.

Basel II

This study provides interesting new findings on the behavior of banks in the light of the 1988 Basel Capital Accord. From a supervisory perspective, the introduction of a more risk-sensitive capital framework such as Basel II raises several questions.

First, my findings with respect to the coordination of capital and risk adjustments depend on the relative cost of capital and asset risk. This relative cost is mainly determined by the steepness of the risk-weight function. The risk-weight function is rather crude under the 1988 Basel Capital Accord and, hence, most of the consultation period for Basel II has been devoted to refining the risk-weight function. As a result, the risk-weight function will be steeper, thereby rendering asset risk more costly. It will be interesting to analyze banks' behavior ten years from now. My hypothesis is that, ceteris paribus, banks will adjust capital even faster and that the coordination of capital and risk adjustment will be two-way or even one-way, running from asset risk to capital and not from capital to asset risk.

Second, from a supervisory perspective, it is interesting whether banks' capital buffers will fluctuate more strongly over the business cycle under Basel II. While, under the 1988 Basel Capital Accord, the risk-weights were constant over the business cycle, the risk-weights will fluctuate procyclically over the business cycle under Basel II. Hence, the question whether banks' capital buffers will fluctuate more strongly over the business cycle under Basel II has two dimensions that can be logically separated. First, how strongly will the regulatory minimum capital requirements fluctuate over the business cycle? And second, what does this mean for banks' capital buffers?

With respect to the first question, simulation studies have widely been used. They predict that capital requirements will indeed fluctuate strongly over the business cycle. Another approach is to look at QIS data and use the different macroeconomic situations in different countries in a cross-section regression analysis. The results also predict that capital requirements will fluctuate strongly over the business cycle (Nier 2005).

With respect to the second question, simulation studies can only show how banks are expected to adjust their loan supply from a theoretical perspective. Further, QIS data do not provide any information on this question, as QIS data are based on the assumption of a constant portfolio composition. Hence, a possible approach is to assume that the introduction of Basel II will not lead to a structural break in the behavior of banks and to apply findings with respect to banks' reaction to changes in their capital buffer based on Basel I data. Admittedly, this assumption is very strong. But against the background of lacking alternatives, it is widely made by the literature.

Along these lines, Chapter 4 of this study finds that low-capitalized German banks do not decrease risk-weighted assets in a business cycle downturn by more than well-capitalized banks. This finding implies that their low capitalization does not force banks to retreat from lending. In contrast, Gambacorta and Mistrulli (2004) find that low-capitalized Italian banks react more strongly to the business cycle than their well-capitalized peers. Based on BankScope data on 600 banks from 31 countries, Zicchino and Nier (2005) find that capital does not have a direct effect on loan growth, but that banks with low capital ratios react more strongly to loan losses and the business cycle than their well-capitalized peers.

In sum, the studies cited predict that, with the introduction of Basel II, risk-weights and, thus, regulatory capital requirements will increase during a business cycle downturn, thereby decreasing banks' capital buffers. However, the empirical evidence on whether this leads to a contraction in banks' loan supply is inconclusive, as the studies cited come to contradictory conclusions. In addition, empirical studies show that banks' capital buffers may even increase during a business cycle downturn, as loan demand decreases (Ayuso et al. 2004; Chapter 4). Thus, predictions about the effect of Basel II on bank lending over the business cycle seem to be problematic.

Third, from a supervisory perspective, it is interesting whether the third pillar of Basel II will help market discipline to flourish and to supersede charter value as a disciplining device. Nier and Baumann (2006) find, based on a large cross-country panel data set, that market discipline has a negative effect on banks' risk-taking already under the 1988 Basel Capital Accord. Further, Furlong and Kwan (2005) attribute the diminishing disciplining effect of charter value in the United States over the 1990s to the fact that market discipline proliferated in the same period.

Here again, we will have to wait some years to empirically assess the question whether the introduction of Basel II will foster the proliferation of market discipline. The answer to this question has the potential to revolutionize today's supervisory doctrine. As Repullo (2004) puts it: "It is well known that an increase in bank competition that erodes the present value of the banks' future rents (their franchise or charter value) reduces their incentives to behave prudently." Hence, supervisors around the globe have been trying to limit the degree of competition. But if the link between competition and charter value is weak, as Chapter 5 suggests, and if, in addition, market discipline is an alternative disciplining device made more effective by Basel II, supervisors may want to rethink their doctrine.

References

Acharya, V., I. Hasan, and A. Saunders (2006). Should Banks Be Diversified? Evidence from Individual Bank Loan Portfolios. Forthcoming in the *Journal of Business* 79.

Aggarwal, R., and K.T. Jacques (2001). The Impact of FDICIA and Prompt Corrective Action on Bank Capital and Risk: Estimates Using a Simultaneous Equations Model. *Journal of Banking and Finance* 25: 1139–1160.

Alonso-Borrego, C., and M. Arellano (1996). Symmetrically Normalised Instrumental Variable Estimation Using Panel Data. *Journal of Business and Economic Statistics* 17: 36–49.

Altman, E.I., B. Brady, A. Resti, and A Sironi (2005). The Link between Default and Recovery Rates: Theory, Empirical Evidence, and Implications. *Journal of Business* 78: 2203–2228.

Andrews, D., and B. Lu (2001). Consistent Model and Moment Selection Procedures for GMM Estimation with Application to Dynamic Panel Data Models. *Journal of Econometrics* 101: 123–164.

Arellano, M., and S. Bond (1991). Some Tests of Specification for Panel Data: Monte Carlo Evidence and an Application to Employment Equations. *Review of Economic Studies* 58: 277–297.

Avery, R.B, and A.B. Berger (1991). Risk-Based Capital and Deposit Insurance Reform. *Journal of Banking and Finance* 15: 847–874.

Ayuso, J., D. Pérez, and J. Saurina (2004). Are Capital Buffers Procyclical? Evidence from Spanish Panel Data. *Journal of Financial Intermediation* 13: 249–264.

Baltensperger, E., and H. Milde (1987). *Theorie des Bankverhaltens*. Berlin: Springer.

Bank for International Settlements (2003). 73rd Annual Report. BIS, Basel.

Barth, J.R., G. Jr. Caprio, and R. Levine (2001). The Regulation and Supervision of Banks around the World: A New Database. In R.E. Litan and R. Herring (eds.), *Brooking-Wharton Papers on Financial Services*. Washington, D.C.: Brookings Institution.

Basel Committee on Banking Supervision (2001). The New Basel Capital Accord: An Explanatory Note. Basel.

Basel Committee on Banking Supervision (2003). Markets for Bank Subordinated Debt and Equity in Basel Committee Member Countries. Basel Committee on Banking Supervision Working Paper 12. Basel.

Benston, G., and G. Kaufman (1996). The Appropriate Role of Bank Regulation. *Economic Journal* 106: 688–697.

Benston, G., R. Eisenbeis, P. Horvitz, E. Kane, and G. Kaufman (1986). *Perspectives on Safe and Sound Banking: Past, Present, and Future.* Cambridge: MIT Press.

Berger, A.N. (1995). The Relationship between Capital and Earnings in Banking. *Journal of Money, Credit, and Banking* 27: 432–456.

Berger, A.N., R.J. Herring, and G.P. Szegö (1995). The Role of Capital in Financial Institutions. *Journal of Banking and Finance* 19: 393–430.

Besanko, D., and G. Kanatas (1996). The Regulation of Bank Capital: Do Capital Standards Promote Bank Safety? *Journal of Financial Intermediation* 5: 160–183.

Bhattacharya, S., A.W.A. Boot, and A.V. Thakor (1998). The Economics of Bank Regulation. *Journal of Money, Credit, and Banking* 30: 745–770.

Black, F., and M. Scholes (1973). The Pricing of Options and Corporate Liabilities. *Journal of Political Economy* 81: 637–659.

Black, F., M.H. Miller, and R.A. Posner (1978). An Approach to the Regulation of Bank Holding Companies. *Journal of Finance* 51: 379–412.

Blundell, R., and S. Bond (1998). Initial Conditions and Moment Restrictions in Dynamic Panel Data Models. *Journal of Econometrics* 87: 115–143.

Bond, S. (2002). Dynamic Panel Data Models: A Guide to Micro Data Methods and Practice. *Portuguese Economic Journal* 1, 141–162.

Boot, A., and S.I. Greenbaum (1993). Bank Regulation, Reputation, and Rents: Theory and Policy Implications. In C. Mayer and X. Vives (eds.), *Capital Markets and Financial Intermediation.* Cambridge: Cambridge University Press.

Bordo, M., A. Redish, and H. Rockoff (1995). A Comparison of the United States and Canadian Banking Systems in the Twentieth Century: Stability v. Efficiency. In M. Bordo and R. Sylla (eds.), *Anglo-American Financial Systems: Institutions and Markets in the Twentieth Century.* New York: Irwin.

Borio, C., C. Furfine, and P. Lowe (2001). Procyclicality of the Financial System and the Financial Stability: Issues and Policy Options. BIS Paper 1: 1–57. Basel.

Buch, C.M. (2000). Capital Market Integration in Euroland: The Role of Banks. *German Economic Review* 1: 443–464.

Buch, C.M. (2002). Financial Market Integration in the US: Lessons for Europe? *Comparative Economic Studies* 44: 46–71.

Buch, C.M. (2003). Information or Regulation: What Drives the International Activities of Commercial Banks? *Journal of Money, Credit, and Banking* 35:851–869.

Buch, C.M., and S.M. Golder (2000). Foreign Competition and Disintermediation: No Threat to the German Banking System? *Quarterly Review* 53: 107–133.

Buch, C.M., A. Schertler, and N. von Westernhagen (2006). Heterogeneity in Lending and Sectoral Growth: Evidence from German Bank-Level Data. Forthcoming as Bundesbank Discussion Paper (Series 2), Frankfurt.

Buser, S., A. Chen, and E. Kane (1981). Federal Deposit Insurance, Regulatory Policy, and Optimal Bank Capital. *Journal of Finance* 36: 51–60.

Capie, F. (1995). Prudent and Stable (but Inefficient?): Commercial Banks in Britain, 1890–1940. In M. Bordo and R. Sylla (eds.), *Anglo-American Financial Systems: Institutions and Markets in the Twentieth Century*. New York: Irwin.

Carletti, E. and P. Hartmann (2003). Competition and Stability: What's Special about Banking? In P. Mizen (ed.), *Monetary History, Exchanges Rates and Financial Markets: Essays in Honour of Charles Goodhart*. Vol. 2. Cheltenham: Edward Elgar.

Chessen, J. (1987). Risk-Based Capital Comes to the Fore. *Issues in Bank Regulation* 10 (4): 3–15.

DeAngelo, H., and R.W. Masulis (1980). Optimal Capital Structure under Corporate and Personal Taxation. *Journal of Financial Economics* 8: 3–29.

Demirgüç-Kunt, A., E. Detragiache, and P. Gupta (2000). Inside the Crisis: An Empirical Analysis of Banking Systems in Distress. IMF Working Paper WP/00/156. Washington, D.C.

Demsetz, R., M. Saidenberg, and P. Strahan (1996). Banks with Something to Lose: The Disciplinary Role of Franchise Value. *FRBNY Economic Policy Review* 2: 1–14 (October).

De Nicolo, G. (2000). Size, Charter Value and Risk in Banking: An International Perspective. International Finance Discussion Paper 689. Board of Governors of the Federal Reserve System, Washington, D.C.

Deutsche Bundesbank (2003). Report on the Stability of the German Financial System. *Monatsbericht* 55 (12): 5–53. Frankfurt am Main.

Dewatripont, M., and J. Tirole (1994). *The Prudential Regulation of Banks*. Cambridge: MIT Press.

Diamond, D.W., and P.H. Dybvig (1986). Banking Theory, Deposit Insurance, and Bank Capital Regulation. *Journal of Business* 59: 55–67.

Diamond, D.W., and R. Rajan (2000). A Theory of Bank Capital. *Journal of Finance* 6: 2431–2465.

Doornik, J., M. Arellano, and S. Bond (2002). Panel Data Estimation Using DPD for Ox. Via Internet <http://www.doornik.com/download/dpd.pdf>.

Dothan, U., and J. Williams (1980). Banks, Bankruptcy and Public Regulation. *Journal of Banking and Finance* 4: 65–88.

Estrella, A. (2004). The Cyclical Behaviour of Optimal Bank Capital. *Journal of Banking and Finance* 28: 1469–1498.

Flannery, M.J. (1991). Pricing Deposit Insurance When the Insurer Measures Bank Risk with an Error. *Journal of Banking and Finance* 15: 975–998.

Freixas, X., and J.-C. Rochet (1997). *Microeconomics of Banking*. Cambridge: MIT.

Furlong, F. T. and M. C. Keeley (1989). Capital Regulation and Bank Risk–Taking: A Note. *Journal of Banking and Finance* 13: 883–891.

Furlong, F. and S. Kwan (2005). Market-to-Book, Charter Value, and Bank Risk-Taking – A Recent Perspective. Paper presented at the Basel Committee Research Task Force Conference on Banking and Financial Stability at the Oesterreichische Nationalbank, Vienna, April 2005.

Galai, D., and R. Masulis (1976). The Option Pricing Model and the Risk Factor of Stock. *Journal of Financial Economics* 3: 53–81.

Gambacorta, L., and Mistrulli, P. E. (2004). Does Bank Capital Affect Lending Behavior? *Journal of Financial Intermediation* 13: 436–457.

Gennotte, G., and D. Pyle (1991). Capital Controls and Bank Risk. *Journal of Banking and Finance* 15: 805–824.

Giammarino, R., T. Lewis, and D. Sappington (1993). An Incentive Approach to Banking Regulation. *Journal of Finance* 48: 1523–1542.

Green, R.C. (1984). Investment Incentives, Debt, and Warrants. *Journal of Financial Economics* 12: 115–136

Gropp, R., and J. Vesala (2004). Deposit Insurance, Moral Hazard and Market Monitoring. European Central Bank Working Paper 302. ECB, Frankfurt am Main.

Hart, O.D., and D.M. Jaffee (1974). On the Application of Portfolio Theory to Depository Financial Intermediaries. *Review of Economic Studies* 41: 129–147.

Hartmann-Wendels, T., A. Pfingsten, and M. Weber (1998). *Bankbetriebslehre*. Berlin: Springer-Verlag.

Hauser, H.M. (2000). SMEs in Germany: Facts and Figures 2000. Institut für Mittelstandsforschung, Bonn.

Hellmann, T., K. Murdock, and J. Stiglitz (2000). Liberalization, Moral Hazard in Banking, and Prudential Regulation: Are Capital Requirements Enough? *American Economic Review* 90: 147–165.

Hoggarth, G., A. Milne, and G. Wood (1998). Alternative Routes to Banking Stability: A Comparison of UK and German Banking Systems. *Financial Stability Review* 5: 55–68.

Im, K.S., M.H. Pesaran, and Y. Shin (2003). Testing for Unit Roots in Heterogeneous Panels. *Journal of Econometrics* 115: 53–74.

Jacques, K., and P. Nigro (1997). Risk-Based Capital, Portfolio Risk, and Bank Capital: A Simultaneous Equations Approach. *Journal of Economics and Business* 49: 533–547.

Jensen, M.C., and W.H. Meckling (1976). Theory of the Firm: Managerial Behavior, Agency Costs and Ownership Structure. *Journal of Financial Economics* 3: 305–360.

Judson, R.A., and A. Owen (1999). Estimating Dynamic Panel Data Model: A Guide for Macroeconomists. *Economics Letters* 65: 9–15.

Kahane, Y. (1977). Capital Adequacy and the Regulation of Financial Intermediaries. *Journal of Banking and Finance* 1: 207–218.

Kane, E. (1985). *The Gathering Crisis in Federal Deposit Insurance.* Cambridge: MIT Press.

Kane, E. (1989). *The S&L Insurance Crisis: How Did It Happen?* Washington, D.C.: Urban Institute Press.

Kareken, J.H., and N. Wallace (1978). Deposit Insurance and Bank Regulation: A Partial Equilibrium Exposition. *Journal of Business* 51: 413–438.

Keeley, M. (1990). Deposit Insurance, Risk, and Market Power in Banking. *American Economic Review* 80: 1183–1200.

Keeley, M.C., and F.T. Furlong (1990). A Reexamination of Mean-Variance Analysis of Bank Capital Regulation. *Journal of Banking and Finance* 14: 69–84.

Keeton, W.R. (1989). The New Risk-Based Capital Plan for Commercial Banks. *Federal Reserve Bank of Kansas City Economic Review* 74: 40–60.

Kim, D., and A.M. Santomero (1988). Risk in Banking and Capital Regulation. *Journal of Finance* 43: 1219–1233.

Kishan, .R.P., and T.P. Opiela (2000). Bank Size, Bank Capital, and the Bank Lending Channel. *Journal of Money, Credit and Banking* 32 (1): 121–141.

Kiviet, J.F. (1995). On Bias, Inconsistency and Efficiency of Various Estimators in Dynamic Panel Data Models. *Journal of Econometrics* 68: 53–78.

Koehn, M., and A.M. Santomero (1980). Regulation of Bank Capital and Portfolio Risk. *Journal of Finance* 35: 1235–1244.

Kraus, A., and R.H. Litzenberger (1973). A State Preference Model of Optimal Financial Leverage. *Journal of Finance* 28: 911–922.

Leland, H.E., and D.H. Pyle (1977). Informational Asymmetries, Financial Structure, and Financial Intermediation. *Journal of Finance* 32: 371–387.

Levin, A., C.-F. Lin, and C.-S. Chu (2002). Unit Root Tests in Panel Data: Asymptotic and Finite Sample Properties. *Journal of Econometrics* 108: 1–24.

Lindquist, K.-G. (2004). Banks' Buffer Capital: How Important Is Risk? *Journal of International Money and Finance* 23: 493–513.

Lowe, P. (2002). Credit Risk Measurement and Procyclicality. BIS Working Paper 116. BIS, Basel.

Marcus, A.J. (1983). The Bank Capital Decision: A Time Series Cross-Section Analysis. *Journal of Finance* 38: 1217–1232.

Marcus, A.J. (1984). Deregulation and Bank Financial Policy. *Journal of Banking and Finance* 8: 557–565.

Marcus, A.J., and I. Shaked (1984). The Valuation of FDIC Deposit Insurance Using Option-Pricing Estimates. *Journal of Money, Credit, and Banking* 16: 446–460.

Merton, R.C. (1977). An Analytic Derivation of the Cost of Deposit Insurance and Loan Guarantees. *Journal of Banking and Finance* 1: 3–11.

Merton, R.C. (1978). On the Cost of Deposit Insurance When There Are Surveillance Costs. *Journal of Business* 51: 439–452.

Miles, D. (1995). Optimal Regulation of Deposit Taking Financial Intermediaries. *European Economic Review* 7: 1365–1384.

Miller, M.H. (1977). Debt and Taxes. *Journal of Finance* 32: 261–275. Via Internet <http://ssrn.com/abstract=576062>.

Milne, A. (2004). The Inventory Perspective on Bank Capital. Mimeo.

Milne, A., and E. Whalley (2001). Bank Capital Regulation and Incentives for Risk-Taking. Via Internet <http://staff.city.ac.uk/~amilne/research/Rfs.pdf>.

Modigliani, F., and M.H. Miller (1958). The Cost of Capital, Corporate Finance, and the Theory of Investment. *American Economic Review* 48: 261–297.

Myers, S.C., and N.S. Majluf (1984). Corporate Financing and Investment Decisions When Firms Have Information That Investors Do Not Have. *Journal of Financial Economics* 13: 187–222.

Nickell, S. (1981). Biases in Dynamic Models with Fixed Effects. *Econometrica* 49: 1417–1426.

Nier, E. (2005). Cyclicality of Basel II Capital Requirements – Analysis of QIS 3 Data. Mimeo. Basel Research Task Force.

Nier, E., and U. Baumann (2006). Market Discipline, Disclosure and Moral Hazard in Banking. Forthcoming in the *Journal of Financial Intermediation.*

Oellerking, C. and M. Holzgrabe (1990). Sparkassen und Genossenschaftsbanken im Spannungsverhältnis zwischen Moral und Ökonomie: Strukturelemente, Organisationsgrundsätze und Geschäftspolitik. *Europäische Hochschulschriften*, Peter Land Verlag, Frankfurt.

Orgler, Y.E., and R.A. Taggart, Jr. (1983). Implications of Corporate Capital Structure Theory for Banking Institutions. *Journal of Money, Credit, and Banking* 15: 212–221.

Peek, J., and E. Rosengren (1995).The Capital Crunch: Neither a Borrower nor a Lender Be. *Journal of Money, Credit, and Banking* 27: 625–638.

Pyle, D.H. (1984). Deregulation and Deposit Insurance Reform. *Federal Reserve of San Francisco Economic Review*, Spring, 5–15.

Repullo, R. (2004). Capital Requirements, Market Power, and Risk-Taking in Banking. *Journal of Financial Intermediation* 13: 156–182.

Rime, B. (2001). Capital Requirements and Bank Behaviour: Empirical Evidence for Switzerland. *Journal of Banking and Finance* 25: 789–805.

Rochet, J.-C. (1992). Capital Requirements and the Behaviour of Commercial Banks. *European Economic Review* 36: 1137–1178.

Roodman, D. (2005). xtabond2: Stata Module to Extend xtabond Dynamic Panel Data Estimator. Center for Global Development. Washington, D.C. http://econpapers.repec.org/software/bocbocode/s435901.htm.

Ross, S.A. (1977). The Determination of Financial Structure: The Incentive-Signalling Approach. *Bell Journal of Economics* 8: 23–40.

Sander, H., and S. Kleimeier (2004). Convergence in Euro-Zone Retail Banking? What Interest Rate Pass-Through Tells Us about Monetary Policy Transmission, Competition and Integration. *Journal of International Money and Finance* 23: 461–492.

Santomero, A.M., and J.D. Vinso (1977). Estimating the Probability of Failure for Commercial Banks and the Banking System. *Journal of Banking and Finance* 1: 185–205.

Santos, J.A.C. (2000). Bank Capital Regulation in Contemporary Banking Theory: A Review of the Literature. BIS Working Paper 90. BIS, Basel.

Saunders, A., E. Strock, and N.G. Travlos (1990). Ownership Structure, Deregulation, and Bank Risk Taking. *Journal of Finance* 45: 643–654.

Sealey, C.W., Jr. (1985). Valuation, Capital Structure, and Shareholder Unanimity for Depository Financial Intermediaries. *Journal of Finance* 38: 857–871.

Sharpe, W.F. (1978). Bank Capital Adequacy, Deposit Insurance and Security Values. *Journal of Financial and Quantitative Analysis* 13: 701–718.

Shrieves, R., and D. Dahl (1992). The Relationship between Risk and Capital in Commercial Banks. *Journal of Banking and Finance* 16: 439–457.

Staikouras, C., and G. Wood (2000). Competition and Banking Stability in Greece and Spain. *Journal of International Banking Regulation* 1(2): 7–24.

Stiglitz, J.E., and A. Weiss (1981). Credit Rationing in Markets with Imperfect Information. *American Economic Review* 71: 393–411.

Suarez, J. (1994). Closure Rules, Market Power, and Risk-Taking in a Dynamic Model of Bank Behavior. LSE Discussion Paper 196. LSE, London.

Tirole, J. (1994). On Banking and Intermediation. *European Economic Review* 38: 469–487.

Van den Heuvel, S.J. (2003). The Bank Capital Channel of Monetary Policy. University of Pennsylvania. Mimeo. Philadelphia.

Windmeijer, F. (2005). A Finite Sample Correction for the Variance of Linear Efficient Two-Step GMM Estimators. *Journal of Econometrics* 126: 25–51.

Zellner, A., and H. Theil (1962). Three Stages Least Squares: Simultaneous Estimation of Simultaneous Equations. *Econometrica* 30: 54–78.

Zicchino, L., and E. Nier (2005). Bank Weakness and Bank Loan Supply. Mimeo.

KIELER STUDIEN · KIEL STUDIES

Kiel Institute for the World Economy

Editor: *Dennis Snower* · Managing Editor: *Harmen Lehment*

329. **Demand and Supply of Aggregate Exports of Goods and Services. Multivariate Cointegration Analyses for the United States, Canada, and Germany,** *Hubert Strauß*

     Berlin · Heidelberg 2004. 241 pp. Hardcover.

330. **Mehr Wachstum in Europa durch eine Koordination makroökonomischer Politik? Zur Kombination von Geld- und Lohnpolitik sowie zur Steuerharmonisierung in der EU,** *Alfred Boss, Klaus-Jürgen Gern, Carsten-Patrick Meier, Joachim Scheide*

     Berlin · Heidelberg 2004. 141 pp. Hardcover.

331. **The Dynamic Macroeconomic Effects of Public Capital: Theory and Evidence for OECD Countries,** *Christophe Kamps*

     Berlin · Heidelberg 2004. 238 pp. Hardcover.

332. **Privatisierung der Arbeitslosenversicherung: Ein Konzept für Deutschland,** *Hans H. Glismann, Klaus Schrader*

     Berlin · Heidelberg 2005. 232 pp. Hardcover.

333. **Die Lohnansprüche deutscher Arbeitsloser. Determinanten und Auswirkungen von Reservationslöhnen,** *Björn Christensen*

     Berlin · Heidelberg 2005. 208 pp. Hardcover.

334. **Monetary Policy and the German Unemployment Problem in Macroeconomic Models: Theory and Evidence,** *Jan Gottschalk*

     Berlin · Heidelberg 2005. 287 pp. Hardcover.

335. **Ausbau der Flughafeninfrastruktur: Konflikte und institutionelle Lösungsansätze,** *Frank Bickenbach, Lars Kumkar, Henning Sichelschmidt, Rüdiger Soltwedel, Hartmut Wolf*

     Berlin · Heidelberg 2005. 251 pp. Hardcover.

336. **Poverty and Inequality in the Era of Structural Reforms: The Case of Bolivia,** *Julius Spatz*

     Berlin · Heidelberg 2006. 167 pp. Hardcover.

337. **Bank Capital and Risk-Taking: The Impact of Capital Regulation, Charter Value, and the Business Cycle,** Stéphanie M. Stolz

     Berlin · Heidelberg 2007. 150 pp. Hardcover.

More information on publications by the Kiel Institute at http://www.ifw-kiel.de/pub/pub.htm, more information on the Kiel Institute at http://www.ifw-kiel.de

---

Berlin · Heidelberg: Springer-Verlag (springeronline.com)

KIELER STUDIEN · KIEL STUDIES

Kiel Institute for the World Economy

GPSR Compliance

The European Union's (EU) General Product Safety Regulation (GPSR) is a set of rules that requires consumer products to be safe and our obligations to ensure this.

If you have any concerns about our products, you can contact us on ProductSafety@springernature.com

In case Publisher is established outside the EU, the EU authorized representative is:

Springer Nature Customer Service Center GmbH
Europaplatz 3
69115 Heidelberg, Germany

The manufacturer's authorised representative in the EU is Springer Nature Customer Service Centre GmbH, Europaplatz 3, 69115 Heidelberg, Germany. If you have any concerns regarding our products, please contact ProductSafety@springernature.com

Printed and bound by CPI Group (UK) Ltd, Croydon, CR0 4YY
22/09/2026
02221061-0018